WITHDRAWN

The Essential Travel Guide
to the Southern States

This is
My South

CAROLINE EUBANKS

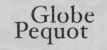

Globe
Pequot

Guilford, Connecticut

Globe Pequot

An imprint of The Rowman & Littlefield Publishing Group, Inc.
4501 Forbes Blvd., Ste. 200
Lanham, MD 20706
www.rowman.com

Distributed by NATIONAL BOOK NETWORK

Most photos by **Caroline Eubanks** with the exception of the following: *Front cover (clockwise):*
Mila Parh/Shutterstock.com (Azaleas at Magnolia Plantation and Garden, SC); **Anthony Heflin/**
Shutterstock.com (Blue Ridge Parkway, NC); **Ron Manville Photography** (Nashville, TN); **Eric**
Urquhart/Shutterstock.com (Mt. Magazine State Park, AR); **Cvandyke/Shutterstock.com** (Bodie
Island Lighthouse, Cape Hatteras National Seashore, NC); **Alexey Stiop/Shutterstock.com**
(Kentucky horses); **Sean Pavone/Shutterstock.com** (Forsyth Park, Savannah, GA); **Fotoluminate**
LLC/Shutterstock.com (New Orleans architecture); **Jason Patrick Ross/Shutterstock.com** (Ala-
bama forest); **f11photo/Shutterstock.com** (paddlewheel boat on the Mississippi River); **Nagel**
Photography/Shutterstock.com (southern live oak). *Back cover:* **Sean Pavone/Shutterstock.
com** (historic architecture, Charleston, SC). *Interior:* p. iii **Ekaterina Iatcenko/Shutterstock.com**;
p. viii **Serge Skiba/Shutterstock.com**; p. 23 **f11photo/Shutterstock.com**; p. 26 **Jason Patrick**
Ross/Shutterstock.com; pp. 43, 45 **Art Meripol/Alabama Tourism Department**; p. 58 **Eric Urqu-**
hart/Shutterstock.com; p. 73 **amadeustx/Shutterstock.com**; pp. 73 (bottom), 76 (top), 83, 84,
86, 87, 88 **Arkansas Department of Parks and Tourism**; p. 78 **Nagel Photography/Shutterstock.**
com; p. 90 **Sean Pavone/Shutterstock.com**; p. 96 **Elizabeth Levy**; p. 122 **Alexey Stiop/Shut-**
terstock.com; pp. 126, 127, 129, 131, 135 (middle right and top left), 136 (left), 137, 138, 145,
146, 149 **www.kentuckytourism.com**; p. 150 **Bram Reusen /Shutterstock.com** (Mammoth Cave
National Park); p. 152 **Fotoluminate LLC/Shutterstock.com**; p. 182 **f11photo/Shutterstock.**
com; p. 187, 190 (top), 198 **Visit Mississippi**; p. 211 **Visit Mississippi Gulf Coast**; p. 212 **Anthony**
Heflin/Shutterstock.com (Blue Ridge Parkway, NC); pp. 218 (top), 239, 241 **Bill Russ—VisitNC.**
com; p. 218 (bottom left), 231, 232 (top), 233 (bottom), 238, 242 **VisitNC.com**; p. 248 **Mila Parh/**
Shutterstock.com; p. 282 **Ron Manville Photography**; p. 314 **Mandritoiu/Shutterstock.com**;
pp. 318, 319 **Bill Crabtree, Jr.**; p. 320 **Nate Dennison**; p. 322, 323 **Virginia Tourism Corporation**;
p. 324 **John Henley**; p. 325 **Jason Barnette**; p. 343 (bottom right) **Judy Watkins**; p.343 (top)
Courtesy of Colonial Williamsburg; p. 343 (bottom left and middle left) **Sarah Hauser**.

British Library Cataloguing in Publication Information Available
Library of Congress Cataloging-in-Publication Data Available

ISBN 978-1-4930-3430-7 (paperback)
ISBN 978-1-4930-3431-4 (e-book)

♾™ The paper used in this publication meets the minimum requirements of
American National Standard for Information Sciences—Permanence of Paper for
Printed Library Materials, ANSI/NISO Z39.48-1992.

Printed in the United States of America

Contents

Blue Ridge Mountains

Welcome to the South!

You may think you know the South for its food, its people, its past, and its stories, but if there's one thing that's certain, it's that the region is far more than one story. It's an ever-evolving place, open to interpretation, defined differently based on who you ask. The size is as large as European nations and just as diverse. The states that make it up are more than just their stereotypes, they're rich in history and culture. Native American tribes such as the Creeks and Cherokees lived here long before the arrival of Europeans, especially the French, English, and Spanish. Slavery brought with it African and Caribbean cultures but at a horrific human cost.

The stories of the South are varied. It's the Korean immigrants in Atlanta and Syrian refugees in Nashville. It's the Gullah language and Ocracoke Brogue, along with the familiar Southern twangs. It's country, bluegrass, hip hop, and even metal. It's greasy spoons and white tablecloth James Beard award winners. Blue laws preventing Sunday sales of alcohol and moonshiners still hiding their riverside stills. It's every side of the political aisle. It's learning what Southern hospitality really means.

So come see for yourself and find your own stories in the South. This isn't just my South, but also yours to discover.

Alabama

The landscape is diverse in "sweet home Alabama," where visitors can go fishing on the many lakes or soak up the sun on the strip of coastline. Don't miss the Barbecue Trail, a map of eateries that focuses on the humble pig, and learn as much as you can about the Civil Rights Movement in Birmingham, Montgomery, and Selma.

Arkansas

Outdoors enthusiasts should head straight to the Ozarks for some of the country's best mountain biking. Northwest Arkansas is a surprising hub for the arts thanks to the Crystal Bridges Museum of Art. History buffs should take a "Billgrimage" to Little Rock and beyond, following the sites related to President Bill Clinton. Hot Springs also has one of the country's most underrated national parks, where visitors can soak in the thermal springs at historic bathhouses.

Georgia

Most travelers pass through the metropolis of Atlanta, which is known as being the home to the 1996 Summer Olympics. It's also where the world's busiest airport is located and where Coca-Cola was invented. Savannah charms visitors with its Spanish moss-covered oak trees, while the Golden Isles are the perfect place to escape.

Kentucky

Imbibe in the Bluegrass State, which is known best for bourbon and horse racing. Lexington is where most of the distilleries are located, but you can't miss the newer urban distilleries in Louisville. Visit the original Kentucky Fried Chicken and the home to the Louisville Slugger before venturing out to the state's lakes for relaxation.

Ernest Zacharevic Mural, Atlanta, Georgia

Louisiana

New Orleans has not only survived since Hurricane Katrina, but now thrives with award-winning restaurants, unique festivals, and *je ne sais quoi*. But don't skip over the rest of the state, stop to enjoy Cajun country in Lafayette, wildlife in Lake Charles, and small town charm in Natchitoches.

Mississippi

Home to the blues, you can't go to Mississippi without catching live music. The Mississippi Delta town of Clarksdale is a great place to start, but Tupelo also has its music history as the birth-place of Elvis Presley. Oxford is the original college town, home to Ole Miss and William Faulkner. The Mississippi Gulf Coast is small, but mighty.

North Carolina

The Tarheel State has some of the country's top educational institutions condensed into the middle of the state, namely Duke, Wake Forest, and the University of North Carolina. Charlotte is known as the home to NASCAR stock racing. Travelers can easily go between the Appalachian Mountains of Asheville and the historic coastline of the Outer Banks if they want the best of both worlds.

South Carolina

Historic Charleston is the darling of the tourism scene, winning countless awards as a destination. Once you've visited the nationally recognized restaurants, you'll start to understand why. The capital city of Columbia is more than just politics, offering a college town atmosphere as well as natural settings on Lake Murray and in Congaree National Park. Greenville is another favorite for outdoors lovers, but Myrtle Beach has a legacy all its own for summer fun.

Tennessee

Music lovers shouldn't miss Nashville and Memphis, perhaps the two cities known best for music worldwide. Elvis fans will make a beeline for Graceland, but be sure to try dry-rub ribs on Beale Street. In Nashville, you can catch a live performance at places like the Grand Ole Opry, but there's always someone playing in the bars on Broadway as well as on the street. Cool off in the Great Smoky Mountains, especially during the months when you might spot a black bear or elk.

Virginia

Drive down the scenic highways of the Blue Ridge Parkway before admiring the street art in Richmond. The historic hometown of Thomas Jefferson is now a college town paradise, complete with a thriving downtown. The Virginia coastline towns of Newport News, Hampton and Virginia Beach are favorites of families.

THINGS TO KNOW

For the purposes of this book, we define "The South" as Alabama, Arkansas, Georgia, Kentucky, Louisiana, Mississippi, North Carolina, South Carolina, Tennessee, and Virginia. If you're flying into this region, you'll likely be going through Atlanta Hartsfield-Jackson International Airport, Charlotte Airport, New Orleans Armstrong International Airport, or Dulles and Reagan airports in Washington DC. Larger airlines such as Delta and American service these airports as well as smaller, regional companies. Within the South, travel between destinations by renting a car, taking the bus, or hopping on a train. All foreign embassies are located in Washington DC. Consular services for some countries can be found in Atlanta, Raleigh, and Charlotte. Contact your government to see where their specific consular services are located.

There are two time zones used in the South, both of which adhere to Daylight Savings. Eastern time zone includes Georgia, South Carolina, North Carolina, Virginia, and parts of Kentucky and Tennessee. Central time includes the rest of Kentucky and Tennessee, Arkansas, Alabama, Mississippi, and Louisiana. Fall and spring are the best times to visit because it isn't yet high tourist season and temperatures have not reached their peaks. Be prepared for humidity if visiting during the summer months. Coastal regions have differing temperatures, as does the Appalachian region. Winters are mild, with little if any snowfall for most of the South.

The Best Small Towns in the South

There's no shortage of small town charm to be found in the region. Detour to a few of our favorites for antiques stores, historic homes, and Southern hospitality at its finest.

Franklin, Tennessee

You wouldn't know that Franklin is located a half hour from bustling Nashville. Founded in 1799, the town is now full of bars, restaurants, and even a historic theatre, earning it the nickname "America's Favorite Main Street." Spend the day or base yourself there while exploring the Music City. Go on a walking tour to learn about the city's past.

Madison, Georgia

Dubbed "the town Sherman refused to burn," Madison survived the March to the Sea during the Civil War, not because the general loved the place, but rather because of a friendship between him and the brother of a local. Madison was later known as "the most cultured and aristocratic town on the stagecoach route from Charleston to New Orleans, as many of the majestic Antebellum homes still stood." Today, it's visited for antiques stores and restaurants as well as the seasonal tour of homes.

Beaufort, South Carolina

Like much of the coastal region, Beaufort took a hit during both the Revolutionary and Civil Wars as well as from hurricanes through the years. But these days, the town is rich in Geechee history, the people of African origin who developed their own language and customs upon arriving in the remote islands of the area. The town was also used as the location of the film *The Big Chill*.

Gadsden, Alabama

Located east of Birmingham, Gadsden is a former hub for boat, tire, and steel production. The water is still important as Neely Henry Lake, Noccalula Falls Park, and the Coosa River attract outdoors lovers. The downtown area has locally owned shops and restaurants and even a craft brewery.

Natchitoches, Louisiana

The thing the town of Natchitoches (Nack-uh-tish) is perhaps best known for, other than it's hard-to-pronounce name, is the film *Steel Magnolias*, which was filmed here. The town is set along the river, which is lined with majestic oak trees. Visitors can check out the museums or enjoy the thriving downtown shops and restaurants. Don't miss the annual Natchitoches Christmas Festival when light displays cover the park.

The Best Destinations for Outdoors Lovers

Get out into the great outdoors on your trip South to see beyond the cities. Home to one of the world's oldest mountain ranges, there's no better place to lace up your boots.

Chattanooga, Tennessee

Frequently voted by outdoors magazines as one of the best places to live, this city is often overlooked by travelers who instead go to the Smokies. The former railroad hub is a hot spot for bouldering and rock climbing. The Stone Fort and Rocktown are favorite venues for the former, while Foster Falls is appropriate for intermediate climbers. Pros head to the Tennessee Wall, a rock face with over 600 possible routes. Beginners can try their luck at the climbing wall underneath the bridge at Coolidge Park, open seasonally.

Bentonville, Arkansas

Arkansas has plenty of mountain biking trails, especially those in Hot Springs, but it's the Slaughter Pen trail in Bentonville that was created in 2006 by the Walton family, founders of Wal-Mart, to encourage employees to move there. It features over 20 miles of trails on their land with connections to other sections. There's something here for every level of biker.

Columbus, Georgia

The banks of the Chattahoochee River's border with Alabama attract whitewater rafters from all over who come here to try out the course created for the 1996 Olympics. It's the longest urban whitewater rafting course in the world, created by Georgia Power to let out water at varying points throughout the day. There are class four and above rapids as well as smaller ones. Spectators can watch the excitement from the Riverwalk or even zip line above it.

Staunton, Virginia

The hills of Virginia are ideal for cyclists, set between the Blue Ridge Parkway, Shenandoah National Park, and the Allegheny Mountains. Visitors can zip down scenic Skyline Drive or past Charlottesville's wineries. Campsites are also easy to find, with the Appalachian Trail passing through nearby.

Huntsville, Alabama

North Alabama overall is great for outdoors lovers, from the waterfalls of Desoto Falls State Park to the underground caves found nearby. But the Huntsville area is home to Monte Sano State Park, the site of a former mineral springs resort. Today, it's known for its miles of hiking trails, zip lining, mountain biking, and camping.

Classic Restaurants You Can't Miss

There's nothing quite like visiting a restaurant that has been serving their signature dish as long as you've been alive. Some eateries may look like dives, but will surprise you.

The Varsity
Atlanta, Georgia

Called "America's largest drive in," The Varsity (61 N. Ave., Atlanta; thevarsity.com; 404-881-1706) has been feeding hungry Georgia Tech students, politicians, tourists, and locals since 1928. Diners can still get carhop service or eat in the expansive restaurant that is covered with memorabilia and pictures of famous visitors. Don't let the yells of "What'll ya have?" intimidate you, but confidently step up with your order of chili dogs, frozen orange drinks, and onion rings.

Ben's Chili Bowl
Washington DC

Opened in 1958 by newlyweds Ben and Virginia Ali, Ben's Chili Bowl (1213 U St. NW, Washington DC; benschilibowl.com; 202-667-0909) has a long history of serving politicians, celebrities, and locals. No one eats for free except for Barack Obama, who is now depicted in a mural outside. The restaurant has been honored with a James Beard Award for the bowls of chili served up to patrons at the booths and counter.

Bowen's Island Restaurant
Charleston, South Carolina

Coastal South Carolina has plenty of seafood eateries, but Bowen's Island Restaurant (1870 Bowens Island Rd., Charleston; bowensisland.com; 843-795-2757) is an institution. Opened in 1946 by May and Jimmy Bowen, the ramshackle concrete buildings covered in the inked names of guests have since survived two devastating fires. May and Jimmy's grandson Robert Barber carries on their legacy with oysters by the shovel, fried seafood plates, and local beer.

Loveless Cafe
Nashville, Tennessee

Loveless Cafe (8400 Hwy. 100, Nashville; lovelesscafe.com; 615-646-9700), Nashville's most iconic restaurant, is off the beaten path near the Natchez Trace Parkway. Lon and Annie Loveless opened the roadside cafe and motel in 1951 and became well known for their biscuits. Ownership has changed over the years, but the recipes haven't. You can watch "The Biscuit Lady" knead the dough through a glass window.

Antoine's
New Orleans, Louisiana

The Big Easy has many historic restaurants, but Antoine's (713 Saint Louis St., New Orleans; antoines.com; 504-581-4422) is over 175 years old, making it the oldest continuously family-owned restaurant in the US. Generations of people have all worked at the restaurant, serving celebrities and dignitaries, presidents and popes. Classic dishes include Oysters Rockefeller and gumbo.

Taylor Grocery
Taylor, Mississippi

In a small town outside of the college town of Oxford is the South's best catfish. Taylor Grocery (2084 Old Taylor Rd., Taylor; taylor grocery.com; 662-236-1716) was originally a local grocery store selling odds and ends, today it is a restaurant, but retains much of its decor along with the signatures of previous diners. Belly up to a table covered in a red and white checkered tablecloth and dig into whole fried catfish. Live music is a highlight on weekends.

Famous Louise's Rock House Restaurant
Linville Falls, North Carolina

Upon arriving at the parking lot of Famous Louise's Rock House Restaurant (23175 Linville Falls Hwy., Linville Falls; no website; 828-765-2702), you'll see where it gets its name: It's covered in rocks. A favorite spot for hikers to fuel up before or after a trip, this landmark sits on three county lines near the Blue Ridge

Parkway. In addition to the seafood and home cooking on the menu, their homemade pies can't be missed.

The Pancake Shop
Hot Springs, Arkansas

Breakfast is the most important meal of the day, especially when you can have pancakes the size of your head. The Pancake Shop (216 Central Ave., Hot Springs; pancakeshop.com; 501-624-5720) is the best place to dine before a day of sightseeing and exploring the national park. Opened in 1940 as Mason's Pancake Shop, the restaurant still serves the same recipe of flapjacks, which are best paired with coffee and ham.

Big Bob Gibson's BBQ
Decatur, Alabama

A waving neon pig welcomes diners to Big Bob Gibson's (1715 6th Ave. SE, Decatur; bigbobgibson.com; 256-350-6969), a North Alabama landmark. Now operated by Bob's descendants, the restaurant dates back to 1925 when it was little more than a roadside stand. Some of the employees have been working there for generations, starting as dishwashers and working their way up. Don't miss the pulled pork with Alabama White Sauce and one of the homemade pies for dessert.

Brown Hotel
Louisville, Kentucky

If you've never heard of a Hot Brown sandwich, you might not know what to expect, but the dish was created at the Brown Hotel (335 W. Broadway, Louisville; brownhotel.com; 502-583-1234), Louisville's most iconic hotel since 1923. Chef Fred K. Schmidt concocted the creation as a late-night dining option, an open-faced turkey sandwich coated in Mornay sauce with bacon and pimento. Dozens of versions have popped up around the city, but the dish should only be enjoyed at the original location, in the space where countless debutante balls and Kentucky Derby parties have taken place.

National Parks to Visit in the South

In addition to the national monuments and historic sites, the South has some of the most national parks of any area in the country. These include winding trails, underground caverns, scenic drives, and protected wildlife. Some have lodging options while others are better for day visits. Each has something different to offer, so bring your parks pass and sense of adventure!

Great Smoky Mountains
Tennessee

The Great Smoky Mountains National Park (nps.gov/grsm/index.htm) is the country's most-visited park, bordering Tennessee and North Carolina at over 500,000 acres. This area suffered a devastating fire in 2016, but is back on the rise thanks to support from the local community and residents such as Dolly Parton. Here you will find black bears and elk among the easy-to-spot species, as well as unique species of plant life. Seeing the misty haze over Clingman's Dome will help you understand the park's name. Stop by the Cades Cove Visitors Center to plan your excursion and don't miss the Roaring Fork Motor Trail. The towns of Gatlinburg and Pigeon Forge are nearby, allowing visitors to stay in hotels or camp within the park.

Hot Springs
Arkansas

The area now known as Hot Springs National Park (nps.gov/hosp/index.htm) has been protected since long before the National Parks System was created, the park claims to be older than Yellowstone. It officially became a park in 1921, including the over 5,000 acres known for their thermal springs as well as downtown Hot Springs. While the natural springs themselves are no longer open apart from bathhouses and resorts, the park offers opportunities for hiking and mountain biking. In Hot Springs proper, the site of the country's first resort and first baseball spring training, the historic structures have been preserved. Learn about why legends like Al Capone frequented the town, then head to Quapaw Bathhouse, one of the restored bathing facilities to enjoy a soak. Accommodations are located in town as well as at the Gulpha Gorge Campground.

Mammoth Cave
Kentucky

What sets Mammoth Cave National Park (nps.gov/maca/index. htm) apart from the rest is its massive size, at over 50,000 acres. It's the world's longest cave system, but only 400 miles have been explored. Located near Bowling Green, the park offers ranger-led tours to showcase the limestone stalagmites and stalactites as well as gypsum formations. Rare animals live within its caves, including rare sightless cave fish, bats, and salamanders. Above ground, the park has nearly 70 miles of hiking trails on both sides of the Green River, which you can access by ferry. Tours of the caves are operated every day except for Christmas, but make a reservation to avoid missing out. The park has a few camp-grounds to choose from as well as The Lodge at Mammoth Cave.

Shenandoah
Virginia

A short drive from Washington DC, Shenandoah is known for its 200,000 acres of waterfalls, viewpoints, and scenic Skyline Drive (nps.gov/shen/index.htm). Hikers flock here for the 500 miles of trails, especially during the fall color. Ambitious athletes can summit Old Rag Mountain, the park's most popular and most difficult hike. Fishing, horseback riding, and rock climbing are also available. Shenandoah has a number of lodging options, including cabins and lodges, some of which are open seasonally. Campers can stay at traditional campsites or in the backcountry.

Congaree
South Carolina

As the nation's newest national park, established in 2003, Conga-ree (nps.gov/cong/index.htm) was once land used for logging, but the over 20,000 acres of bald cypresses were saved by locals who pushed for preservation. The floodplain allows visitors to kayak through, but when the area is dry enough, visitors can walk along the boardwalks via five hiking trails appropriate for all fitness levels. The Congaree is home to countless species of animals, including whitetail deer, opossum, and blue heron. In addition to the bald cypresses that dot the landscape, loblolly pines, hickories, and cabbage palmetto can also be seen. The park is around 20 miles from downtown Columbia, which has a wide range of accommodations, but Congaree also has two official campsites and free backcountry camping.

Scenic Drives

The best way to really experience the South is through the great American road trip and the region has some of the best scenic drives around. Don't worry about being in a hurry here, as there are scenic turnoffs on every one of these roads.

Blue Ridge Parkway

Originally a project of the Depression-era works administration under Franklin Delano Roosevelt, the scenic highway stretches over 80,000 acres and 400 miles between North Carolina and Virginia and was finally completed after 52 years in 1987. It links between the Appalachian Mountains near Cherokee, through the Great Smoky Mountains, and into Shenandoah National Park's Skyline Drive before ending in Rockfish Gap. Travelers stop in the small towns along the way, taking advantage of the music, food, and arts of Appalachia. There are also countless recreation areas to stop and explore.

Natchez Trace Parkway

Built on the origins of a Native American trading route, the Natchez Trace Parkway was built by the Civilian Conservation Corps in the 1930s. The two-lane road runs 400 miles between Nashville, Tennessee and Natchez, Mississippi. The winding pathways shaded by trees make it popular with cyclists and motorcyclists, but it's also steeped in Native American history. Unlike other scenic drives, this one passes through larger destinations such as Florence, Tupelo, home to the official parkway visitor center, and Jackson. A highlight includes Tom's Wall, a memorial to those who perished on the Trail of Tears.

US Coastal 17

A welcome alternative to the massive I-95, US Route 17 runs parallel from Winchester, Virginia, south to Punta Gorda, Florida. For much of the journey, it's little more than a two-lane road through rural states, but in places like Charleston, it's a main road through the city. It passes through five states, only a few miles from the ocean most of the way. Quirky landmarks dot the road, such as the "World's Smallest Church" in South Newport, Georgia.

Louisiana's Great Mississippi River Road

If you plan on visiting the state's grand plantations and mansions, you'll certainly drive down the River Road, named for the waterway that transported building materials and, later, sugar and other crops, to cities to be sold. This road is where you'll see the iconic images of majestic oak tree–lined roads. It stretches over 70 miles outside of New Orleans to Baton Rouge.

Mississippi's Great River Road

Like the one in Louisiana, Mississippi's scenic byway follows the winding curves of the namesake river, but it also serves as the road along the Blues Highway, starting in Memphis and continuing south until it hits Vicksburg. The road itself can be bumpy and rural, only notable in some stretches for its familiar Blues Trail markers. But other areas can't be missed for their music history and unique local food.

The Most Unique Events

If there's one thing the South knows how to do, it's celebrate. Some events have connections to religious holidays, while others center around a beloved food item. Plan your visit around one of these quirky festivities!

Mardi Gras
New Orleans, Louisiana

See what they mean when they say, "Let the good times roll" in this annual festival, which lasts longer than just Fat Tuesday. Catch the parades around the city, organized by local krewes.

Tupelo Elvis Festival
Tupelo, Mississippi

The hometown of Elvis Presley hosts this yearly festival where "tribute artists" from around the world compete to win a spot at the prestigious Elvis Week in Memphis.

Vidalia Onion Festival
Vidalia, Georgia

The quintessential small town festival, this one celebrates the sweet onion that is known by name. Festivities include a beauty pageant, live music, a fun run, and a cook off to showcase the vegetable.

Southeastern Wildlife Expo
Charleston, South Carolina

Held every February, this event brings in celebrities like conservationist, Jack Hanna, for activities that include cooking demonstrations, gallery walks, and the beloved "Dock Dogs" competition.

Kentucky Derby
Louisville, Kentucky

The "fastest two minutes in sports" is so much more than the actual horse race, but is steeped in traditions. Seeing the outfits is a big part of it, along with the food and drinks only found on Derby Day.

St. Patrick's Day
Savannah, Georgia

Did you know that the coastal Georgia city is home to one of the nation's largest celebrations of the Irish holiday? The river is dyed green and downtown bars offer live music, Irish dancing, and plenty of beer.

Dragoncon
Atlanta, Georgia

Every Labor Day weekend, the city is taken over by the nation's largest fan-run convention for pop culture, including science fiction, gaming, comics, and more. Don't miss the parade, which has impressive cosplay from your favorite movies and shows.

Natchitoches Christmas Festival
Natchitoches, Louisiana

Founded in 1927, this holiday festival is one of the nation's oldest. The town displays lights along the Cane River and hosts live music, a pageant, parade, and craft show.

World Grits Festival
St. George, South Carolina

Held in a rural community outside of Charleston, this place consumes more of the hominy dish than anywhere else in the world. The festival includes their "Rolling in the Grits" competition, arts and crafts booths, and plenty of dishes to sample.

International Biscuit Festival
Knoxville, Tennessee

The humble of dish is given elevated status at this event, which includes live music, a pageant, and, of course, biscuit-baking competitions.

Gingerbread House Festival
Asheville, North Carolina

Every holiday season, the world's most impressive gingerbread houses take over the lobby spaces of the historic Grove Park Inn. Guests and the public can both see the creations.

Delta Hot Tamale Festival
Greenville, Mississippi

The dish that the region is best known for is celebrated with tamale-tasting tents and competitions, live music, a parade, a pageant, and a tamale-eating contest.

Dirty Dancing Festival
Lake Lure, North Carolina

Fans of the film's famous lake scene can't miss a visit to the place where it was filmed. The schedule includes dance lessons and competitions, guest panels, and a lakeside screening of the movie.

Grandfather Mountain Highland Games
Linville, North Carolina

The area was settled by Scots-Irish immigrants who continue their traditions today with Celtic music, competitions and games, and a parade of tartans.

Oktoberfest
Helen, Georgia

The town in the North Georgia Mountains was transformed into its current Alpine kitsch in 1968 and hosts annual Oktoberfest celebrations as a nod to its German inspiration. The Festhalle hosts dancing and drinking all month.

Mayberry Days
Mt. Airy, North Carolina

The small town that inspired Mayberry on the Andy Griffith Show honors its native son every year with special guests, a barbecue cook-off, and performances.

Can't-Miss Day Trips

There are so many smaller destinations within a short drive from more known ones. Borrow a car for the afternoon to explore farther, taking the back roads. Here are a few of our favorite day trips, all less than three hours from the main city.

Day Trip from Atlanta: Senoia

An hour south of downtown, this small town is perhaps best known for being the home of *The Walking Dead*. The town had become run down until production moved there, breathing new life into the shops and restaurants. Film fans can go on tours, pose with famous filming locations, and even grab a bite at Nic and Norman's, owned by actor Norman Reedus and producer Greg Nicotero. Shop for unique gifts at Beyond the Door.

Day Trip from Savannah: Bluffton

Across the border in South Carolina is the coastal community of Bluffton, named for the Palmetto Bluff. Majestic oak trees are draped in Spanish moss along the downtown streets, retaining its small town atmosphere despite proximity to Beaufort and Savannah. Visit the restaurants and shops within the Inn at Palmetto Bluff, built among the ruins of a mansion.

Day Trip from Charleston: Georgetown

Halfway between Charleston and Myrtle Beach is the colonial trading port of Georgetown. Originally settled by Native Americans and the Spanish before the British, the historic district dates back to 1729. Two signers of the Declaration of Independence hailed from the town. Browse the downtown shops before visiting the Rice Museum to learn about the area's important role in the nation's rice production.

Day Trip from Memphis: Oxford

The quaint college town where William Faulkner once roamed is the perfect day trip from the energy of Beale Street. Visit his home at Rowan Oak, check out the campus of Ole Miss, and browse for books in Square Books, one of the region's best independent bookstores. Dine at one of the city's restaurants, including a handful owned by John Currence.

Day Trip from Jackson: Natchez

Leave the capital city bound for the Mississippi River to the 300-year-old city. Tour one of the many grand mansions that are open to tours. Longwood is a must-see, the only octagonal home and one that was left unfinished after the Civil War started, leaving tools and building materials to gather dust. Dine at the historic King's Tavern, which is reportedly haunted, and sample rum at Charboneau Rum Distillery, owned by the same family. If you have time, grab a drink at Under the Hill Saloon and leave your name on a dollar bill to be tacked onto the ceiling.

Day Trip from Louisville: Frankfort

People often forget that Louisville isn't actually the capital of Kentucky, but rather Frankfort is. The city is also home to the Buffalo Trace Distillery, which has operated continuously, even during Prohibition, thanks to their "medicinal" whiskey. This is also where Pappy Van Winkle and Blanton's products are made, stop by for a tasting and tour. Downtown Frankfort has a number of museums and restaurants you can enjoy after your visit.

Day Trip from Little Rock: Hope

Once you've visited the Clinton Presidential Library in Little Rock, see the small town where the future leader grew up, which he famously referred to as "a little town called Hope."

Tour the President William Jefferson Clinton Birthplace Home National Historic Site where Clinton lived with his grandparents and mother. The town has a few smaller museums as well as antiques shops.

Day Trip from New Orleans: Grand Isle

Swamp and plantation tours make popular day trips from the Big Easy, but for a truly unique day trip, head south into the remote corners of the bayou. Grand Isle State Park is the only inhabited barrier island in the state. The area is known for its beaches and wildlife spotting. Historic Grand Isle has been named one of the top fishing spots in the world.

Day Trip from Nashville: Sewanee

Home to the University of the South, this stunning campus seriously resembles Hogwarts, especially since upperclassmen actually can wear robes to class. Snap some photos at the All Saints Chapel before checking out the downtown shops and restaurants or walking the miles of trails that surround the campus.

Day Trip from Birmingham: Florence

Set in the heart of Muscle Shoals, Florence has a thriving downtown with locally owned restaurants such as Odette alongside Billy Reid's headquarters and boutique. Court Street Market has cafes and independent shops. Visit the recording studios that made your favorite hit songs, the local brewery, or even a house designed by Frank Lloyd Wright.

Day Trip from Charlotte: Boone

Escape to the mountains for the afternoon to this quirky college town. Pay your respects at the statue of Doc Watson before wandering down King Street. During ski season, you can hit the nearby slopes or live the après life in one of the favorite local watering holes. Catch a performance of *Horn in the West*, a seasonal outdoor drama.

Day Trip from Richmond: Lynchburg

Get away to the Blue Ridge foothills where Thomas Jefferson once built his second home. Its mountainous location makes it ideal for hiking, especially around Peaks of Otter and Smith Mountain Lake, the state's largest. The historic downtown has shops, restaurants, and art galleries.

An Essential Southern Playlist

There's no denying how greatly Southern music has impacted the rest of the country. Each state and region has its own style. There's the Mississippi and Arkansas blues; Old Time music in North Carolina; bluegrass in Kentucky and Virginia; zydeco and jazz in Louisiana; country in Tennessee; and modern rock, rap, and hip-hop in Georgia. All of the artists mentioned in this playlist hail from the region and some might surprise you.

- "These Arms of Mine," Otis Redding
- "When the Saints Go Marching In," Louis Armstrong
- "Birmingham," Shovels and Rope
- "Jolene," Dolly Parton
- "Back Down South," Kings of Leon
- "Wagon Wheel," Old Crow Medicine Show
- "Home," Marc Broussard
- "Suspicious Minds," Elvis
- "The Thrill is Gone," BB King
- "Deep River Blues," Doc Watson
- "Hold On," The Alabama Shakes
- "Ms. Jackson," OutKast
- "Time," Hootie and the Blowfish
- "Oh My Sweet Carolina," Ryan Adams
- "Stand by Your Man," Tammy Wynette
- "Call Me," St. Paul and the Broken Bones

The Nashville music scene

- "Love Shack," the B-52s
- "Get on Up," James Brown
- "Zip City," Drive by Truckers
- "Georgia on My Mind," Ray Charles
- "My Town," Montgomery Gentry
- "Crash," Dave Matthews Band
- "Dream a Little Dream of Me," Ella Fitzgerald
- "Folsom Prison Blues," Johnny Cash
- "Hit 'Em Up Style," The Carolina Chocolate Drops
- "Cripple Creek," Earl Scruggs
- "Stay Fly," Three 6 Mafia
- "Coal Miner's Daughter," Loretta Lynn
- "Ramblin'," Marshall Tucker Band
- "Bring It On Home To Me," Sam Cooke

An Essential Southern Reading List

Some of the nation's best writers have hailed from the South, so settle in with a good book before you visit.

- *Fried Green Tomatoes at the Whistle Stop Cafe* by Fannie Flagg
- *The Watsons Go to Birmingham* by Christopher Paul Curtis
- *To Kill a Mockingbird* by Harper Lee
- *Forrest Gump* by Winston Groom
- *Their Eyes Were Watching God* by Zora Neale Hurston
- *Gone with the Wind* by Margaret Mitchell
- *Midnight in the Garden of Good and Evil* by John Berendt
- *The Color Purple* by Alice Walker
- *The Heart is a Lonely Hunter* by Carson McCullers
- *Dead Until Dark* by Charlaine Harris
- *Twelve Years a Slave* by Solomon Northup
- *All the King's Men* by Robert Penn Warren
- *As I Lay Dying* by William Faulkner
- *The Help* by Kathryn Stockett
- *Cold Mountain* by Charles Frazier
- *South of Broad* by Pat Conroy
- *The Secret Life of Bees* by Sue Monk Kidd
- *Bastard Out of Carolina* by Dorothy Allison
- *Porgy* by DuBose Heyward
- *A Death in the Family*, James Agee
- *The Firm* by John Grisham
- *The Wettest County in the World* by Matt Bondurant

An Essential Southern Watch List

The South has been captured on the big and small screens for many years, but we've chosen a few favorites that tell the real and fictional stories from the region.

- *Selma*
- *Driving Miss Daisy*
- *Coal Miner's Daughter*
- *Secretariat*
- *Interview with a Vampire*
- *Steel Magnolias*
- *A Streetcar Named Desire*
- *A Time to Kill*
- *My Dog Skip*
- *O Brother Where Art Thou?*
- *Bull Durham*
- *The Patriot*
- *The Big Chill*
- *The Notebook*
- *Hustle & Flow*
- *The Blindside*
- *Walk the Line*
- *Hidden Figures*
- *Lawless*

Alabama forests

Alabama

You've heard Lynyrd Skynyrd sing about the state, but what do you really know about "Sweet Home Alabama?" Originally home to Native Americans, the state joined the US in 1819 after the arrival of Europeans. During the Civil War, Montgomery was the first capital of the Confederacy and is the state's capital still. Alabama was ground zero for the Civil Rights Movement, home to significant events such as the Montgomery Bus Boycott, Bloody Sunday, and Martin Luther King Jr.'s Letter from the Birmingham Jail. It was also the unlikely home of the US rocket program, with the *Saturn V* being developed in Huntsville. The coast was hit hard with modern hurricanes and the 2010 Deepwater Horizon oil spill. The state's ties to music span from the early days of jazz to the present. Artists such as the Rolling Stones and Aretha Franklin came to the Muscle Shoals area to record hit songs, while artists such as The Alabama Shakes and St. Paul and the Broken Bones have made it big after forming locally.

15 Things to Taste in Alabama

There's no way to limit the delicious dishes you'll eat around Alabama to 15 items, but when traveling through the state, be sure to brake for these.

1. Pulled pork with white barbecue sauce, **Big Bob Gibson's** (1715 6th Ave. SE, Decatur; bigbobgibson.com; 256-350-6969)

2. Roasted chicken, **Odette** (120 N. Court St., Florence; odette alabama.com; 256-349-5219)

3. Goulash, **Hildegard's** (2357 Whitesburg Dr. SE, Huntsville; hildegardsgermancuisine.com; 256-512-9776)

4. Chicken salad, **Claunch Cafe** (400 S. Main St., Tuscumbia; 256-386-0222)

5. Fried catfish, **Old Greenbrier Restaurant** (27028 Old Hwy. 20, Madison; oldgreenbrier.com; 256-351-1800)

6. Wood-fired lamb, **Hot and Hot Fish Club** (2180 11th Ct. S, Birmingham; hotandhotfishclub.com; 205-933-5474)

7. Hereford beef tenderloin, **Acre** (210 E. Glenn Ave., Auburn; acreauburn.com; 334-246-3763)

8. Hot dog with Chris's sauce, **Chris's Hot Dogs** (138 Dexter Ave., Montgomery; chrishotdogs.com; 334-265-6850)

9. Fried Green Tomato BLT, **Rama Jama** (1000 Paul W. Bryant Dr., Tuscaloosa; 205-750-0901)

10. Chicken Parmesan, **Tally Ho Restaurant** (509 Mangum Ave., Selma; tallyhoselma.com; 334-872-1390)

11. Oyster Sampler, **Wintzell's Oyster House** (605 Dauphin St., Mobile; wintzellsoysterhouse.com; 251-432-4605)

12. Royal Reds, **King Neptune's** (1137 Gulf Shores Pkwy., Gulf Shores; kingneptuneseafoodrestaurant.com; 251-968-5464)

13. Bushwhacker, **Flora Bama** (17401 Perdido Key Dr., Orange Beach, Pensacola; florabama.com; 850-492-0611)

14. Beignets, **Panini Pete's** (42 1/2 South Section St., Fairhope; paninipetes.com; 251-929-0122)

15. Pulled pork, **BBQ Shack** (2122 S. Brannon Stand Rd., Dothan; 334-678-6817)

North Alabama

The cities and towns of the Alabama mountains are where you'll find the most natural beauty in the state, from freshwater lakes to breathtaking waterfalls, state parks and national forests, and even underground caves. The lakes themselves line the Tennessee River, some created through dams by the Tennessee Valley Authority. It was this land that was settled by Native Americans and where the Confederacy set up depots during the Civil War. Huntsville became a place for scientists and engineers to relocate during the "Space Race" to work with Wernher Von Braun. Traveling through this region offers quaint small towns such as Gadsden and Madison as well as the city skyline of Huntsville, all accessible via country roads and major highways. The city has a small airport, but is also accessible from the major airports in Birmingham, Nashville, and Atlanta.

REMEMBERING THE TRAIL OF TEARS

The first Native American tribes settled in the area now known as Alabama over 10,000 years ago. This includes the Chickasaw, Choctaw, and Creek peoples as well as the Cherokee. Even with the arrival of Europeans, tribes developed a mostly peaceful trading relationship. Their connection with the land taught settlers how to live in their new home. In the case of tribes in northern Alabama, there was also a connection with the "singing river," better known as the Tennessee River.

In the 1800s, President Andrew Jackson pushed for the removal of Native people in Alabama and much of the South to reservations in the West. Treaties were ignored and in 1838, 60,000 Native Americans were removed from their homelands. Thousands died on the thousand-mile journey, earning it the name "The Trail of Tears." The original route they took through north Georgia, into Alabama, and onward can be seen in historic markers in this region from Fort Payne to Tuscumbia. There is no longer a Native American presence in Alabama, but the legacy of these tribes continues in the names of places such as Oneonta.

⊙ Can't-Miss Landmarks

» Learn about the state's rich musical history at the **Alabama Music Hall of Fame** (617 US 72 W., Tuscumbia; alamhof.org; 256-381-4417). Included are the walkway of stars, the hall itself which features paintings of notable music industry members, and exhibits on everyone from the band Alabama to Lionel Richie. Walk through a real tour bus and see the inked pages that became your favorite songs.

» Visitors to the Muscle Shoals area can now tour the recording studios that brought in world-renowned artists. **FAME Recording Studio** (603 Avalon Ave., Muscle Shoals; fame2.com; 256-381-0801) and **3614 Jackson Highway** (3614 N. Jackson Hwy., Shef-field; msmusicfoundation.org; 256-394-3562) were where songs like "Wild Horses" and "When a Man Loves a Woman" were recorded with what became known as the Muscle Shoals Sound.

» In Florence, the **WC Handy Home** (20 W. College St., Florence; 256-760-6434) tells of the Father of the Blues in his former one-room cabin decorated how it was when he lived there. Exhibits

Alabama Music Hall of Fame

(top) Welcome sign to Muscle Shoals (bottom) downtown Florence

showcase his guitar, piano, and trumpet as well as the sheet music for his famous works such as "Beale Street Blues." He was not only a musician, but also a composer, songwriter, and publisher.

» **Ivy Green** (300 E. Commons St. N., Tuscumbia; helenkeller birthplace.org; 256-383-4066) is the name of the Tuscumbia home where a young deaf and mute Helen Keller met her teacher Annie Sullivan, who would become her friend and educator for her entire life. Here you'll see memorabilia from Keller's life.

» The **US Space and Rocket Center** (1 Tranquility Base, Huntsville; rocketcenter.com; 800-637-7223) is an essential stop to see where the American space program took place. In addition to the massive exhibits that feature real rockets and space suits, the center is home to Space Camp and the Marshall Space Center, accessible by tour. Give yourself a minimum of three hours here.

(top) US Space and Rocket Center (bottom) Lowe Mill Arts and Entertainment Center

» A former mill, **Lowe Mill Arts and Entertainment Center** (2211 Seminole Dr. SW, Huntsville; lowemill.net; 256-533-0399) is now made up of locally owned shops, artist studios, and restaurants. Many events are held here, including live music and food trucks on weekends.

» Featured on countless travel shows, the **Unclaimed Baggage Center** (509 W. Willow St., Scottsboro; unclaimedbaggage.com; 256-259-1525) is easily the state's most unique store. The company buys pallets of items that were lost by airlines and never claimed. You can find everything from clothing to electronics to souvenirs from distant lands.

Off the Beaten Path

» **Frank Lloyd Wright's Rosenbaum House** (601 Riverview Dr., Florence; wrightinalabama.com; 256-718-5050) is one of the only designs of his in the region and the only one in Alabama. Called one of the purest examples of Wright's Usonian design, a local family commissioned the home in 1939. Now operated as a

Frank Lloyd Wright's Rosenbaum House

museum by the city, the home has been restored with its original furnishings.

» Right off the Natchez Trace Parkway near Florence lies **Tom's Wall** (13890 Lauderdale County 8, Florence; ifthelegendsfade. com; 256-764-3617), a man-made rock wall of stones from the river. Built by Tom Hendrix for his ancestors who were removed on the Trail of Tears. Legend has it that his great-great-grandmother returned to her homeland by following the "singing river." Visitors have brought their own rocks and offerings to leave at the wall.

» Spend the day in the **Huntsville Botanical Garden** (4747 Bob Wallace Ave. SW, Huntsville; hsvbg.org; 256-830-4447), a themed garden with a diverse selection of wildflowers and plants. Open year-round, highlights include the Children's Garden and the butterfly house at the Nature Center.

» **Alabama Constitution Village** (109 Gates Ave. SE, Huntsville; earlyworks.com/alabama-constitution-village; 256-564-8100) is a recreated living history museum in Huntsville that documents where the state's delegates discussed the Constitutional Convention and signed the document.

» Located in the band's hometown of Fort Payne, the **Alabama Fan Club and Museum** (101 Glenn Blvd. SW, Fort Payne; thealabamaband.com/fanclub.html; 256-845-1646) offers exhibits on the music superstars, their production and promotion offices as well as a gift shop with official merchandise.

» Constructed in the 1930s by Brother Joseph Zoettl, a Benedictine monk of St. Bernard Abbey, **Ave Maria Grotto** (1600 Saint Bernard Ave. SE, Cullman; avemariagrotto.com; 256-734-4110) is called "Jerusalem in Miniature." The four-acre park features 125 structures of the Holy Land.

» Detour to rural Danville for the **Jesse Owens Museum** (7019 CR 203, Danville; jesseowensmemorialpark.com; 256-974-3636), a space devoted to the African-American athlete that stood up

Tom's Wall

to Hitler at the 1936 Olympic Games. Inside is a replica of his birth home and memorabilia related to his life.

» The **Scottsboro Boys Museum & Cultural Center** (428 W. Willow St., Scottsboro; scottsboro-multicultural.com; 256-912-0471) honors a dark period in Alabama's history, when a group of African-American boys were wrongfully accused for a crime and sentenced to death. But by 1950, all were freed and later pardoned. The story was later said to have inspired Harper Lee's *To Kill a Mockingbird*. The museum, set in a former church, holds items from the infamous trial.

» Located at the Ottis and Evelyn Burrow Center for the Fine and Performing Arts at Wallace State Community College, the **Evelyn Burrows Museum** (801 Main St. NW, Hanceville; burrow-museum.org; 256-352-8457) holds over 5,000 pieces of decorative art, focusing on porcelain items.

» **The Indian Mound and Museum** (1028 S. Court St., Florence; 256-760-6427) is constructed on a traditional mound built in the style of the Cherokee, Chickasaw, and Creek nations, making it the Tennessee Valley's largest domiciliary mound. The museum has Native American artifacts from over 10,000 years ago.

» North Alabama is lucky to have a number of remaining covered bridges, many constructed in the Town Lattice design. **Clarkson Covered Bridge** (1240 CR 1043, Cullman; cullmancountyparks.com/clarkson.html; 256-739-2916) was built in Cullman in 1904. **The Gilliland-Reese Covered Bridge** (Noccalula Falls Park, Gadsden; noccalulafallspark.com; 256-549-4663) was built in 1899 before being relocated to Noccalula Falls State Park near Gadsden. **Swann Covered Bridge** (1590 Swann Bridge Rd., Cleveland, (205-274-2153) near Cleveland reopened to traffic after being restored in 2012. Built in 1930, **Old Easley Covered Bridge** (Easley Bridge Rd., Oneonta) is one of the more modern bridges, while nearby **Horton Mill Covered Bridge** (AL Hwy. 75, Oneonta) was completed in 1934.

» Caves dot the northern Alabama countryside, each offering something different. **Rattlesnake Saloon** (1292 Mt. Mills Rd., Tuscumbia; rattlesnakesaloon.net; 256-370-7220) is a remote bar and restaurant inside a cavern that hosts live music. **Cathedral Caverns State Park** (637 Cave Rd., Woodville; alapark.com/cathedral-caverns-state-park; 256-728-8193) near Huntsville first opened to visitors in 1950 and has one of the largest stalagmites in the world. **Rickwood Caverns State Park** (370 Rickwood Park Rd., Warrior; alapark.com/rickwood-caverns-state-park; 205-647-9692), between Cullman and Birmingham, offers guided tours of its sprawling cave tunnels.

» Fishermen flock to the lakes of northern Alabama, especially Guntersville and Neely Henry. Home to the **Alabama Bass Trail** (alabamabasstrail.org), it's a year-round destination for the sport. Grab a brochure from any visitor center for a map of lakes and listings of guiding services, tackle shops, marinas, and information on fishing licenses.

» **Noccalula Falls** and **Desoto Falls** are two favorite parks for their namesake waterfalls, hiking trails, and campsites. Joe Wheeler, Monte Sano, Lake Guntersville, and Bucks Pocket are additional state parks in the area where visitors can connect with the state's natural surroundings. **Alabama State Parks** website (alapark.com) offers information on camping reservations, maps, and more.

» Beyond the state parks, **Dismals Canyon** (901 CR 8, Phil Campbell; dismalscanyon.com; 205-993-4559) is a privately operated nature park south of Florence, rich in biodiversity and bioluminescence, waterfalls, and shaded trails. Open since 1954, **Natural Bridge Park** (CR 3500, Haleyville; 205-486-5330) features a sandstone archway that is the longest natural bridge east of the Rocky Mountains. **Cherokee Rock Village** (2000 CR 70, Leesburg; ccparkboard.com; 256-523-3799) has 14 miles of hiking trails, rock formations, bird watching opportunities, rock climbing, and geocaching as well as camping. **Bankhead National Forest** (Alabama 33, Double Springs; www.fs.usda.gov/alabama) spans over a large part of North Alabama, made up of six recreation areas made for fishing, camping, hiking, and swimming. Located in Decatur, the 35,000-acre **Wheeler National Wildlife Refuge** (Visitors Center Road, Decatur; fws.gov/wheeler; 256-350-6639) is where wintering waterfowl flock every year.

⚑ Tours for Every Interest

» Find out where the local spots are with **Guntersville Bass Guides** (guntersvillebassguides.com, 256-698-6593), a guiding service on Lake Guntersville. The owners have over 15 years of experience and know the lake better than anyone.

» The **Downtown Dish Huntsville Food Tour** (huntsvillefood-tours.com, 800-656-0713) showcases the city's historic neighborhoods and favorite local eateries. Snack on samples along the way, led by natives of the city over the course of two and a half hours.

» Learn about the dark side of the Rocket City with **Huntsville Ghost Walk** (huntsvilleghostwalk.com, 256-509-3940), which operates seasonal ghost-themed walking and trolley tours of historic neighborhoods. They're led by paranormal experts.

» See the Tennessee River from the water with **Forrest Paddle Boarding** (forrestpaddleboarding.com, 256-690-7000), an outfitter local to Huntsville. They offer rentals and private lessons.

» **Haunted History of the Shoals** (florenceghostwalk.com, 256-810-5618) also offers a creepy look inside northern Alabama, this time in the Shoals towns of Florence and Sheffield. The guide is the author of dozens of spooky books, so she knows ghosts.

Five Unique Sleeps in North Alabama

Hotels are a dime a dozen, but northern Alabama has some truly unique places to lay your head at night.

» On the same land as Rattlesnake Saloon in Tuscumbia is **Seven Springs Lodge** (1532 Mt. Mills Rd., Tuscumbia; rattlesnakesaloon .net/lodge; 256-370-7218), a property with more than 20,000 acres, campsites for tents and RVs, and cabins, including one in a former grain silo. You can even bring your own horse and ride on their trails.

» **St. Bernard Retreat Center** (1600 St. Bernard Dr., Cullman; stbernardabbey.com/accommodations; 256-734-8291) is a real-life Benedictine monastery that welcomes visitors for quiet reflection and overnight visits. Forty-six rooms have two twin beds, private bathrooms, and telephones, but leave your laptop behind in favor of contemplation.

» **DeSoto State Park's Historic Lodge** (7104 Desoto Pkwy. NE, Fort Payne; alapark.com/desoto-state-park; 256-845-0051) was constructed by the Civilian Conservation Corps in the 1930s. It has motel rooms, a restaurant, and nearby cabins and campsites as well as easy access to restaurants and shops in Mentone.

» **Gorham's Bluff** (101 Gorham Dr., Pisgah, gorhamsbluff.com; 256-451-2787) is a luxurious inn set in a historic mansion atop Sand Mountain. Accommodation options include their lodge rooms and cottages and access to the property's restaurant, amphitheater, and other facilities. But you'll need to bring your own alcohol, as the inn is located in a dry county.

» **Dismals Canyon** (901 CR 8, Phil Campbell; dismalscanyon. com; 205-993-4559) has campsites and rustic cabins decorated in quilts and antiques that provide guests with easy access to the park's facilities and trails.

Central Alabama

A classic case of industry, central Alabama was once known for cotton and later for steel and iron. The rivers that flowed from the mountains to the north brought the resources needed. The Confederacy was established in Montgomery, which would go on to be the capital of the state. Even after the devastation of the Civil War, these foundries thrived as did cotton plantations, but the arrival of the boll weevil insect in 1910 caused problems for the industry. Also in this region are the state's finest centers for higher learning, including the Tuskegee Institute, the University of Alabama, and Auburn University. During the Civil Rights Movement, Selma, Montgomery, and Birmingham were the sites of notable events. Montgomery may be the capital, but Birmingham is no second city, nicknamed "Magic City," as it's home to the state's major airport.

I HAVE A DREAM

While the modern Civil Rights Movement took place throughout the South, it was in Alabama where many of the major events took place. After the Civil War was over and the region took to rebuilding, "Jim Crow" laws were established to prevent equal opportunities and rights for African-Americans. This included voting, riding public transportation, and even dining at restaurants. In the 1960s, activist groups such as the Student Nonviolent Coordinating Committee started a series of non-violent protests and boycotts to force white politicians to repeal the laws. It was here that Rosa Parks was arrested for refusing to give up her seat in Montgomery and later where Martin Luther King Jr. penned his famous letter from the Birmingham Jail. The Alabama Civil Rights Trail highlights these important landmarks around the state today, reminding visitors the long road to gain equality. Pick up a map or download their smartphone app for more information.

⊙ Can't-Miss Landmarks

>> **The Birmingham Civil Rights Institute** (520 16th St. N., Birmingham; bcri.org; 205-328-9696) is a must-visit for those interested in learning about the city's not-so-distant past. The museum showcases the area's role in the movement such as

Rosa Parks and her individual protest as well as Dr. King's incarceration in Birmingham. Across the street in Kelly Ingram Park, see the statues based on the events of the Children's Crusade when protesters were attacked with fire houses and dogs. There's a mobile phone tour and map that helps shed light on what took place here.

(top) Kelly Ingram Park (bottom) 16th Street Baptist Chruch

» On the other side of the street is **16th Street Baptist Church** (1530 6th Ave. N., Birmingham; 16thstreetbaptist.org; 205-251-9402), a still-operational congregation that was the site of a bombing by a KKK member that killed four African-American girls. There's a small museum with information about the girls and the church. Tours visit the worship hall, where a stained-glass window was donated by the people of Wales.

» Formerly a blast furnace, **Sloss Furnaces National Historic Landmark** (20 32nd St. N., Birmingham; slossfurnaces.com; 205-254-2025) is now a park that offers tours of the 1800s facility and hosts events such as the annual Sloss Music and Arts Festival. It's the only museum of its kind in the US.

» Gearheads and novices alike will enjoy the **Barber Motorsports Museum** (6040 Barber Motorsports Pkwy., Leeds; barbermuseum.org; 205-699-7275), located on the outskirts of Birmingham. The sprawling museum has thousands of motorcycles, from early motorized bicycles to experimental bikes. Also onsite is a Porsche test track and a racing park.

» Race fans will know **Talladega Superspeedway** (3366 Speedway Blvd., Talladega; talladegasuperspeedway.com) as the home to some of the fastest races in NASCAR. Set on a former Air Force base, the park hosts a number of yearly events and is the longest racing oval in the stock car racing association. Will Ferrell's *Talladega Nights: The Ballad of Ricky Bobby* was filmed here. Visit the International **Motorsports Hall of Fame** (3198 Speedway Blvd., Talladega; motorsportshalloffame.com; 256-362-5002) to learn even more about the sport.

» Visit the attraction that honors the famous country star at the **Hank Williams Museum** (118 Commerce St., Montgomery; thehankwilliamsmuseum.net; 334-262-3600). Here you can see the 1952 Cadillac in which he took his famous last ride as well as memorable suits and stage costumes and his guitars. Music fans can also see his boyhood home in Georgiana.

Barber Motorsports Museum

» Montgomery's **Rosa Parks Library and Museum** (252 Montgomery St., Montgomery; troy.edu/rosaparks; 334-241-8615) honors the role the local woman played in the Civil Rights Movement, starting with her refusal to give up her seat to a white passenger. The exhibits focus on her life and the movement. Nearby historic markers show where she boarded the bus and was arrested.

» **The First White House of the Confederacy** (644 Washington Ave., Montgomery; firstwhitehouse.org; 334-242-1861) was home to Jefferson Davis and his family from February to May of 1861 when the capital of the Confederacy moved to Richmond. It's furnished with period pieces and is open for tours.

» **Dexter Avenue King Memorial Baptist Church** (454 Dexter Ave., Montgomery; dexterkingmemorial.org; 334-263-3970) was where Martin Luther King Jr. served as pastor from 1954 to 1960. Don't miss the nearby parsonage where he and his wife lived, as well as the **Civil Rights Memorial** (400 Washington Ave., Montgomery; splcenter.org/civil-rights-memorial) at the Southern Poverty Law Center. At the **Freedom Rides Museum** (210 S. Court St., Montgomery; freedomridesmuseum.org; 334-414-8647), learn about the work of the "Freedom Riders."

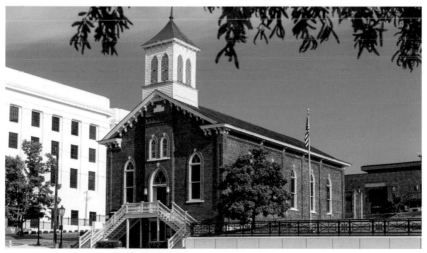

Dexter Avenue King Memorial Baptist Church

» The town of Tuskegee is known best for the **Tuskegee Institute National Historic Site** (1212 W. Montgomery Rd., Tuskegee; nps.gov/tuin/index.htm; 334-727-3200), which details the history of the African-American school founded by Booker T. Washington. George Washington Carver was one of the well-known alumni, honored on his own at the George Washington Carver Museum (Campus Rd., Tuskegee; nps.gov/tuin/index.htm; 334-727-3200). Also on the National Park-affiliated campus is The Oaks (905 W. Montgomery Rd., Tuskegee; nps.gov/museum/exhibits/tuskegee/btwoaks.htm), the home of Washington.

» Nearby, the **Tuskegee Airmen National Historic Site** (1616 Chappie James Ave., Tuskegee; nps.gov/tuai/index.htm; 334-724-0922) recognizes the group of African-Americans who served in the military as pilots, navigators, and technicians during a time of racial segregation. Two museums feature World War II–era planes flown by the airmen.

» Set in the former rehearsal and recording studio for the band, **The Commodores Museum** (208 E. Martin Luther King Hwy., Tuskegee; 334-724-0777) includes the group's stage costumes, recording equipment, and other items of memorabilia.

» The Civil Rights legacy is strong in Selma, home to the **Edmund Pettus Bridge** (nps.gov/semo/learn/historyculture/edmund-winston-pettus-bridge.htm). Named for a Grand Dragon of the KKK, the bridge was the site of Bloody Sunday, an event where protesters were attacked by police officers.

» The **Selma to Montgomery National Historic Trail** (nps.gov/semo/index.htm) features a number of attractions, including interpretive centers in Selma, Lowndes, and Montgomery. While in Selma, don't miss the National Voting Rights Museum and Institute (6 US Hwy. 80 E., Selma, nvrmi.com, 334-526-4340), which has exhibits on the people who fought for equal voting rights for all.

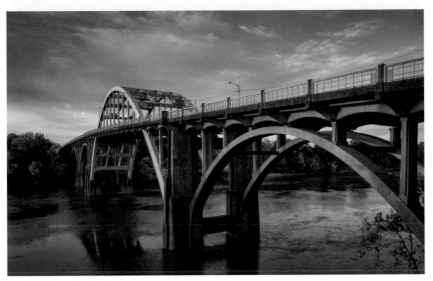

Edmund Pettus Bridge

 **Off the Beaten Path**

» Located near Birmingham's minor league baseball stadium, the **Negro Southern League Museum** (120 16th St. S., Birmingham; birminghamnslm.org; 205-581-3040) is a free but worthwhile museum devoted to the African-American leagues in the region. Exhibits include uniforms and memorabilia as well as interactive displays.

» Climb (or drive) to the top of the city to **Vulcan Park and Museum** (1701 Valley View Dr., Birmingham; visitvulcan.com; 205-933-1409) for the best views in Birmingham. The hilltop park is a reminder of the steel industry, set in the shadow of the famous statue, the largest cast iron variety in the world. There's an observation deck under it as well as a museum.

» Also in Birmingham, the **Alabama Jazz Hall of Fame** (1701 4th Ave. N., Birmingham; jazzhall.com; 205-327-9424) highlights the contributions of artists with ties to the state, including Lionel Hampton and Sun Ra. The museum has a number of displays with photos, instruments, and more.

>> **Red Mountain Park** (2011 Frankfurt Dr., Birmingham; red-mountainpark.org; 205-202-6043) is one of many places near Birmingham where you can connect with nature. The 1,200-acre space is one of the nation's largest urban parks. Here, you can enjoy 10 miles of trails, a zip line canopy course, and a ropes course obstacle challenge. They also have onsite accommodations.

>> **The Birmingham Museum of Art** (2000 Reverend Abraham Woods Jr Blvd., Birmingham; artsbma.org; 205-254-2565) has an impressive and extensive collection of paintings, sculpture, photography, and the largest collection of Wedgwood items outside of their native England. Admission is free.

>> Located in nearby Vance at their manufacturing plant, the **Mercedes Benz Visitors Center** (6 Mercedes Dr., Vance; mbusi.com/visitorcenter/vc-museum; 888-286-8762) is the only one of its kind in the US. Inside, visitors find a museum with early vehicles such as horse-drawn carriages as well as the German company's line of luxury automobiles.

>> See the city where a young Zelda Sayre met future husband F. Scott Fitzgerald in Montgomery at the **F. Scott and Zelda Fitzgerald Museum** (919 Felder Ave. # 919, Montgomery; the-fitzgeraldmuseum.org; 334-264-4222). The home was where the Fitzgeralds lived with their child around the time of the death of Zelda's father. Inside are exhibits on the couple and the "Jazz Age" period.

>> **The Sprawling Museum of Alabama** (624 Washington Ave., Montgomery; museum.alabama.gov; 334-242-4435) is the most comprehensive when it comes to educating on the history and culture of the state. Exhibits include Native American tribes, the Civil War, the cotton industry, and the Civil Rights Institute.

>> Central Alabama's finest art museum is the **Montgomery Museum of Fine Art** (1 Museum Dr., Montgomery; mmfa.org; 334-240-4333), which boasts a collection of American paintings, regional artwork, and artwork from Africa. In Tuscaloosa,

the **Sarah Moody Gallery of Art** (103 Garland Hall, Tuscaloosa; art.ua.edu/gallery/smga; 205-348-1890) at the University of Alabama as a collection of contemporary works as well as exhibitions on self-taught Southern artists. Rival Auburn University has the **Jule Collins Smith Museum of Art** (901 S. College St., Auburn; jcsm.auburn.edu; 334-844-1484), made up of six galleries of works from around the region from traditional to contemporary.

» Dating back to AD 1000, **Moundville Archaeological Park** (634 Mound Pkwy., Moundville; moundville.ua.edu; 205-371-2234) was inhabited by Native American tribes in central Alabama. Today, the park contains mounds as well as artifacts found through archaeological digs.

» **Heart of Dixie Railroad Museum** (1919 9th St., Calera; hodrrm. org; 205-757-8383) showcases Alabama's railroad tradition, including steam engines and trains dating back to the 1800s. The museum itself is set inside two historic railroad depots.

» Football fans will enjoy Tuscaloosa's **Paul W. Bryant Museum** (300 Paul W. Bryant Dr., Tuscaloosa; bryantmuseum.com; 205-348-4668), named for the University of Alabama's famous coach. Exhibits focus on all of the school's athletics teams, including early sports at the school, and include a replica of "Bear" Bryant's office and even his iconic houndstooth hat.

» Located in Anniston, the **Berman Museum of World History** (840 Museum Dr., Anniston; bermanmuseum.org; 256-237-6261) is a surprising collection started by a local man that includes artwork, weaponry, and historical documents from around the globe. Highlights include wares from the Qing Dynasty and Adolf Hitler's personal silver tea service.

» Central Alabama's great outdoors provide plenty of opportunities to enjoy them. The **Horseshoe Bend National Military Park** (11288 Horseshoe Bend Rd., Daviston; nps.gov/hobe/index. htm; 256-234-7111) is a Civil War battlefield with a 2.8-mile nature trail and a boat ramp on Lake Martin. **Brierfield Ironworks**

Historical State Park (240 Furnace Pkwy., Brierfield; brierfield-ironworks.com; 205-665-1856) and **Tannehill Ironworks Historical State Park** (12632 Confederate Pkwy., McCalla; tannehill.org; 205-477-5711) are both former iron foundries with hiking and nature trails. **Talladega National Forest** (9901 Alabama 5, Brent; www.fs.usda.gov/detail/alabama/about-forest/districts; 205-926-9765) and **Cheaha State Park** (19644 AL-281, Delta, alapark.com/cheaha-state-park; 256-488-5111) are also worth a visit, especially for Cheaha Mountain, the state's highest peak.

» **Five Mile Creek Canoe and Company** (brooksidealabama.com, click on Recreation, 205-910-4746) operates kayaking excursions from the town of Brookside. The creek is located 20 minutes from downtown Birmingham and also has camping facilities.

» To experience the Birmingham area's rock climbing and rappelling, book with **Idlewild Adventure Company** (goidlewild.com, 256-273-9596). They lead trips for beginner climbers and team building activities to Palisades Park, Sand Rock, and Yellow Bluff.

» **Limestone Tubing** (205-926-9672) in Brierfield and **Floating Fun** (floatingfun.net, 256-589-4418) in Oxford both run tubing excursions in central Alabama. **Canoe the Cahaba** (205-874-5623) in Helena allows you to explore the Tallapoosa and Cahaba rivers by canoe.

▶ Tours for Every Interest

» Tour the Birmingham facility where **Golden Flake** (goldenflake.com/tours, 800-239-2447) products are made, known as the South's original potato chip. Visitors can learn about the company and taste one of the chips straight off the production line.

» **Red Clay Tours** (redclaytourism.com, 205-240-3829) offers themed tours around the Magic City, including general history tours, brewery tours, barbecue tours, and Civil Rights tours. Each ticket price includes transportation and a guide.

» There are more than a few spooky experiences in Central Alabama. **Birmingham Ghost Walk** (bhamhistory.com, 205-440-2720), **Haunted Hearse Montgomery Tours** (334-514-4457), and **Haunted Tuscaloosa Tours** (hauntedtuscaloosatours.com) all visit the state's creepiest locations.

» While the **Robert Trent Jones Golf Trail** (rtjgolf.com) isn't a tour, it is one of the most popular attractions for sports enthusiasts.

😴 Five Unique Sleeps in Central Alabama

» Originally Birmingham's grand hotel that hosted Hank Williams, **The Redmont Hotel** (2101 5th Ave. N., Birmingham; redmontbirmingham.com; 205-957-6828) has reopened for a new generation of guests to enjoy. Historic elements have been retained and the property has an in-house coffee shop and rooftop bar.

» **Pursell Farms** (386 Talladega Springs Rd., Sylacauga; pursellfarms.com; 256-208-7600) is the perfect getaway, offering activities such as golf, Orvis shooting grounds, an in-house spa, and a chef-inspired restaurant. Accommodations include private cottages, cabins, lodge rooms, and even historic homes as well as an inn.

» Set in a stunning Victorian mansion, **Hotel Finial** (1600 Quintard Ave., Anniston; hotelfinial.com; 256-236-0503) has won countless awards for its Southern hospitality. The property has 61 guest rooms and five suites as well as complimentary breakfast and an in-house bar.

» **Cheaha State Park**'s hotel (19644 AL-281, Delta; alapark.com /cheaha-state-park; 256-488-5111) is located atop the highest point in the state with 30 basic and affordable rooms. The park also has campsites, bluffside cabins, and chalets.

» The **Wind Creek Casino** (100 River Oaks Dr., Wetumpka; windcreekwetumpka.com; 866-946-3360) boasts a AAA-Four Diamond hotel, complete with deluxe rooms and suites, multiple dining options, and top-notch entertainment.

The Coast and Southern Alabama

Southern Alabama and its coast along the Gulf of Mexico have been influenced by the French, British, and Spanish. In fact, a fort was constructed in what is now Mobile in 1702 and it later became the capital of French Louisiana, a fact of which you'll be reminded walking the streets that are reminiscent of the French Quarter in New Orleans. Carnival celebrations first took place in 1830 and they live up to their motto of "born to celebrate." Just across the bay lies Fairhope, one of the area's most scenic towns, and farther down is Gulf Shores and Orange Beach, two of the region's best beach communities. Settled in the 1800s as a part of the Mississippi territory, they later became part of Alabama's small strip of coastline. The seafood industry and tourism

THE BAR THAT SPANS TWO STATES

Originally built equally between the Alabama and Florida state lines in 1962, the Flora-Bama Lounge & Oyster Bar (17401 Perdido Key Dr., Pensacola, FL 32507; florabama.com; 850- 492-0611) is a local institution. While it now sits on the Florida side after hurricane damage, you can't miss a visit to this dive, equal parts live music venue, store, oyster bar, package store, and, on Sundays, it's even a church! Since its founding, the Flora-Bama has earned mentions everywhere from Jimmy Buffett songs to John Grisham's novel The Pelican Brief. Don't mind the bras strung up on the walls or the bull riding sometimes held in the parking lot. Grab yourself a cold beer or bushwhacker, a local frozen cocktail, for the full experience. Bachelorette parties are frequently found here as well.

Mobile Carnival Museum

are major employers, which were affected by the 2010 oil spill and frequent hurricanes. But the area is used to these situations and the clean-up effort was swift. The beaches are open for business, as well as towns like Fairhope, Dothan, Monroeville, and Enterprise. Mobile has a regional airport, but nearby Pensacola, Florida, services more flights.

 Can't-Miss Landmarks

» Alabama has a long history of Mardi Gras celebrations that pre-date those in New Orleans. Visitors can learn about local krewes and traditions at the **Mobile Carnival Museum** (355 Government St., Mobile; mobilecarnivalmuseum.com; 251-432-3324), the only one of its kind. Rooms are filled with the lavish attire previously worn by court members and colorful floats that make their way through the historic city.

» More than your average museum, **Gulf Quest** (155 Water St., Mobile, gulfquest.org; 251-436-8901) has sprawling floors filled with everything connected to the Gulf of Mexico and maritime life on the Alabama coast. Highlights include life-size shipping containers like the ones found in Mobile's port, a simulation of hurricane conditions, and remote-controlled boats.

» Learn about Mobile's beginnings as French, British, and Spanish settlements at **Fort Conde** (150 S. Royal St., Mobile; colonialmobile.com; 251-802-3092), a smaller replica of what once defended the city. The unique seven-point design held cannons and other weapons and now showcases period artifacts. Also nearby is **Fort Morgan** (110 AL-180, Gulf Shores; fort-morgan. org), used in the Battle of Mobile Bay as well as in later conflicts.

Fort Conde

» The *USS Alabama* **Battleship Memorial Park** (2703 Battleship Pkwy., Mobile; ussalabama.com; 251-433-2703) is a 75-year-old warship that now has a permanent home in the Mobile Bay. The ship originated in Virginia but was used in World War II before becoming a national historic landmark. The facility has exhibits on military history and even a submarine.

» Set on the winding waterways of Gulf Shores and Orange Beach, the **Branyon Backcountry Trail** (3801 Orange Beach Blvd., Orange Beach; backcountrytrail.com; 251-981-1180) was built in 2003 with paved trails for biking and walking, playgrounds, and bathrooms along the way. Bike and Segway rentals and tours are available nearby and there's even a resident alligator.

» Nearby, **Bon Secour National Wildlife Refuge** (12295 Alabama 180, Gulf Shores; fws.gov/refuge/Bon_Secour; 251-540-7720) can't be missed if you want to see the unique species of birds, turtles, and even the endangered Alabama Beach Mouse. **Gulf State Park Pier** (20800 E. Beach Blvd., Gulf Shores; alapark.com/gulf-state-park-fishing-and-education-pier; 251-948-7275) also has miles of walking and biking paths and countless recreation opportunities including fishing, golf, and tennis.

» The **Monroe County Courthouse** (65 N. Alabama Ave., Monroeville; monroe.alacourt.gov) is an unlikely landmark, but literary fans flock here for its connections to writers Harper Lee and Truman Capote. The building itself inspired the scene in Lee's *To Kill a Mockingbird*, but the town has a self-guided trail made up of spots tied to the authors.

 Off the Beaten Path

» Learn about the early life of a baseball legend at the **Hank Aaron Museum** (755 Bolling Brothers Blvd., Mobile; www.milb.com/content/page.jsp?ymd=20150114&content_id=106435746&sid=t417&vkey=team1), a modest three-room dwelling where he grew up. Exhibits showcase his rise to fame as well as the baseball traditions of coastal Alabama. The museum is on the campus of Mobile's minor league baseball team.

» Coastal Alabama's arts traditions are best viewed at the **Alabama Contemporary Art Center** (301 Conti St., Mobile; alabamacontemporary.org; 251-208-5671), which includes works by Alabama natives and notable regional artists such as Thornton Dial. The **Mobile Museum of Art** (4850 Museum Dr., Mobile; mobilemuseumofart.com; 251-208-5200) features more traditional works with a permanent collection of African, Asian, European, and American works. Dothan is home to the **Wiregrass Museum of Art** (126 Museum Ave., Dothan; wiregrassmuseum.org; 334-794-3871), which was created in reaction to an article

Dauphin Street, Mobile

calling the town one of the worst places to live in America. The museum proves that isn't the case with exhibitions focusing on the visual arts in the South and the US.

» Because of Mobile's long history that predates the US, a number of grand historic homes are still standing and are open to visitors. **Oakleigh** (300 Oakleigh Pl., Mobile; historicoakleigh. com; 251-432-1281) is a favorite of travelers, a Greek Revival mansion protected from Civil War damage. The complex also includes interpretive panels, a Creole cottage, and historical archives. The **Bragg-Mitchell Mansion** (1906 SpringHill Ave., Mobile; braggmitchellmansion.com; 251-471-6364) is another one of Mobile's grandest, built in 1855. It's another Greek Revival home and is open for tours. **Bellingrath Gardens and Home** (12401 Bellingrath Gardens Road, Theodore; bellingrath.org; 251-973-2217) boasts stunning gardens, set in neighboring Theodore, and the house is furnished almost exactly as it was when the Bellingrath family lived there in the 1930s.

» Hop aboard the ferry to **Dauphin Island** (dauphinisland.org), a barrier island in Mobile Bay. Here you can get up close with nature and disconnect. You can visit the Audubon Bird Sanctuary, an over 100-acre space for both native and migrating birds. The Estuarium features species found in the area. Fort Gaines was used during the Civil War.

» Easily one of Alabama's quirkiest landmarks, the **Boll Weevil Monument** (Main St., Enterprise) recognizes the insect that nearly brought down King Cotton. Built in 1919, the statue has long amused road trippin' travelers.

▶ Tours for Every Interest

» Learn about the ecosystems of the coast on a boat trip with **Wild Native Tours** (wildnativetours.com, 251-272 4088), naturalist-led excursions of Bon Secour National Wildlife Refuge. The company also leads kayaking tours. You never know when you might spot a dolphin.

» **Beachnriver Kayak Rentals** (beachnriverkayakrentals.com, 251-971-8359), based in Foley, has self-guided tours on the Bon Secour River as well as rentals. **Sunshine Canoes** (sunshine canoerentals.com, 251-367-4144) traverses the waters of the Mobile-Tensaw Delta and beyond.

» Based on Dauphin Island, **Action Outdoors** (actionoutdoors. org, 251-861-2201) is one of many companies that provides educational experiences about this special part of the South. Dolphin Fun Dolphin Cruises in Orange Beach (dolphincruises. net, 251-971-1893) is another. Or you can charter a fishing excursion with Capt Mike's Deep Sea Fishing (captainmike online.com, 251-861-5302) on Dauphin Island.

» If you just want to spend an afternoon on the water, join a trip with **Back Bay Sailing Adventures** (backbaysailing.com, 251-550-9774) or Orange Beach Sailing Charters (sailob.com /Cruises.htm, 251-981-7245), both located in Orange Beach.

» If you're looking for a view not quite like any other, **Orange Beach Helicopters** (new.orangebeachhelicopters.com, 855-496-2747) runs tours from the Caribe Resort for the best photos of the crystalline ocean.

💤 Five Unique Sleeps in Southern and Coastal Alabama

Every budget can find a suitable place to stay in southern and coastal Alabama.

» In downtown Mobile, the **Battle House Renaissance Mobile Hotel & Spa** (26 N. Royal St., Mobile; renaissance-hotels.marriott.com/battle-house-renaissance-mobile-hotel-spa; 251-338-2000) is a local landmark, a grand hotel with a domed atrium that dates back to 1908. Notable past guests include Oscar Wilde, Jefferson Davis, and Woodrow Wilson.

» Across the bay accessible by ferry, Dauphin Island allows travelers to get immersed in nature. **Dauphin Island Park and Beach Board** (109 Bienville Blvd. Dauphin Island; dauphinisland.org/camping; 251-861-2742) has plenty of tent and RV campsites with Wi-Fi, boat launches, and a dog park.

» Condominium rentals are the most common option in Gulf Shores and Orange Beach, but **Turquoise Place** (26302 Perdido Beach Blvd., Orange Beach; turquoiseplace.spectrumresorts.com; 877-720-5864) is the finest, offering resort amenities such as pools and concierge services with residential kitchens and balconies overlooking the sugar sand beaches.

» Located in Enterprise, the **Rawls Hotel** (116 S. Main St., Enterprise; rawlsbandb.com; 334-308-9387) has a storied past, dating back to 1903 and rumored to be haunted. It has its own fine-dining restaurant and four guest rooms.

Fishing boats along the coastline

» **Magnolia Springs Bed & Breakfast** (14469 Oak St., Magnolia Springs; magnoliasprings.com; 251-965-7321) is the perfect small-town getaway and is a short drive from both Mobile and the Gulf beaches. The house itself was built in 1897 and today includes cozy guest rooms and three-course breakfasts daily.

Mt. Magazine State Park

Arkansas

Known as the Natural State, Arkansas sits somewhere between "Southern" and "Midwestern." Native Americans gained a deep understanding of the land, influencing the names of places and finding natural hot springs. Explorer Hernando De Soto first explored the area in 1541. Stretching from the Mississippi River to the east to the Ozark Mountains of the west, the area was acquired in the Louisiana Purchase and officially became a state in 1836. Like many of its neighboring states, Arkansas relied on the plantation model and slave labor up until the Civil War. During the Civil Rights Movement, the state was brought to the national stage during the protests against the desegregation of Little Rock Central High School. The state's most well-known native is President Bill Clinton, who was born famously in "a little town called Hope." The Walmart Corporation is also based in Arkansas and has been involved in a cultivation of the arts and philanthropy.

15 Things to Taste in Arkansas

There's no way to limit the delicious dishes you'll eat around
Arkansas to 15 items, but when traveling through the state,
be sure to brake for these.

1. Chicken fried steak, **AQ Chicken House** (1207 N. Thompson St.,
   Springdale; aqchickenhouse.net; 479-751-4633)

2. Catfish dinner, **Jo Jo's Catfish Wharf** (151 Jacks Resort Rd.,
   Mountain View; jacksresort.com/menu; 870-585-2121)

3. Peach cobbler, **Bean Palace** (11045 War Eagle Rd., Rogers;
   wareaglemill.com/bean-palace; 866-492-7324)

4. The Classic, **Crepes Paulette** (213 NE A St., Bentonville;
   crepespaulette.com; 479-250-1110)

5. Herman's Famous Garlic Chicken, **Herman's Rib House** (2901 N.
   College Ave., Fayetteville; hermansribhouse.com; 479-442-9671)

6. Buttermilk pancakes, **Pancake Shop** (216 Central Ave., Hot
   Springs; pancakeshop.com; 501-624-5720)

7. Hubcap burger, **Cotham's** (1401 W. 3rd St., Little Rock; cothams
   .com; 501-370-9177)

8. Chopped pork sandwich, **Sims Bar-B-Que** (2415 Broadway, Little
   Rock; simsbbqar.com; 501-372-6868)

9. Whole Spread tamale plate, **McClard's Bar-B-Q** (505 Albert Pike
   Rd., Hot Springs; mcclards.com; 501-623-9665)

10. Fried green beans, **Tailgater's Burger Company** (101 S. Main St.,
    Hope; 870-777-4444)

11. Hot tamales, **Rhoda's Famous Hot Tamales** (714 Saint Mary St.,
    Lake Village; 870-265-3108)

12. Pulled pork sandwich, **Jones' Bar-B-Q Diner** (219 W. Louisiana
    St., Marianna; 870-295-3807)

13. Strawberry Shortcake, **Bulldog Restaurant** (3614 AR-367, Bald
    Knob; bulldogrestaurantbaldknob.com; 501-724-5195)

14. Blue Plate Special, **Wilson Cafe** (2 N. Jefferson St., Wilson;
    eatatwilson.com; 870-655-0222)

15. Buffet, **Parachute Inn** (10 North Sky Watch, Walnut Ridge;
    870-886-5918)

Northwest

If you've ever seen images of Arkansas, they were likely taken in the stunning communities of the northwest part of the state, referred to as NWA. Dozens of unique towns are clustered around the major highways, including Bentonville, Fayetteville, Springdale, Rogers, Fort Smith, Bella Vista, and Eureka Springs. The town of Fayetteville is home to the University of Arkansas and has a thriving downtown full of local businesses. The Walmart Corporation is based in Bentonville and has left its mark in the form of an award-winning art museum, paved bike paths, and other resources for their employees. Quirky Eureka Springs feels like an Old West town, complete with historic architecture and a storied past. The region has also become the surprising home to craft breweries, which can be visited on the Fayetteville Ale Trail. Bella Vista was founded as a summer resort in 1915. The area is best explored by car. Bentonville has a small regional airport, but Little Rock's international airport is only a few hours away.

BIKE THE OZARKS

With miles of trails and facilities, Northwest Arkansas has become a hot spot for fans of mountain biking. Slaughter Pen Bike Park alone boasts 20 miles of single-track designs. Another trail surrounds Lake Fayetteville and connects to the Razorback Greenway, which riders can take all the way to Bentonville. Inside the Ozark-St. Francis National Forest, the Syllamo Trail has been named an "Epic Route" by the International Mountain Bicycling Association with 50 miles of trails in varying degrees

of difficulty. Pick up a Bicycling in Arkansas brochure for a list of all the state's top trails. You can bring your own bike or rent one from the outfitters in communities such as Mountain View and Fayetteville.

⊙ Can't-Miss Landmarks

» Easily one of the nation's finest art museums, the **Crystal Bridges Museum of American Art** (600 Museum Way, Bentonville; crystal bridges.org; 479-418- 5700) is full of familiar pieces from artists such as Warhol and Rockwell. Established by Alice Walton, the modern building sits on a natural spring and is surrounded by paved hiking trails.

(top) Crystal Bridges Museum of American Art (bottom) Walmart Museum

» At the **Walmart Museum** (105 N. Main St., Bentonville; walmartmuseum.com; 479-273-1329) visitors can learn about the company's rise from small town five and dime store to international corporation. Inside, you'll find Sam Walton's recreated office and items from their locations worldwide.

» In the college town of Fayetteville, the **Clinton House Museum** (930 W. Clinton Dr., Fayetteville; clintonhousemuseum.org; 479-444-0066) interprets the time period when Bill and Hillary Clinton lived in the home. See a replica of Hillary's wedding dress as well as campaign items from both Clintons.

» In a case of pure Ozarks kitsch, the **Great Passion Play** (935 Passion Play Rd., Eureka Springs; greatpassionplay.org; 479-253-9200) is a Christian-focused outdoor play held every summer. Even if you're not visiting during performances, make the drive to see the Christ of the Ozarks statue and a piece of the Berlin Wall.

Clinton House Museum

» Set on acres of stunning property in Rogers, **War Eagle Mill** (11045 War Eagle Rd.; wareaglemill.com; 866-492-7324) is an active gristmill with its own restaurant and a small museum. Wander the grounds for endless photo opportunities.

War Eagle Mill

» **Pea Ridge National Military Park** (15930 US 62, Garfield; nps. gov/peri/index.htm; 479-451-8122) was the site of a pivotal Civil War battle in which more than 26,000 soldiers fought to decide the fate of Missouri and the West. The sprawling park is one of the nation's most intact battlefields. Wander the trails in search of wildlife and catch the film at the visitor center.

» The scenic **Arkansas and Missouri Railroad** (306 E. Emma, Springdale; amrailroad.com; 479-751-8600) travels through the Ozarks from Springdale, Van Buren, and Fort Smith. Grab a seat in the cars with big windows for the full experience.

» Don't miss the **Buffalo National River** (170 Ranger Rd., St Joe; nps.gov/buff/index.htm; 870-439-2502), the nation's first des- ignated river. It runs for 135 miles and has acres of trails and waterways for canoeing. Dozens of outfitters run tours of the river and cabins and campgrounds allow visitors to stay in the heart of the park.

⬤ Off the Beaten Path

» Bella Vista's **Mildred B. Cooper Memorial Chapel** (504 Memorial Dr., Bella Vista; cooperchapel.com; 479-855-6598) was designed by famed Arkansas architect, E. Fay Jones. The wood and glass structure is the perfect place for quiet contemplation. Eureka Springs' **Thorncrown Chapel** (12968 US 62, Eureka Springs; thorncrown.com; 479-253-7401), designed by the same architect, is also worth the detour.

» Honoring service members from the Revolutionary War to the present, the **Veterans Wall of Honor** (103 Veterans Way, Bella Vista; veteransmonumentbellavistaar.org) in Bella Vista has over 4,500 granite tablets with hand carved names of those lost.

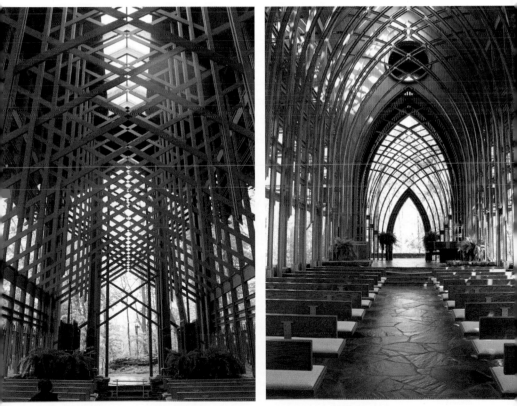

(left) Thorncrown Chapel (right) Mildred B. Cooper Memorial Chapel

>> In addition to the gardens at Crystal Bridges, Bentonville also boasts the 1875 **Peel Mansion Museum and Heritage Gardens** (400 S. Walton Blvd., Bentonville; peelcompton.org /peel; 479-254-3870) as well as **Compton Gardens** (312 N. Main St., Bentonville; peelcompton.org/compton; 479-254-3870). The native gardens offer plant life found in Arkansas. Tours of the mansion are also available.

>> The **Museum of Native American History** (202 SW O St., Bentonville; monah.us; 479-273-2456) details the tribes that lived on the land over 14,000 years ago. Among the collections are tools and artifacts, early pottery, and even a wooly mammoth skeleton.

>> Visit the **Daisy Airgun Museum** (202 W. Walnut St., Rogers; daisymuseum.com; 479-986-6873) to learn about the vintage rifle company known for the Red Ryder series. A museum has early models of their rifles and is staffed mostly by former Daisy employees.

>> Set in Eureka Springs, **Quigley's Castle** (274 Quigley Castle Rd., Eureka Springs; quigleyscastle.com; 479-253-8311) is a nearly all stone home designed by the wife of a lumber mill worker in 1943. The unusual exterior is now covered with stones collected by Elise Quigley as a child, including fossils, crystals, and arrowheads.

>> Certainly one of the state's creepier attractions, the **Arkansas Tuberculosis Sanatorium Museum** (256 Carey Rd., Booneville; 479-675-5009) opened as a treatment facility in 1910 and was one of the nation's largest. The building itself is an architectural gem and the museum describes the facility's history and patients.

>> Operated by the US Forest Service, **Blanchard Springs Caverns** (704 Blanchard Springs Rd., Fifty Six; blanchardsprings.org; 870-757-2211) near Mountain View runs guided tours of the cave. It's inhabited by bats and salamanders, so keep your eyes peeled.

» In Fayetteville, the **Botanical Garden of the Ozarks** (4703 N. Crossover Rd., Fayetteville; bgozarks.org; 479-750-2620) highlights the region's plant life with 40 acres made up of 12 themed gardens and a butterfly house.

» The **Arkansas Air Museum** (4290 S. School Ave., Fayetteville; arkansasairandmilitary.com; 479-521-4947) documents the state's aviation history with a hangar full of classic airplanes. This space was used as one of the nation's headquarters for World War II training.

» The best place to learn about the history and traditions of this part of the state is at the **Ozark Folk Center State Park** (1032 Park Ave., Mountain View; ozarkfolkcenter.com; 870-269-3851). The center showcases the music and arts culture with workshops, a gallery, and monthly concerts. They also have one of the region's best restaurants.

» Northwest Arkansas is also home to the state's wine regions. Altus and Wiederkehr Village are the best starting place for tours and tastings. Visit the **Arkansas Historic Wine Museum** (101 N. Carbon City Rd., Paris; 479-963-3990; cowiewinecellars. com) before sampling the varieties at **Chateau Aux Arc Vineyards** (8045 AR-186, Altus; chateauauxarc.com; 479-468-4400) and **Keels Creek Winery** (3185 E. Van Buren, Eureka Springs; keelscreek.com; 479-253-9463).

» The state also boasts 52 state parks (arkansasstateparks.com), including the ones in the Ozarks. **Hobbs State Park** near Rogers has over 12,000 acres, making it one of the state's largest. **Devil's Den State Park** has a lake built by the Civilian Conservation Corps and stunning waterfalls. **Mt. Magazine State Park** is located atop the state's highest point.

▶ Tours for Every Interest

» Visit the best wineries and breweries in the Ozarks with **Hogshead Tours** (hogsheadtours.com, 479-263-4957), which transports guests in classic automobiles. They include tastings at each location.

» Enjoy Bentonville's most beloved restaurants with **BiteSeeing Food Tours** (biteseeingfoodtours.com, 479-689-7174), which stops for five tastings that offer enough food for a full meal. Special diets can also be accommodated with advance notice.

Eureka Springs

» Learn about the city's "checkered past" with **Bentonville Mystery History Tours** (bentonville-tours.com, 479-212-0935), including tales from the Civil War and Jesse James' Wild West.

» Hunt ghosts with EMF meters with **Haunted Eureka Springs** (hauntedeurekasprings.com, 479-310-5266), which discusses the history of hauntings in the mountain town.

» **Buffalo Outdoor Center** (buffaloriver.com, 870-861-5514) operates zip line tours of the national river's treetops as well as day and multi-day float trips. The company also offers boat rentals and overnight accommodations.

Downtown Eureka

Five Unique Sleeps
in Northwest Arkansas

» There's nowhere quite like **The Crescent Hotel and Spa** (75 Prospect Ave., Eureka Springs; crescent-hotel.com; 855-725-5720), an 1886 Victorian hotel overlooking Eureka Springs. Rumored to be haunted, the restored hotel has both traditional hotel rooms and cottages.

» A wholly different experience is offered in safari lodges at **Turpentine Creek Wildlife Refuge** (239 Turpentine Creek Ln., Eureka Springs; turpentinecreek.org; 479-253-5841), a big cat rescue facility. Rooms are outfitted with cozy beds, artwork, snacks, and immediate access to the park.

» While the hotel is a part of a chain, **21C Museum Hotel Bentonville** (200 NE A St., Bentonville; 21cmuseumhotels.com /bentonville; 479-286-6500) is unique in its setting, a small town with a rich arts culture. Enjoy the modern rooms; the lobby gallery space; and The Hive, their award-winning restaurant.

21C Museum Hotel

» Unlike your average college town accommodations, the **Inn at Carnall Hall** (465 Arkansas Ave., Fayetteville; innatcarnallhall. com; 479-582-0400) is a 49-room inn on campus that dates back to 1906. Once a women's dormitory, amenities include complimentary Wi-Fi, coffee, and access to the city's trail network.

» Set in Petit Jean State Park, the state's first, **Mather Lodge** (1285 Petit Jean Mountain Rd., Morrilton; petitjeanstatepark. com/accommodations/mather-lodge.aspx; 877-879-2741) is the only state lodge to be built by the Civilian Conservation Corps. It contains 24 guest rooms with a dining hall as well as cabins. Nearby, you can enjoy hiking, fishing, and horseback riding.

Little Rock and Surrounds

Central Arkansas and the capital city of Little Rock is where all travelers to the state should start their journeys, as it's where much of the history begins, with both urban and rural settings. Little Rock was named by a French explorer traveling the Arkansas River in 1722. Hunters and trappers settled along local tribes. The former territory became an important trading post due to its riverside location. The city was home to a Civil War battle and government intervention during the desegregation of a local high school during the Civil Rights movement. The capital is also home to the state's major airport. To the southwest, Hot Springs was the site of an early Native American quarry for weapons but was later known as "America's First Resort Town." Everyone from athletes to gangsters to celebrities came to the thermal pools for healing. Hot Springs National Park was one of the first to be nationally protected, long before the establishment of the National Parks System. There's also Ouachita National Forest in this region, which stretches west into Oklahoma.

"BILLGRIMAGE"

Past US presidents hail from other parts of the South, but Arkansas is the only one to have a trail related to presidential historic sites. They've even set up a passport to get stamps at each location. President William J. Clinton lived in the state for most of his life and still visits. Start your "Billgrimage" in the capital city of Little Rock, where he worked as a private practice lawyer, served as state attorney general, and later became governor. His presidential library is a must-see. Next up is Hot Springs, to the south, where he moved with his family and later graduated from high school. Hope is the site of Clinton's childhood home. And the college town of Fayetteville is where Clinton taught law at the University of Arkansas and where he married his wife, Hillary. Their former home is now a museum.

★ Can't-Miss Landmarks

» Start your trip at the **Clinton Presidential Center and Park** (1200 President Clinton Ave., Little Rock; clintonlibrary.gov; 501-374-4242), which features 20,000 square feet of exhibit space with interactive panels such as the Oval Office replica and a museum on his life. The facility also houses the offices of the Clinton Foundation and the University of Arkansas Clinton School of Public Service.

» The Civil Rights Movement legacy carries on at the **Central High Museum and Visitor's Center** (1500 S. Park St., Little Rock; nps.gov/chsc/index.htm; 501-447-1400), where, in 1957, national troops were dispatched to assist in desegregation after the governor tried to block it. Part of the larger national historic site, programming focuses on the movement that led up to the event.

(top) Clinton Presidential Center (bottom) Central High Museum and Visitor's Center

» The **Old State House Museum** (300 W. Markham St., Little Rock; oldstatehouse.com; 501-324-9685) was built in 1833 in the Greek Revival style as the state's first capitol. It is also where Bill Clinton delivered acceptance speeches. It became a museum in 1947 and is the oldest surviving state capitol west of the Mississippi.

» Built in the Neoclassical style between 1899 and 1915, the **Arkansas State Capitol** (500 Woodlane St., Little Rock; gov/sos-virtualtour; 501-682-3000) is open to guided and self-guided tours. The grounds feature monuments to the Little Rock Nine, fallen firefighters, and Vietnam veterans.

» **Hot Springs National Park** (369 Central Ave., Hot Springs; nps.gov/hosp/index.htm; 501-620-6715) is the main draw to the town of the same name. It includes miles of hiking trails and most of downtown, including Bathhouse Row. Visit the Fordyce Bathhouse Visitor's Center for background on the Victorian bath-houses and the park itself.

Hot Springs

Quapaw Baths & Spa

» There are few functioning bathhouses on **Bathhouse Row**, but Quapaw Baths & Spa and Buckstaff Bathhouse have both thermal pools and modern spa services in restored historic buildings.

» If you're interested in Hot Springs' criminal element, **The Gangster Museum of America** (510 Central Ave., Hot Springs; tgmoa.com; 501-318-1717) documents legends such as Al Capone, Bugsy Siegel, and Lucky Luciano who spent time gambling, drinking, and relaxing in the town. The building itself has previously served as both a drive-through mortuary and bordello.

» In the town of Hope, everything ties back to President Clinton. Start at the **Hope Visitors Center and Museum** (100 E. Division St., Hope; http://hopearkansas.net/pView.aspx?id=6502& catid=583; 870-722-2580), set in a 1912 railroad depot. It has exhibits on the town's history and its native son.

William Jefferson Clinton Birthplace

At the **President William Jefferson Clinton Birthplace Home National Historic Site** (117 S. Hervey St., Hope; clintonchildhoodhomemuseum.com; 870-777-4455), tour the home where Clinton lived with his grandparents and mother.

» **Crater of Diamonds State Park** (209 State Park Rd., Murfreesboro; craterofdiamondsstatepark.com; 870-285-3113) is the country's only diamond-bearing site open to the public. Visitors can search for real diamonds and learn about the famous gems discovered in the park.

» Headquartered in Hot Springs, **Ouachita National Forest** (fs.usda.gov/ouachita) spans over 1 million acres in western Arkansas and Oklahoma. Trails vary in length and difficulty. The Talimena National Scenic Byway is the best way to see the park by car.

⬤ Off the Beaten Path

» Don't let the name fool you, the **Esse Purse Museum** (1510 Main St., Little Rock; essepursemuseum.com; 501-916-9022) is more than fashion, it illustrates women's history through handbags. The permanent collection covers 10 decades of items and the traveling exhibits tie it all together.

Esse Purse Museum

» Learn about Territorial Arkansas at the **Historic Arkansas Museum** (200 E. 3rd St., Little Rock; historicarkansas.org; 501-324-9351), which is made up of pre–Civil War homes. Exhibits include Bowie knives and contemporary art created in Arkansas. The museum also hosts living history days and reenactments.

» The **Arkansas Arts Center** (501 E. 9th St., Little Rock; arkansasartscenter.org; 501-372-4000) holds a collection that spans 600 years of Western art, including works by Claude Monet and Diego Rivera. In addition, they showcase unique exhibitions on ceramics and furniture design.

» Established by a local philanthropist, **Garvan Woodland Gardens** (550 Arkridge Rd., Hot Springs; garvangardens.org; 501-262-9300) sits on 210 acres on Lake Hamilton. Highlights include the Japanese garden and the Anthony Chapel, which was designed by a student of Fay Jones.

» Baseball fans can do the self-guided **Hot Springs Historic Baseball Trail** (hotspringsbaseballtrail.com), which shows where legends like Cy Young, Babe Ruth, and Hank Aaron trained.

» Home to some of the largest Native American mounds in the Lower Mississippi River Valley, **Toltec Mounds Archaeological State Park** (490 Toltec Mounds Rd., Scott; arkansasstateparks.com/toltecmounds; 501-961-9442) interprets the period between AD 650 and 1050. See the artifacts found at the site inside the visitor center.

» Named for George Washington, **Historic Washington State Park** (103 Franklin St., Washington; historicwashingtonstatepark.com; 870-983-2625) is a living history town restored to how it looked in 1824. Davy Crockett once passed through the town and it's believed to be where the Bowie knife was created.

Garvan Woodland Gardens

► Tours for Every Interest

» Explore Little Rock on two wheels with **Bobby's Bike Hike** (littlerock.bobbysbikehike.com, 501-613-7001), which offers tours for families, covering craft beer, the city's historic neighborhoods, and all things pork. Your day includes helmets, bikes, and samples on applicable tours. Rentals are also available.

» Like its counterparts in other states, **Arkansas Brews Cruise** (arkansas brewscruise.com, 501-410-6078) brings craft beer fans to Little Rock's best breweries for samples and information about their operations.

Arkansas Brews Cruise

» **404 Tour Co.** (404tour.com, 501-404-0404) visits Little Rock landmarks via Segway, including the Clinton Presidential Park.

» **Haunted Tours of Little Rock** (hauntedtoursoflittlerock.com, 501-681-3857) and **Hot Springs Haunted Tour** (hotspringshaunted-tours.com, 501-339-3751) visit the spooky sites of the respective cities, including cemeteries and historic homes, telling their stories along the way.

» Hot Springs' own **Adventureworks** (adventureworks.com /adventurepark-hotsprings-ziplines, 501-262-9182) runs zip line tours on their 12 lines through the protected forest. Adrenaline junkies can even zip at night.

» **A Bite of Hot Springs** (abiteofhotsprings.com, 501-781-0978) is a food tour that visits downtown eateries by foot. Enjoy six samples from the city's best restaurants on the Bites & Flights Tour.

Little Rock

» Fishermen can seek out **Xtreme Strike Guide Service** (xtremestrikeguideservice.com, 501-627-6181), one of the fishing charter services that operates around Hot Springs and Lake Ouachita.

💤 Five Unique Sleeps in Little Rock and Surrounds

» Called the "front porch of Little Rock," the historic **Capital Hotel** (111 W. Markham St., Little Rock; capitalhotel.com; 501-374-7474) was built in 1876 and has a wide range of room types. One Eleven, its in-house restaurant, is run by an award-winning chef.

» Budget travelers can stay in the **Firehouse Hostel and Museum** (1201 Commerce St., Little Rock; firehousehostel.org; 501-476-0294), the city's first, located in a former firehouse. It has dorm rooms, a communal kitchen, and is a member of Hostelling International.

» **Lookout Point Lakeside Inn** (104 Lookout Circle, Hot Springs; lookoutpointinn.com; 501-525-6155) is a welcome getaway in the form of a bed and breakfast on Lake Hamilton. Each cozy room is decorated to a different theme and the inn also has onsite condos.

» As the state's only resort state park, **DeGray Lake Resort State Park** (2027 State Park Entrance Rd., Bismarck; degray.com; 501-865-5850) has endless outdoors opportunities, including the famed Iron Mountain Bike Trail System and DeGray Lake. The lodge has 96 guest rooms with standard amenities and a central location within the park, but it's the yurts that offer the ideal combination of a hotel and camping.

» While not a hotel, **Stoneflower** (704 Stony Ridge Rd., Heber Springs; stoneflower.info; 479-200-5371) is a rental home like no other found in Arkansas. This cottage was designed by Fay Jones and built in 1965. This architectural gem has a queen bed, natural stone walls, and large windows overlooking the forest.

The Delta

The area that follows the Mississippi River is known as the Arkansas Delta and has connections to significant moments in American history. In the upper Delta, the Military Road was used as the path of troop movement for the Trail of Tears, where Arkansas tribes were sent into Oklahoma. Franklin D. Roosevelt's New Deal programs brought impoverished farmers to what became the Dyess Colony in 1934. In the lower Delta, the Arkansas Post was established in 1686 by a French explorer. It later became the capital of the territory and a target for Sherman's troops during the Civil War. The towns of Rohwer and Jerome were used as internment camps for Japanese-Americans during World War II. The Memphis airport across the state line is the easiest airport to fly into to explore this part of Arkansas.

KING BISCUIT TIME

Mississippi isn't the only one with a Delta. The river of the same name runs along the eastern border of Arkansas, contributing to its similar history in terms of cuisine and music. Hot tamales can be found just as easily as the blues. Notable artists with ties to the area include Johnny Cash, who was born in the Arkansas Delta, and the Beatles, who traveled through Walnut Ridge for rest and relaxation. The twin cities of Helena and West Helena are home to the King Biscuit Blues Festival and King Biscuit Time, the longest-running daily blues radio show in the US, which influenced generations of artists. The area was once full of juke joints, but few remain today. Markers on the Arkansas Blues Trail indicate significant places in music history, including Bubba's Blues Corner, a legendary music store, and Little Rock's Dreamland Ballroom.

⊙ Can't-Miss Landmarks

» Located in the historic Dyess Colony, the **Johnny Cash Boyhood Home** (110 Center Dr., Dyess; dyesscash.astate.edu; 870-764-2274) was where the musician lived with his family. The museum is operated by Arkansas State University and has been restored to the period when the New Deal program was happening.

» The **Delta Cultural Center** (141 Cherry St., Helena; deltacul turalcenter.com; 870-338-4350) is the best place to learn about 27 counties in this part of the state and is also where the King Biscuit Radio program is recorded. Exhibits cover the music legacy of the Delta, the Civil War, and early settlement. The center also manages a number of historic buildings downtown.

Johnny Cash Boyhood Home

Rowher Japanese American Relocation Center

» The Arkansas Delta was the site of two World War II internment camps for Japanese-Americans, the stories of which are
told at the WWII Japanese-American Internment Museum. The
Rowher Japanese American Relocation Center (100 South
Railroad St., McGehee; rohwer.astate.edu; 870-222-9168) has a
small museum in a former train depot. Actor George Takei was
held here as a child. Little remains from the original facility, with
historic markers placed in both Rowher and Jerome.

» Learn about the musicians who toured the Arkansas Delta at
the **Rock 'N Roll Highway 67 Museum** (201 Hazel St., Newport;
depotdays.org/rock-n-roll-highway-67-museum; 870-523-1009),
including Elvis Presley, Jerry Lee Lewis, and Roy Orbison.
The museum has posters from the performances as well as
instruments.

» **Freedom Park** (700 Biscoe St., Helena; 870-338-4350) has exhibits related to the Civil War and the Underground Railroad. Panels tell of the journey slaves took to get to freedom. This is the state's first site to be included in the National Park Service's National Underground Railroad Network to Freedom program.

 Off the Beaten Path

» Located in a former Kress building in downtown Blytheville, the **Delta Gateway Museum** (210 W. Main St., Blytheville; deltagatewaymuseum.weebly.com; 870-824-2346) interprets the fertile agricultural region known as the Delta, including its foodways, ecosystem, and cultures.

» Ernest Hemingway's family ties are found at the **Hemingway-Pfeiffer Museum and Educational Center** (1021 W. Cherry St., Piggott; hemingway.astate.edu; 870-598-3487). His wife's parents lived in northeast Arkansas and the writer worked on *A Farewell to Arms* from their converted barn, which has been restored to how it looked in the 1930s.

» The Delta of Arkansas is known for its scenic byways, including **Crowley's Ridge Parkway** (fhwa.dot.gov/byways /byways/2588/maps), the state's first. It has a number of state parks and historic landmarks along the way on its stretch between Missouri and Arkansas. The **Great River Road** (fhwa. dot.gov/byways/byways/2279/directions) passes through 10 states, including Arkansas.

» Learn about the early days of the Arkansas territory at **Davidsonville Historic State Park** (8047 Highway 166 S., Pocahontas; arkansasstateparks.com/davidsonville; 870-892-4708), the settlement that was home to the area's first post office. Wander the nature trails or hit the water for fishing and boating.

» **Arkansas State University's Museum** (320 University Loop, Jonesboro; astate.edu/museum; 870-972-2074) interprets

(above) Hemingway-Pfeiffer Museum and Educational Center (right) Arkansas State University Museum

the people and history of Northeast Arkansas and the Mississippi River Delta with exhibits on the Arkansas frontier and the pre-historic creatures that lived there. The university also operates the **Bradbury Art Museum** (201 Olympic Dr., Jonesboro; bradburyartmuseum.org; 870-972-2567), which hosts changing exhibitions of contemporary art.

» See the works of local and regional artists at **Arts Center of Grand Prairie** (108 W. 12th St., Stuttgart; grandprairiearts.com; 870-673-1781), which also offers workshops, classes, and theater productions. The **Museum of the Arkansas Grand Prairie** (921 E. 4th St., Stuttgart; grandprairiemuseum.org; 870-673-7001) is a history museum with exhibits on the area from the 1800s to 1921.

» The **Forrest L. Wood Crowley's Ridge Nature Center** (600 E. Lawson Rd., Jonesboro; crowleysridge.org; 870-933-6787) has over 200 miles of trails that are home to native wildlife.

Craighead Forest Park

Interpretive panels and self-guided exhibits inform visitors about the area. Nearby, **Craighead Forest Park** (4910 S. Culberhouse Rd., Jonesboro; jonesboro.org/197/Craighead-Forest-Park; 870-933-4604) offers camping, fishing, and running trails. **Delta Heritage Trail State Park** (5539 US 49, West Helena; arkansasstateparks.com/deltaheritagetrail; 870-572-2352) has its own "rails to trails" path for biking and walking.

» See where early Native American tribes lived at the **Parkin Archeological Park** (60 State Highway 184, Parkin; arkansasstateparks.com/parkinarcheological; 870-755-2500) where one of the mounds remains. **Hampson Archeological Museum State Park** (2 Lake Dr., Wilson; arkansasstateparks.com/hampsonmuseum; 870-655-8622) has artifacts found in the Delta region.

» The **Beatles Sculpture** (SW 2nd St., Walnut Ridge) celebrates the "Fab Four" and their short visit to Arkansas. The **Guitar Walk at Cavenaugh Park** (SW Front St., beatlesattheridge.com/attractions/guitar-walk) features nine plaques for artists who have contributed to the area's music traditions.

» Pine Bluff's **Arkansas Railroad Museum** (1700 Port Rd., Pine Bluff; arkansasrailroadmuseum.org; 870-535-8819) has a collection of historic steam engines, including the steam locomotive built in the Cotton Belt Shops. Today, it has 17 tracks and two display rooms full of train-centric memorabilia.

» **John H. Johnson Cultural Center** (Courthouse Square, Arkansas City; 870-877-2426) is set in the childhood home of the publisher of *Jet* and *Ebony* magazines, who established Johnson Publishing Company in Chicago in 1942.

Beatles sculpture

» Considered to be the most haunted place in the state, the **Allen House** (705 N. Main St., Monticello; allenhousemonticello .com; 870-224-2271) is still a private residence that offers tours. It's been featured on countless shows for its sinister past.

» The **Arkansas Entertainers Hall of Fame** (One Convention Center Plaza, Pine Bluff; arkansasentertainershalloffame.com; 870-536-7600) covers the musicians, authors, artists, and notable residents of the state, including John Grisham and Johnny Cash.

▶ Tours for Every Interest

» **Quapaw Canoe Company** (island63.com/helena.cfm; 662-627-4070) operates throughout the Mississippi River Delta, including outposts in Natchez and Clarksdale, but their Helena location sits on the main channel, offering canoe rentals for day or overnight trips.

» **Delta Heritage Tours** (deltaheritagetours.net; 870-995-2698) runs tours under different themes related to Arkansas, including the Civil War, music, agriculture, and history. The Heart and Soul tour is their most popular, covering soul food and gospel music.

ⓏZ Unique Sleeps in the Arkansas Delta

» **The Inn at Piggott** (193 W. Main St., Piggott; theinnatpiggott. com; 870-598-8888) is located in the town of the same name's original bank, built in 1925 and later bought by Paul Pfeiffer, father-in-law of Ernest Hemingway. Now a nine-room bed and breakfast, the cozy inn is within walking distance of local attractions and has hosted guests such as Andy Griffith.

» **Hotel Rhea** (117 W. Main St., Walnut Ridge; thehotelrhea.com; 870-637-4901) was built in 1904 but was later destroyed by a fire. The current incarnation is set inside the former drugstore and has been designed to look similar to how it did at the time of opening, although with modern conveniences in the four rooms.

» Set in the eastern section of the Ozarks, **Shady River Getaway** (1835 Stoney Point Rd., Pocahontas; shadyriverark.com; 870-248-0859) sits on the Eleven Point River with cozy cottages and treehouses. Guests can enjoy tubing, kayaking, and fishing on the river as well as hiking and bird watching nearby.

» **Delta Resort & Spa** (8624 Bucksducks Rd., Tillar; deltaconfer encecenter.com; 877-GO-DELTA) is a popular spot for hunters but is also a great place to disconnect. The hotel complex has 130 rooms, which houses guests enjoying the sporting clay courses, spa treatments, and in-house restaurants.

» Camping is available at **Mississippi River State Park** (2955 State Hwy. 44, Marianna; arkansasstateparks.com/mississippi river; 870-295-4040) at the Bear Creek Lake Recreation Area with tent and RV sites with a boat dock and bathhouse. Nearby activities include fishing, swimming, and nature spotting.

Forsyth Park

Georgia

The Peach State is known for its genteel cities such as Savannah and the bustling metropolis of Atlanta, but there's so much more to see. Founded as one of the 13 colonies in honor of King George of England, the area saw settlements crop up on the coast. Over time, the railroad established cities inland, including Atlanta, Macon, and Augusta. In fact, Atlanta was originally named Terminus for being the endpoint of a rail line, but was changed to its current version as a nod to the Western & Atlantic railroad. The state rose to recognition during the 1996 Centennial Olympic Games in the capital city. Throughout the state, you'll find a variety of landscapes, from the marshes of the coast to the swamps of the south, the highlands to the north, and the plains of central Georgia.

15 Things to Taste in Georgia

There's no way to limit the delicious dishes you'll eat around Georgia to 15 items, but when traveling through the state, be sure to brake for these.

1. Fried chicken, **Paschal's Restaurant** (180 Northside Dr. SW #B, Atlanta; paschalsatlanta.com; 404-525-2023)

2. International dishes, various restaurants (Buford Highway, welovebuhi.com)

3. Peach cobbler, **Mary Mac's Tea Room** (224 Ponce De Leon Ave. NE, Atlanta; marymacs.com; 404-876-1800)

4. Chicken salad, **Swan Coach House** (3130 Slaton Dr. NW, Atlanta; swancoachhouse.com; 404-261-0636)

5. Frozen orange, **The Varsity** (61 North Ave. NW, Atlanta; thevarsity.com; 404-881-1706)

6. Spaetzle, **Bodensee Restaurant** (64 Munich Strasse, Helen; bodenseerestaurant.com; 706-878-1026)

7. Family style Southern food, **Dillard House** (768 Franklin St., Dillard; dillardhouse.com; 706-746-5348)

8. Greek chicken, **Grapes and Beans** (42 E. Savannah St., Cleveland; grapesandbeans.com; 706-212-0020)

9. Dahlonega Gold Bar, **Paul Thomas Chocolates** (102 Public Square N., Dahlonega; paulthomaschocolates.com; 706-864-6333)

10. Black Forest Torte, **Hofers** (8758 N. Main St., Helen; hofers.com; 706-878-8200)

11. Barbecue at **Southern Soul** (2020 Demere Rd., St. Simon's Island; southernsoulbbq.com; 912-638-7685)

12. Black-eyed peas, **Mrs. Wilkes Boarding House** (107 W. Jones St., Savannah; mrswilkes.com; 912-232-5997)

13. Fresh oysters, **The Grey** (109 Martin Luther King Jr Blvd., Savannah; thegreyrestaurant.com; 912-662-5999)

14. Fisherman's Bowl, **Indigo Coastal Shanty** (1402 Reynolds St., Brunswick; indigocoastalshanty.com; 912-265-2007)

15. Wild Georgia Shrimp and Grits, **Driftwood Bistro** (Villas by the Sea, 1175 N. Beachview Dr., Jekyll Island; driftwoodbistro.com; 912-635-3588)

Atlanta Metro

Originally known as Terminus, it was here that the Western and Atlantic railroads ended. Sherman's troops burned much of the city to the ground during the Civil War, but it rose from the ashes, naming the phoenix as the unofficial Atlanta mascot. The city of Atlanta is a sprawling metropolis made up of dozens of unique neighborhoods. Flying into the airport, you might be surprised to see just how green it is, often referred to as a "city in a forest." Locals break it up into two zones, "inside the perimeter" and "outside the perimeter," based on the location to highway I-285, which runs in a circle around the city.

"Y'ALLYWOOD"

The state of Georgia has been used in film and television projects for decades, but it was a system of tax incentives passed in 2005 that put the state on the map. The benefits are something with which both sides of the aisle can agree, bringing in $7 billion dollars a year in revenue from projects such as *The Walking Dead*, *Stranger Things*, the Tyler Perry projects, and Marvel films. In addition to the influx to the economy, Georgia's, and especially Atlanta's, role in the film industry has created new experiences for fans. Easy to visit filming locations in the city include the Swan House, the Georgia Aquarium, and Piedmont Park. Atlanta Movie Tours offers guided tours (see below) to the filming locations of locally lensed movies and television shows. If you have time, it's worth a road trip to Senoia, Grantville, and Douglasville to see even more. Keep a lookout for those yellow production code signs. You never know when you might spot your favorite stars!

◉ Can't-Miss Landmarks

〉 There's no shortage of well-known museums and attractions to keep you busy during your visit to Atlanta. Most are located around Centennial Olympic Park, site of the 1996 Summer Games. If you plan on visiting many of these attractions during your visit, you can save money on combination tickets with the **Atlanta CityPASS** (citypass.com/atlanta), which includes five attractions for one price. They're available for purchase online and at the venues that accept them.

〉 Start at the **Georgia Aquarium** (225 Baker St. NW, Atlanta; georgiaaquarium.org; 404-581-4000), one of the world's largest aquariums, which opened in 2005 in partnership with corporate sponsors. The Smithsonian-affiliated facility has hundreds of species of fish and mammals, including sea otters, beluga whales, and whale sharks. Exhibits are organized into the type of habitat in which the animals exist. The aquarium focuses on research and conservation. Beyond what you can expect from other aquariums, the Georgia Aquarium has STEM initiatives for children, opportunities to swim and dive in the tanks, and diverse programming and events.

〉 Across the park named Pemberton Place for the Coca-Cola chemist is the **World of Coca Cola** (121 Baker St. NW, Atlanta; worldofcoca-cola.com; 404-676-5151), moved from its Underground Atlanta location. The new-and-improved facility traces the roots of the company from small-town pharmacy remedy to internationally known brand. In addition to the beloved tasting room where you can sample Coca Cola products from around the world, you can learn about the company's famous advertisements and role in the art community. And it's here that the secret recipe for the soda is kept! Just don't get any ideas about breaking into the vault.

〉 The newest addition to Centennial Olympic Park is the **Center for Civil and Human Rights** (100 Ivan Allen Jr. Blvd. NW, Atlanta; civilandhumanrights.org; 678-999-8990). The expansive museum

(top) Georgia Aquarium Ocean Explorer, (bottom) Center for Civil and Human Rights

has exhibits on the Civil Rights Movement and the South's role in it, especially as the home of Martin Luther King Jr. But there are also exhibits on modern civil and human rights struggles, like those of refugees, LGBTQ people, and those with disabilities. Check out the changing exhibits while you're exploring.

» Another attraction to make its way to the downtown corridor is the College Football Hall of Fame and Chick-fil-a Fan Experience (250 Marietta St. NW, Atlanta; cfbhall.com; 404-880-4800). It replicates the experience of a college football game, which is like a religion in the South. Choose your team upon entering the attraction and your school's insignia will be saved onto your All-Access Pass, a reusable card where you can also save game scores. Exhibits showcase the players, coaches, and memorable traditions surrounding these teams. You can also try out your skills on the Indoor Playing Field before looking for familiar names in the hall of fame.

» There's no better view of the park than from the top of **SkyView** (168 Luckie St. NW, Atlanta; skyviewatlanta.com; 678-949-9023), a Ferris Wheel that soars 20 stories above. Take a ride in one of 42 climate-controlled pods, each of which offers panoramic views of Atlanta day and night. They also offer a VIP experience with stylish seats, less people in each pod, a glass floor, and a longer flight time.

» Go behind the scenes on the **CNN Studio Tour** (190 Marietta St. NW, Atlanta; tours.cnn.com; 404-827-2300) to fully experience Ted Turner's 24-hour cable news network. While many shows are based elsewhere, Atlanta is still the company's headquarters. You might catch *Morning Express with Robin Meade* filming. The tour includes the control room and newsroom.

» There are many more attractions outside of the Centennial Olympic Park corridor. Start with the **Martin Luther King Jr. National Historic Site** (450 Auburn Ave. NE, Atlanta; nps.gov/malu/index.htm; 404-331-5190 x5046) in historic Sweet Auburn, the downtown neighborhood where King grew up and worked.

(clockwise, from top) College Football Hall of Fame, SkyView, Martin Luther King Birthplace, Martin Luther King Jr. National Historic Site, CNN Center

(clockwise, from top) Zoo Altanta,
High Museum, High Museum
Modern Wing, Atlanta Botanical
Garden and Atlanta Botanical
Garden Orchid House

Tour the National Park System–run site before seeing Ebenezer Baptist Church, King's Boyhood Home, the Center for Nonviolent Social Change, and other historic structures in the neighborhood. Tours of his home must be arranged in advance.

» **Zoo Atlanta** (800 Cherokee Ave. SE, Atlanta; zooatlanta.org; 404-624-9453) in Grant Park is the city's oldest attraction, starting as a circus that ran out of money. In later years, the Candler family, of Coca-Cola fame, donated their private menagerie to the collection, including leopards, llamas, and monkeys. Today, the emphasis is on education for this AZA-accredited facility. The giant pandas, Western lowland gorillas, and kangaroos are among the favorite animals of visitors.

» Get a dose of culture at the **High Museum of Art** (1280 Peachtree St. NW, Atlanta; high.org; 404-733-4400), the leading art museum in the region. The High was founded in 1905 on the land of a local family. Collections range from African art to modern sculptures. Past exhibits have brought in the Louvre's most famous works, the Terra Cotta Soldiers from China, and American sneaker culture.

» Located within Midtown's Piedmont Park, the city's largest green space, **Atlanta Botanical Garden** (1345 Piedmont Ave. NE, Atlanta; atlantabg.org; 404-876-5859) showcases plants from around the region and the world. The 30-acre space also boasts Chihuly glass sculptures and programming for both adults and families. The Canopy Walk allows visitors to walk among the treetops, and the Fuqua Orchid Collection is a favorite of visitors.

» Named for an 1800s neighborhood of Atlanta, **Fernbank Museum of Natural History** (767 Clifton Rd., Atlanta; fernbankmuseum.org; 404-929-6300) in Decatur is surrounded by the largest old-growth urban Piedmont forest in the country. The beloved museum is perhaps best known for its collection of dinosaurs, including the Argentinosaurus and Giganotosaurus. Fernbank also has a big screen theater that shows nature documentaries.

(left) Jimmy Carter Presidential Library and Museum, (right) Margaret Mitchell House

» Learn about the man who went from small town peanut farmer to president at the **Jimmy Carter Presidential Library and Museum** (441 Freedom Pkwy. NE, Atlanta; jimmycarterlibrary. gov; 404-865-7100), located near Little Five Points. The exhibits start with Carter's early life and continue into his life in office, later highlighting his work worldwide with the Carter Center. Be sure to check out the Oval Office replica.

» There's no better place to learn about the city than at Buckhead's **Atlanta History Center** (130 W. Paces Ferry Rd. NW, Atlanta; atlantahistorycenter.com; 404-814-4000). Founded in 1926, the complex includes the Swan House, the majestic former home of the Inman family. Also on the campus are a Civil War museum, a replica farm, and the Centennial Olympic Games Museum. The center also operates the **Margaret Mitchell House** (979 Crescent Ave. NE, Atlanta; atlantahistorycenter.com/explore/destinations/margaret-mitchell-house; 404-249-7015) in Midtown.

» **Stone Mountain** (1000 Robert E. Lee Blvd., Stone Mountain; stonemountainpark.com; 800-401-2407) is a massive exposed piece of quartz monzonite that reaches over 1,600 feet. It has a relief carving of Confederate generals completed by Gutzon Borglum, most famous for his work on Mount Rushmore. Visitors can hike to the top or take an aerial tram before exploring the park's trails and attractions.

◉ Off the Beaten Path

Beyond the top attractions in the city are under-the-radar museums and cultural offerings worth a visit.

» Located across the street from The High, the **Museum of Design Atlanta** (1315 Peachtree St. NW, Atlanta; museumofdesign.org; 404-979-6455), known as MODA, seeks to educate visitors about creativity and design. Exhibits focus on these elements and programming appeals to all ages, like their classes on 3D printing and young professional-friendly nights with beer and Legos.

» **Porsche Driving Experience** (1 Porsche Dr., Atlanta; porsche-driving.com/porsche-experience-center-atlanta; 888-204-7474) in Hapeville is the North American headquarters for the well-known sports car company. Here you can learn more about the company's products, dine in its restaurant, or take a car for a drive on the test track.

» Also in Hapeville, the **Delta Flight Museum** (1060 Delta Blvd. B-914, Atlanta; deltamuseum.org; 404-715-7886) showcases the airline's rise from small-town farming airline to international

(clockwise) Museum of Design Atlanta, Delta Flight Museum

company. Aviation geeks will enjoy the vintage aircrafts and the Boeing 747 that Delta employees banded together to purchase. The museum is located inside their historic hangar.

>> The **Atlanta Beltline** (beltline.org) has totally transformed the way Atlantans get around. Originally the idea of a local graduate student, the former rail line has been turned into a popular walking and biking path. The Eastside Trail, which runs between Old Fourth Ward and Piedmont Park, is the most frequently traveled portion, but new sections are being added every year.

>> Kids will love the **Center for Puppetry Arts** (1404 Spring St. NW, Atlanta; puppet.org; 404-873-3391), an award-winning facility that offers family-friendly programming. They also have a museum of puppets with exhibits from Jim Henson's productions as well as puppets from around the world.

>> Atlanta's Jewish history is told at the **Breman Museum** (1440 Spring St. NW, Atlanta, thebreman.org; 678-222-3700). Exhibits discuss the Holocaust and early Jewish business leaders in Atlanta. The museum also features changing exhibits on Jewish culture and issues.

>> Historic Sweet Auburn is the ideal home for **APEX** (135 Auburn Ave. NE, Atlanta; apexmuseum.org; 404-523-2739), the African-American Panoramic Experience. This is the only

(left to right) Eastside Trail of the Atlanta Beltline, Atlanta Beltline, Breman Museum

museum in the area devoted completely to African-American history and sharing stories of the diaspora.

» An hour north of Atlanta, the **Tellus Museum** (100 Tellus Dr., Cartersville; tellusmuseum.org; 770-606-5700) grew from a humble rock and mineral museum to the region's top science museum. Browse the exhibits featuring fossils, early machines, and space-themed artifacts.

» Also in Cartersville, the **Booth Museum of Western Art** (501 N. Museum Dr., Cartersville; boothmuseum.org; 770-387-1300) has the largest collection of exhibited works in the state, showcasing Western-themed paintings, photography, and sculptures.

» Located on the campus of the Centers for Disease Control in Decatur, the **David J. Sencer CDC Museum** (1600 Clifton Rd., Atlanta; cdc.gov/museum/index.htm; 404-639-0830) covers the organization's work. Past exhibits of this Smithsonian-affiliated museum have also featured information on weaponized diseases, global health crises, and the role of science.

» The original regional rails to trails project, the **Silver Comet Trail** (Mavell Road Trailhead, Smyrna) runs between the suburbs of Atlanta all the way to Alabama. The 61.5-mile trail is paved, ideal for short walks with your family or long bike rides.

» Jonesboro is known as the unofficial inspiration for *Gone with the Wind*. Here you'll find the **Road to Tara Museum** (104 N. Main St., Jonesboro; atlantastruesouth.com/gone-with-wind/road-to-tara-museum; 770-478-4800), which has exhibits on both the famous Margaret Mitchell novel and its big screen interpretation.

» **Kennesaw Mountain National Battlefield Park** (900 Kennesaw Mountain Dr., Kennesaw; nps.gov/kemo/index.htm; 770-427-4686) was the site of a real-life Civil War battle. In addition to the visitor center, which provides background information on the battle, visitors can roam the miles of trails.

▶ Tours for Every Interest

Atlanta offers more than your average bus tour. There's something to suit just about every interest.

» Thanks to the rise of film tourism in the state, **Atlanta Movie Tours** (atlantamovietours.com, 855-255-3456) visits the filming locations of blockbuster hits like *The Hunger Games*, *The Walking Dead*, and the Marvel universe, including *Ant Man* and *Captain America: Civil War*.

» Bring your appetite on **Atlanta Food Walks** (atlantafoodwalks.com, 470-223-2203), which combines city history with tasty local dishes. The Downtown Southern Food Walk goes through street-art-covered Five Points and historic Sweet Auburn, while the Grant Park Past & Future Food Walk explores the area around Oakland Cemetery.

» See the city on two wheels with **Bicycle Tours of Atlanta** (biketoursatl.com, 404-273-2558). They offer general tours of Atlanta's best neighborhoods, a street-art-focused tour, and even a tour at night! Bikes and other gear are provided.

(top) Road to Tara Museum, (bottom) Sweet Auburn Curb Market

» Taste the best brews of the beer-loving city with **Atlanta Brews Cruise** (brewscruise.com/atlanta; 404-384-6006). Every tour can be different, but you can visit Sweetwater, Monday Night, and Red Brick, as well as smaller brewpubs such as Wrecking Bar and Five Seasons.

Five Unique Sleeps in Atlanta Metro

The Atlanta area has so many hotel options from which to choose with all of the big-name brands represented. But there are also unique spots that can only be found in the city.

» The **Georgian Terrace** (659 Peachtree St. NW, Atlanta; the-georgianterrace.com; 866-845-7551) opened in 1911 and has since hosted guests such as Walt Disney, F. Scott Fitzgerald, and Calvin Coolidge. The historic hotel has been updated with a modern atrium and the amenities to go with it like a basement speakeasy.

» Pet owners will appreciate the **Highland Inn** (644 N. Highland Ave. Northeast, Atlanta; thehighlandinn.com; 404-874-5756), a cozy property that lets you stay with your four-legged friends. It's surrounded by bars and restaurants in the walkable Poncey Highland neighborhood.

» The bar's fire pit–filled patio makes the **Artmore Hotel** (1302 W. Peachtree St., Atlanta; artmorehotel.com; 404-876-6100) in Midtown a popular choice for a cocktail or a getaway. The 1924 Spanish Mediterranean building is one of a kind in the city.

» **Stonehurst Place Bed and Breakfast** (923 Piedmont Ave. NE, Atlanta; stonehurstplace.com; 404-881-0722) is one of the city's few under-the-radar inns, located in a 19th-century mansion in Midtown. The luxurious art-filled space has only six rooms, making it an intimate place to get away from the city noise.

» Farther south, the **Inn at Serenbe** (10950 Hutchesons Ferry Rd., Palmetto; serenbeinn.com; 770-463-2610) is a short drive from the airport but feels like a different place entirely. The inn sits on 900 acres of preserved land and within the complex is a top-notch restaurant and beloved local playhouse.

North Georgia Mountains

The towns of the North Georgia mountains have served as a getaway from city life for much of the state's history. Originally settled by Native American tribes, today it's the best place in the state to experience the great outdoors. This includes the Chattahoochee National Forest, Brasstown Bald, Georgia's highest peak, the Blue Ridge Mountains, and the starting point of the famed Appalachian Trail. There's a trail for just about every fitness level, but also enough to do that doesn't require you to lace up your hiking boots. This region of Georgia was also made infamous by the book and subsequent film *Deliverance*, but it was a work of fiction. Less than two hours from Atlanta, this part of Georgia requires a car to explore as transportation hubs are limited. This option will also allow more flexibility.

WHITE LIGHTNING

Mountain dew, white lightning, hooch, and moonshine are all names for the corn whiskey that's been illegally distilled in the mountains in the South. The North Georgia mountains region has its own legacy, especially around Dawson County. The government cracked down over the years, breaking up still operations; but changes in laws led to family recipes being transformed into legal moonshine. Today, visitors can sample the strong liquor at places such as **Dawsonville Moonshine Distillery** (415 Hwy. 53 E., Ste. 120, Dawsonville; dawsonvillemoonshinedistillery.com; 770-401-1211) and **Grandaddy Mimm's Moonshine Distillery and Gift Shop** (161 Pappy's Plaza, Blairsville; mimmsmoonshine.com; 706-781-1829). Try both the corn whiskey styles and the flavored varieties, especially those using Georgia peaches.

◉ Can't-Miss Landmarks and Experiences

〉〉 North Georgia is full of waterfalls and natural landmarks worth checking out. **Anna Ruby Falls** (3455 Anna Ruby Falls Rd., Helen, fs.usda.gov/recarea/conf/recarea/?recid=10517) is one of the most popular with a short but steep walk to the viewing platform. **Amicalola Falls** (418 Amicalola Falls State Park Rd., Dawsonville, amicalolafallslodge.com/ga-state-park) is another, located within a state park, as well as **Cloudland Canyon Falls** (122 Cloudland Canyon Park Rd., Rising Fawn, gastateparks.org/Cloudland-Canyon). **Tallulah Gorge** (338 Jane Hurt Yarn Rd., Tallulah Falls, gastateparks.org/TallulahGorge) has a few trails and falls, but **Minnehaha** (Off Bear Gap Rd., Tallulah Falls, exploregeorgia.org/listing/3199-minnehaha-falls-cnf) is the easiest to hike.

〉〉 This part of the state has the most state parks (gastateparks.org), which provide unique accommodations, dining, and, of course, trails for exploring. Among the best for visitors are **Amicalola Falls**, **Vogel**, **Unicoi**, and **Smithgall Woods**. Take advantage of guided hikes, GPS scavenger hunts, and family-friendly activities.

〉〉 Managed by Georgia State Parks, **Hardman Farm** (143 GA-17, Sautee Nacoochee; gastateparks.org/HardmanFarm; 706-878-1077) is an important place to visit to understand the history of the area around Sautee-Nacoochee. Located here is an Indian burial mound and the former dairy and historic home where the family of Anna Ruby Nichols, namesake of nearby Anna Ruby Falls, lived.

〉〉 The region is also known for its wineries, which span between Dahlonega, Helen, Cleveland, and beyond. Each offers different varieties of wine. **Wolf Mountain** (180 Wolf Mountain Tr., Dahlonega; wolfmountainvineyards.com; 706-867-9862) has a top-notch restaurant and the best views around, while **Yonah Mountain** (1717 GA 255, Cleveland; yonahmountainvineyards.

(clockwise from left) Hardman Farm, Yonah Mountain, Crane Creek Vineyard, Wolf Mountain

com; 706-878-5522) sits in the shadow of its namesake peak. **Crane Creek** (916 Crane Creek Rd., Young Harris; cranecreekvine yards.com; 706-379-1236) is calm and quiet, perfect for small groups. And if you're staying near Helen, **Habersham** (7025 S. Main St., Helen; habershamwinery.com; 706-878-9463) offers tastings throughout the day. If you don't want to drive between the vineyards, **Georgia VIP Wine Tours** (vipsoutherntours.com, 706-348-8747) can transport you.

» No matter what time of year you visit, there's plenty of adventurous activities to enjoy. Zip lines and ropes courses are found throughout North Georgia. **Amicalola Falls State Park** (418 Amicalola Falls Lodge Rd., Dawsonville; amicalolazipline .com; 706-265-1233) and **Unicoi State Park** (1788 GA-356, Helen; unicoizipline.com; 706-878-4740) both have "Screaming Eagle" zip line courses that soar above the trees. **North Georgia Canopy Tours** (5290 Harris Rd., Lula; northgeorgiacanopytours.com; 770-869-7272) and **Nacoochee Adventures** (7019 S. Main St., Helen; nacoocheeadventures.com; 706-878-9477) also operate nearby.

» During the summer months, borrow a tube from one of the local outfitters to float down the Chattahoochee River. **Cool River Tubing** (590 Edelweiss Strasse, Helen; coolrivertubing. com; 706-878-2665) can transport you and your tube. If you're looking for more high octane adventure, try a rafting trip with **Southeastern Expeditions** (7350 US 76, Clayton; southeastern-expeditions.com; 800-868-7238), the company that set up on the Chattooga River after *Deliverance* was released. Fly Fishing is another way to experience the rivers of the region.

Off the Beaten Path

» Home to Cabbage Patch Kids, **Babyland General Hospital** (300 NOK Dr., Cleveland; babylandgeneral.com; 706-865-2171) is where these "babies" are born. Creator Xavier Roberts founded the brand nearby and today visitors can adopt their own dolls.

(clockwise) Goats on the Roof, Babyland General Hospital, Alpine Helen

» As the name implies, **Goats on the Roof** (3026 Hwy. 441 S., Tiger; goats-on-the-roof.com; 706-782-2784) is a bizarre roadside attraction where curious passersby can detour to feed the goats in a pulley system. You can also shop for souvenirs and purchase Amish furnishings and homemade fudge.

» The entire town of **Helen** (helenga.org) could be called "offbeat" thanks to local businesses that in 1969 decided to transform it into an Alpine village. Most structures have a similar design and restaurants serve authentic German fare. They also boast one of the country's biggest Oktoberfest celebrations.

» **The Foxfire Museum** (98 Foxfire Ln., Mountain City; foxfire. org; 706-746-5828) has documented the history of this part of Appalachia. Located in 10 historic pioneer log cabins since 1966, the museum displays folk art, artifacts, and tools from the people who have lived here for the last century.

» Located near Dahlonega, **Chestatee Wildlife Preserve** (469 Old Dahlonega Hwy., Dahlonega; chestateewildlife.com; 678-859-6820) is a non-profit wildlife facility that was used as a filming location in *The Hunger Games*. Established in 1992, most of the over 150 animals were rescued by the Department of Natural Resources.

» Learn about the rich arts history at the **Folk Pottery Museum** (283 GA 255, Sautee Nacoochee; folkpotterymuseum.com; 706-878-3300), which is a part of the Sautee Nacoochee Center, a gallery and arts space. The museum documents the pottery traditions from those of early Native American to the present.

» Dahlonega is known around the state as being home to one of the country's early gold rushes and you can still go panning here at **Consolidated Gold Mine** (185 Consolidated Gold Mine Rd., Dahlonega; consolidatedgoldmine.com; 706-864-8473). If you don't strike it rich, you can see gold covering one of the towers on the campus of the **University of North Georgia** (82 College Circle, Dahlonega; ung.edu; 706-864-1400) or at the **Dahlonega Gold Museum** (1 Public Square N., Dahlonega; gastateparks.org/ DahlonegaGoldMuseum; 706-864-2257).

Five Unique Sleeps in North Georgia

>> Unicoi State Park (1788 Highway 356, Helen; unicoilodge.com; 706-878-2201) in Helen has a wide range of accommodations, but their wine barrel cabins are the most unique. The lofted spaces have kitchens, bedrooms, and even a porch overlooking the lake.

Wine Barrel Cabin Unicoi State Park

>> Adventurous travelers will want to stay a night or two at the **Len Foote Hike Inn** (280 Amicalola Falls State Park Rd., Dawsonville; hike-inn.com; (800) 581-8032), which is only accessible via a five-mile hike through the mountains from Amicalola Falls State Park. But once there, guests are met with comfortable beds and family-style meals, popular with Appalachian Trail thru-hikers.

>> Similarly, the **Barefoot Hills** (7693 U.S. Highway 19 N., Dahlonega; barefoothills.com; 470-788-8044) is popular with hikers for its range of options, starting with the hiker hostel dorms and going up to private cabins and luxurious suites.

>> Embrace the kitsch at Helen's **Valhalla Resort Hotel** (688 Bahn Innsbruck, Helen; valhallaresorthotel.com; 706-878-2200), a castle-like property with suites, a golf course, and an in-house spa.

>> Another favorite is the secluded **Glen Ella Springs Inn** (1789 Bear Gap Rd., Clarkesville; glenella.com; 706-754-7295) in Clarkesville. The inn has 16 guest rooms, a first-class restaurant, and a location ideal for disconnecting.

Georgia Coast

Settlers to Georgia arrived first in the communities on the coast, making this area the oldest. In fact, James Oglethorpe and his group of English settlers came to Yamacraw Bluff near present-day Savannah in 1733. They worked with local tribes and later forts were built in Savannah and St. Simon's Island to defend against the Spanish to the south. The slave trade brought Africans to work on the coastal rice, cotton, and indigo plantations in the 1750s. The coast was also the site of a number of battles over the years, including those in the Revolutionary War. Charming Savannah serves as a hub for travelers looking to explore the Georgia coast, as it is home to one of the country's busiest ports and a mid-sized airport. Savannah is made up of dozens of tree-lined squares on a grid system and is easily walkable. It has been featured in countless films such as *Forrest Gump* and *Midnight in the Garden of Good and Evil*. The hospitality city that served as the state's first capital is also where you go for a good meal at one of the family-style eateries.

GULLAH GEECHEE CULTURES

The people brought over from West Africa in the 1700s settled in the Sea Islands of Georgia and are now known as the "Geechee" people, with "Gullah" representing those who live in South Carolina. Because of the distance between these coastal communities and the rest of the mainland, these groups of people from similar ethnic groups formed a culture that incorporated their traditional dishes, language, and religion. Sapelo Island is Georgia's hub for Geechee culture, especially after St. Simon's and Jekyll Islands have become more developed. Sweet grass baskets made traditionally by these coastal people are a popular souvenir.

📍 Can't-Miss Landmarks and Activities

» Girl scouts and history buffs should add the **Juliette Gordon Lowe Birthplace** (10 E. Oglethorpe Ave., Savannah; juliettegordonlowbirthplace.org; 912-233-4501) to their Savannah itineraries. Visitors will learn about the woman herself, her family life, and what inspired her to start the Girl Scouts. Highlights include early uniforms and her vast art collection.

» **Bonaventure Cemetery** (330 Bonaventure Rd., Thunderbolt; bonaventurehistorical.org; 912-651-6843) is one of the creepier attractions in Savannah, famously mentioned in the book *Midnight in the Garden of Good and Evil*. Notable locals such as Johnny Mercer and Conrad Aiken are buried amongst the Spanish moss-draped trees. You won't find *The Bird Girl* statue, which was featured on the cover of the book, here anymore but many of the graves bear sculptures are markers.

» Also known for its connection with "the book," as it's known locally, is the **Mercer Williams House** (429 Bull St., Savannah; mercerhouse.com; 912-236-6352) that has tried to separate itself

(above) Juliette Gordon Lowe Birthplace,
(right) Bonaventure Cemetery

from the crime that took place there. It was originally built in the 1860s and later owned by a relative of Georgia-born musician Johnny Mercer.

» Perhaps the most photographed spot in Savannah, **Wormsloe State Historic Site** (7601 Skidaway Rd., Savannah; gastateparks. org/Wormsloe; 912-353-3023) welcomes visitors down a majestic avenue of oaks. Once inside, you can walk among the nature trails and around the ruins of the tabby Colonial home of Noble Jones. A museum showcases artifacts from the time period and costumed interpreters share about the history.

◢ Off the Beaten Path

» Savannah is also home to America's only **Prohibition Museum** (209 W. St. Julian St., Savannah; americanprohibitionmuseum. com; 912-220-1249), honoring the city's wild past. Exhibits detail the rise of the Temperance Movement and Carry Nation, passage of the 18th amendment, and the creative ways imbibers got their fix.

» Learn about the endangered species at the **Georgia Sea Turtle Center** (214 Stable Rd., Jekyll Island; georgiaseaturtlecenter. org; 912-635-4444), where turtles are rescued and rehabilitated before being released back into the wild. You can watch turtle feedings throughout the day and catch program lectures. There's also an interactive exhibit about the coastal Georgia ecosystems.

» **Driftwood Beach** (Off Beach View Drive; goldenisles.com /listing/driftwood-beach) on the westernmost point of Jekyll Island is like a natural playground where driftwood branches and sun-bleached trees cover the sand. Photographers set up shots of the sunset while kids climb all over.

» Revolutionary War hero Nathanael Greene's widow constructed **Dungeness**, her home on Cumberland Island. The four-story mansion didn't survive, but a century later, Thomas

(clockwise) Wormsloe State Historic Site, Driftwood Beach, Georgia Sea Turtle Center

Carnegie and his wife built another home on the original foundation. Their version of Dungeness also was destroyed in 1959, but now the ruins are a popular landmark on the island. The **Cumberland Island Seashore** (nps.gov/cuis; 912-882-4336) itself begs to be explored, with its untamed landscapes and wild horses.

» Step back in time at **Reynolds Mansion on Sapelo Island** (1100 Autobahn, Sapelo Island; gastateparks.org/Reynolds-Mansion; 912-485-2299), a former tabby mansion built in 1802 by Thomas Spalding. It was damaged in the Civil War, but was rebuilt later by another owner and then sold to tobacco heir Richard Reynolds. Since his death in 1964, the mansion has served as an estuarine research facility.

» The arts have a home in Savannah, with a number of museums located around the city. The **Telfair Academy** (121 Barnard St., Savannah; telfair.org/visit/Telfair; 912-790-8800) is a Neoclassical mansion that now holds American and European works. The most famous piece there is *The Bird Girl* from the cover of *Mid-*

night in the Garden of Good and Evil. **Jepson Center for the Arts** houses the museum's modern works and the nearby Savannah College of Art and Design has their own space. **SCAD Museum of Art** (601 Turner Blvd., Savannah; scadmoa.org; 912-525-7191) showcases student pieces as well as traveling exhibitions.

Telfair Academy

» The coast is home to a few of Georgia's five remaining lighthouses. **Tybee Island Light Station and Museum** (30 Meddin Dr., Tybee Island; tybeelighthouse.org; 912-786-5801) outside of Savannah is the state's oldest and tallest. Built in 1736, the complex still has original structures such as the Light Keeper's Cottages. To the south, the current **St. Simon's Island Lighthouse Museum** (610 Beachview Dr., Saint Simons Island; coastalgeorgiahistory.org/visit/st-simons-lighthouse-museum; 912-638-4666) was built in 1872 and still operates. Visitors can climb to the top to see the Victorian design and museum.

⚑ Tours for Every Interest

» Dine in Atlanta like a local with **Savannah Taste Experience** (savannahtasteexperience.com, 912-221-4439), a company that offers tours of some of the city's most unique eateries. Among the highlights on their two tours are British savory pies at Pie Society, the fried chicken at The Pirate House, and the famous Conquistador sandwich at Zunzi's.

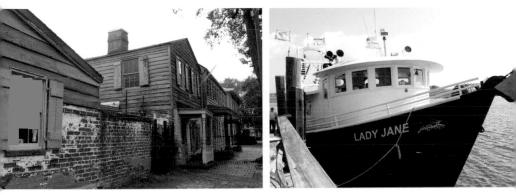

(left) Pirate's House Restaurant, (right) Lady Jane Shrimping Boat

» You don't have to get inside a carriage or hire a private guide to learn about the city's history. **Free Savannah Walking Tours** (freesavannahtours.com, 470-231-9247) operates 90-minute tours led by history buffs who point out landmarks like Chippewa Square and the Forsyth Park fountain. The tours themselves are free, but you'll want to tip your guides.

» Hop aboard the **Lady Jane Shrimp Boat** (shrimpcruise.com, 912-265-5711) with Captain Credle in Brunswick. Here guests can learn about the area's seafood industry and sample fresh shrimp boiled onsite. You might also get to see other creatures such as horseshoe crabs and sea turtles before they are returned to the sea. They also offer a blue dolphin spotting cruise.

💤 Five Unique Sleeps along Georgia's Coast

》 The Georgia coast has all sorts of accommodations, whether you're looking to get back to nature by camping on a sparsely inhabited island or to stay at one of the world's most luxurious resorts, brushing shoulders with the rich and famous.

》 Camping on **Cumberland Island** (101 Wheeler St., St. Marys; nps.gov/cuis/planyourvisit/camping.htm; 912-882-4336) and **Sapelo Island** (Route 1, Box 1500, Darien; gastateparks.org/ReynoldsMansion; 912-485-2299) are surreal experiences, as you can only access the barrier islands by boat.

》 **Little St. Simon's Island** (1000 Hampton River Club Marina Dr., Saint Simons Island; littlestsimonsisland.com; 888-733-5774) has the same opportunities to connect with nature, but in an all-inclusive rustic lodge setting. Visitors can also come for the day.

》 **The Jekyll Island Club** (371 Riverview Dr., Jekyll Island; jekyllclub.com; 855-787-3857) has long been a playground for the well-to-do, including the Rockefellers, Carnegies, and Vanderbilts. It was here that the first transcontinental phone call took place and where the Federal Reserve system was brainstormed.

》 Savannah is known for its historic inns, but it's the **Mansion on Forsyth** (700 Drayton St., Savannah; mansiononforsythpark.com; 912-238-5158) that consistently wins awards for its luxurious hospitality. The former mansion is furnished in antiques and artwork and runs a popular cooking school.

》 If you're looking for a funkier stay, **Thunderbird Inn** (611 W. Oglethorpe Ave., Savannah; thethunderbirdinn.com; 912-232-2661) is reminiscent of the roadside motels of the 1950s. They have old-school toiletries like VO5 and daily breakfast of Krispy Kreme doughnuts.

(top) The Jekyll Island Club, (bottom) Long sandy beach on Jekyll Island

Kentucky horses

Kentucky

Forever connected with horses and bourbon, the "Bluegrass State" of Kentucky was explored by people such as Daniel Boone before becoming a state in 1792. It has long been a place for independence and a "Wild West" attitude, where the Hatfields and McCoys battled it out and where Fort Knox holds the largest gold reserve in the world. Kentucky has been home to Abraham Lincoln and Muhammad Ali, as well as the Shakers religious movement and moonshiners on the run from the law. Even today, in a region still under strict laws managing alcohol production, the state is leading the charge in craft breweries and distilleries as well as hemp production. Western Kentucky is the original home of bluegrass music, but modern musicians flock to Louisville every year for the Forecastle Festival. The towns of Appalachian Kentucky vary greatly from those along the Ohio River.

15 Things to Taste in Kentucky

There's no way to limit the delicious dishes you'll eat around Kentucky to 15 items, but when traveling through the state, be sure to brake for these.

1. BBQ Mutton Plate, **Moonlite BBQ Inn** (2840 W. Parrish Ave., Owensboro; moonlite.com; 270-684-8143)

2. Biscuits and gravy, **Judy's Castle** (1302 US 31 BYP, Bowling Green; 270-842-8736)

3. Barbecue sandwich, **Starnes Barbecue** (1008 Joe Clifton Dr., Paducah; 270-444-9555)

4. Patti Brown, **Patti's 1880s Settlement** (1793 J H O'Bryan Ave., Grand Rivers; pattis1880s.com; 270-362-8844)

5. The Stack, **Boyce General Store** (10551 Woodburn Allen Springs Rd., Alvaton; burgerandpies.com; 270-842-1900)

6. Hot Brown, **The Brown Hotel** (335 W. Broadway, Louisville; brownhotel.com; 502-583-1234)

7. Smoked St. Louis Ribs, **Talbott Tavern** (101 W. Stephen Foster Ave., Bardstown; talbotts.com; 502-348-3494)

8. Fish sandwich, **Suburban Social Club** (3901 South 3rd St., Louisville; suburban740.org/famous-fish-fry; 502-368-3161)

9. Lamb fries, **Halls on the River** (1225 Athens Boonesboro Rd., Winchester; hallsontheriver.com; 859-527-6620)

10. Derby Pie, **Winchell's** (348 Southland Dr., Lexington; winchellsrestaurant.com; 859-278-9424)

11. Cheeseburger, **Corner Cafe** (214 Hamilton Ave., Augusta; 606-756-3219)

12. Tater tot waffle, **Press on Monmouth** (421 Monmouth St., Newport; pressonmonmouthnky.com; 859-261-3397)

13. Meatloaf, **Greyhound Tavern** (2500 Dixie Hwy., Covington; greyhoundtavern.com; 859-331-3767)

14. Spoon bread, **Boone Tavern** (100 Main St. N., Berea; boonetavernhotel.com; 800-366-9358)

15. Fried chicken, **Harland Sanders Cafe** (688 US Highway 25 W., Corbin, 606-528-2163)

Eastern Kentucky

Although a lesser visited part of Kentucky, the Appalachian region in the Eastern side of the state was the area originally explored by Daniel Boone and his contemporaries. The passage to the mountains became known as Cumberland Gap. Forests have been inhabited for thousands of years, leaving behind artifacts and petroglyphs that can still be seen by visitors today. Outdoor enthusiasts flock to the region for its recreation activities. In this section, the towns east of Daniel Boone National Forest are included, as well as the Ohio River communities between Lexington and Cincinnati, where the major airport is located.

KENTUCKY COLONELS

At ease, Soldier. Colonel Sanders isn't the only one. The title of Kentucky Colonel is honorary, the highest bestowed upon citizens by the governor. First used in 1813, it originally involved military service, but later became a society in 1931. Their social events coincided with the Kentucky Derby. A change in leadership attracted more colonels, including celebrities. Notable Kentucky Colonels range from athletes to musicians to game show hosts, both male and female, including Fred Astaire, Betty White, and John Glenn. But there are also citizens in the ranks of the 85,000 colonels. Today, the organization supports local charities.

⊛ Can't-Miss Landmarks

» Visit the Augusta home of the acclaimed actress at the **Rosemary Clooney House** (106 E. Riverside Dr., Augusta; rosemary-clooney.org; 502-384-5346). The star of *White Christmas* and aunt of George Clooney lived in the home from 1980 until her death in 2002. The museum has a large collection of memorabilia from her life and career.

» Deep in Kentucky coal country lies **Butcher Hollow** (Millers Creek Road, Van Lear; 606-789-3397), the birthplace of "Coal Miner's Daughter" Loretta Lynn. Start at nearby Webb's Grocery, which has a collection of memorabilia related to the singer, before arranging a tour of the simple wooden cabin.

» Travelers from all over the world come to Pike County for the **Hatfield McCoy Driving Tour** (tourpikecounty.com; 800-844-7453) to see the sites of the most famous family feud. Brochures and apps send you to former McCoy homes and places related to the generations-long conflict.

Cumberland Falls

» No matter your stance on the environmental impact, there's no denying the role of coal mining in Kentucky's history. Stop by the **Kentucky Coal Mining Museum** (231 Main St., Benham; benhamky.org/museum; 606-848-1530), housed in a former company commissary, to learn about how the industry began. Don't miss the Portal 31 tour of a real mine.

» Eastern Kentucky has miles of breathtaking forest, especially the **Red River Gorge** (1700 Bypass Rd., Winchester; www.fs.usda .gov/detail/dbnf/specialplaces; 859-745-3100) section of **Daniel Boone Forest, Natural Bridge State Park** (2135 Natural Bridge Rd., Slade; parks.ky.gov/parks/resortparks/natural-bridge; 606-663-2214), and **Cumberland Falls** (7351 Hwy 90, Corbin; parks.ky.gov/parks/resortparks/cumberland-falls, 606-528-4121). Waterfalls, rock climbing, hiking, and wildlife are just a few of the draws.

» Stretching into Tennessee and Virginia, **Cumberland Gap National Historical Park** (91 Bartlett Park Rd., Middlesboro; nps. gov/cuga/index.htm; 606-248-2817) is the southeasternmost point in the state. Learn about the historic area at the visitor

Cumberland Gap National Historical Park

center before touring the Hensley Settlement, which retains original buildings from 1903. You can also tour the Gap Cave.

» The **Kentucky Music Hall of Fame** (2590 Richmond St., Mt. Vernon; kentuckymusichalloffame.com; 606-256-1000) honors the performers who left their mark on the state through their songs. Artifacts date back to the 1700s, including belongings from inductees such as Loretta Lynn, Wynonna Judd, and Sam Bush.

🔄 Off the Beaten Path

» Few know about the **Franklin Sousley Monument** (Highway 170, Elizaville; 606-845-1223), which honors the Kentucky native who was one of the men who raised the flag at Iwo Jima, captured in the timeless image. Stop by Elizaville Cemetery to pay your respects.

» Located in the small town of Manchester, the **Ancient Petroglyphs Rock** (Rawlings-Stinson Park, 239 Memorial Dr., Manchester; 606-598-3456) is an unlikely stop where you can see eight Old World alphabets carved into a rock that pre-date the arrival of Columbus.

» This region has the majority of Kentucky's 13 remaining covered bridges. Although most are no longer open to vehicles, **Cabin Creek** (KY 984, Tollesboro; kentuckytourism.com), **Johnson Creek** (KY 1029, Mount Olivet; kentuckytourism.com), **Ringos Mill** (KY 158, Flemingsburg; kentuckytourism.com), **Grange City** (KY 111, Flemingsburg; kentuckytourism.com), and **Goddard** (KY 32, Flemingsburg; kentuckytourism.com) are all open to the public.

» A number of facilities educate visitors about pioneer life in Kentucky. **Mefford's Fort** (Old Main Street, Old Washington Maysville; 606-759-7411) contains a 1787 log cabin constructed out of flatboat pieces, which was home to a family of 15. **Campbell County Log Cabin Museum** (Box 890, Clayridge Road,

Kentucky Artisan Center

Alexandria; 859-635-5913) in Alexandria is open seasonally and has reconstructed log cabins and antique farm equipment. Near Paintsville Lake State Park is the **Mountain HomePlace** (445 KY 2275, Staffordsville; 606-297-1850), a working 1850s farm with a one-room school, blacksmith shop, and barn. Costumed interpreters share the stories of the time period.

» The Appalachian region of Kentucky is known for its arts and handicrafts. The **Godbey Appalachian Cultural and Fine Arts Center** (700 College Rd., Cumberland; southeast.kctcs.edu; 606-589-2145) in Cumberland has exhibits on the art, music, and oral histories as well as classes and performances. The **Kentucky Artisan Center** (200 Artisan Way, Berea; kentucky artisancenter.ky.gov; 859-985-5448) highlights the state's makers in a 25,000-square-foot space of galleries and shops.

» One of the Cincinnati area's top attractions is actually in Kentucky. **Newport Aquarium** (1 Dave Cowens Dr., Newport; newportaquarium.com; 800-406-3474) is an accredited facility that educates visitors on stingrays, alligators, seahorses, penguins, and other marine creatures.

Newport Aquarium

» Where else in the world can you find a museum devoted to ventriloquism? The **Vent Haven Museum** (33 W. Maple Ave., Fort Mitchell; venthaven.org; 859-341-0461) in Fort Mitchell started as a private collection of dummies and memorabilia that now includes over 900 pieces from the 19th century to the present.

» Covington's **Behringer-Crawford Museum** (1600 Montague Rd., Covington; bcmuseum.org; 859-491-4003) sprawls between multiple floors of a 19th-century home. Exhibits feature the early days of settlement on the Ohio River, the importance of the railroad, and the music of the region.

» The **National Underground Railroad Museum** (38 W. 4th St., Maysville; kentuckytourism.com/national-underground-rail-road-museum/2081; 606-564-3200) in Maysville is located in a house that was used to hide runaway slaves. The museum is open seasonally and features exhibits on slavery and the leadup to the Civil War.

» Kentucky's **state park sites** (parks.ky.gov) are also worth a visit. Carter Caves is one of the lesser visited caverns, overshadowed by Mammoth Cave. Big Bone Lick State Park interprets the prehistoric creatures that once roamed the prairies of the Bluegrass State. Bison are frequently spotted here today.

▶ Tours for Every Interest

》 Appalachian Kentucky is ideal for outdoor adventures, especially zip lines. **Tree Top Adventures** (treetopadventureky.com, 606-878-9734) operates in London, while **Screaming Raptor Ziplines** and **Canopy Tour** are part of the **Creation Museum** (creationmuseum.org/zip-lines; 888-582-4253), with some of the longest zip lines in the region. **Black Mountain Thunder Zipline** (blackmountainthunder.com, 606-837-3205) in Harlan County is another favorite, allowing guests to zip at 60 miles per hour. And the **Red River Gorge Zipline** (redrivergorgezipline.com; 606-668-6222) provides the best views around.

》 **Riverside Food Tours** (riversidefoodtours.com; 513-289-0035) operates in both Covington and Cincinnati, showcasing the area's best restaurants. The Mainstrasse food tour is their most popular, embracing the German traditions of the Ohio River.

》 Learn about the surprising history of the Ohio River town on the **Newport Gangster Tour** (americanlegacytours.com/newport-gangster-tour; 859-951-8560), which focuses on mobsters, gamblers, and "ladies of the night." Tours start at the city's dueling piano bar.

》 The species of elk that live in the Appalachian region of Kentucky have diminished over the years, but the state is making efforts to restore them. Tours to see them leave from **Jenny Wiley State Resort Park** (parks.ky.gov/parks/resortparks/jenny-wiley) and include transportation and breakfast.

》 **BB Riverboats** (bbriverboats.com; 800-261-8586) operates dining and sightseeing cruises out of Newport on their riverboats with guided narration and live music.

Five Unique Sleeps
in Eastern Kentucky

» **Christopher's Bed and Breakfast** (604 Poplar St., Bellevue; christophersbb.com; 859-491-9354) is set in a historic church and located less than a mile from downtown Cincinnati. It retains stained-glass windows, Gothic doorways, and hardwood floors in the three guest suites.

» Embrace the kitsch at **Wildwood Inn** (7809 US 42, Florence; wildwoodinnky.com; 859-371-6300), which has themed rooms such as the Arctic Cave, the Happy Days Suite, and the Pirate Ship. It's close to Cincinnati attractions and has an indoor waterfall.

» Set on the campus of Berea College, the historic **Boone Tavern** (100 Main St. N., Berea; boonetavernhotel.com; 800-366-9358) combines old and new with a building that dates back to 1909 that has become LEED certified. Rooms and suites include hand-crafted wood furnishings.

» **Earthjoy Tree Climbing Adventures** (3400 Bridgeville Rd., Brooksville; climbtreeswithearthjoy.com; 859-635-0320) in Germantown has a treehouse featured on *Treehouse Masters* in which guests can spend the night. It's completely furnished but doesn't have cell service, so plan on disconnecting and spending the afternoon soaring through the trees.

» The knotty pine paneling and exposed beams of the DuPont Lodge at **Cumberland Falls State Resort** (7351 Hwy. 90, Corbin; parks.ky.gov/parks/resortparks/cumberland-falls; 606-528-4121) make it a popular choice for non-campers, especially the observation deck overlooking the park. Campsites and cabins are also available.

Lexington, Louisville, and Central Kentucky

Contrary to popular belief, Louisville is not actually the capital of Kentucky. It could, however, certainly be considered its heart. Located on the Ohio River, LOOH-uh-vull (as it is pronounced by locals) is a thriving metropolis, becoming the state's largest city before the Civil War that was inhabited by German and Irish immigrants. Louisville and Lexington both have airports that service the region. Lexington is the state's second-biggest city and, while there are certainly those rolling hills and fenced paddocks where legends like Man O'War and Secretariat roamed, it's also a college town. The University of Kentucky and Transylvania University are the largest. And the Derby isn't the only race in the state, as Keeneland is another local favorite. Harrodsburg was settled in 1774 as an English settlement, later inhabited by the Shakers. Bardstown is the second oldest town in the state, home to most of the distilleries. The capital city of Frankfort also has a few distilleries.

CRAFT IS KING

Central Kentucky has always been associated with alcohol, but these days there's more to it than you think. Old school bourbon distilleries such as **Woodford Reserve** (woodfordreserve. com) and **Buffalo Trace** (buffalotrace.com) still thrive, but it's not just the "good ole boys" and "pappys" distilling bourbon anymore. The spirit must be produced in this part of Kentucky by law to be called "bourbon." Marianne Barnes became the state's first master distiller since Prohibition in 2016, later launching the **Castle & Key** (castleandkey.com) brand. Mother-daughter duo Joyce and Autumn Nethery opened **Jeptha Creed Distilling** (jepthacreed.com). But there's also something for craft beer lovers as breweries have popped up around the state, creating a "Brewgrass Trail" (visitlex.com/about/discover/flavors/brewgrass-trail). **West Sixth** and **Blue Stallion** breweries in Lexington, **Apocalypse** in Louisville, and **Rooster Brewing** in Paris are favorites.

Buffalo Trace Bourbon

◉ Can't-Miss Landmarks

» Home to one of baseball's most iconic items, the **Louisville Slugger Museum and Factory** (800 W. Main St., Louisville; sluggermuseum.com; 877-775-8443) welcomes visitors with a 120-foot exact scale replica of the bat used by legend Babe Ruth. Tours discuss the process of making the bats and the famous players who have used them.

» The city's native son is honored at the **Muhammad Ali Center** (144 N. 6th St., Louisville; alicenter.org; 502-584-9254), a museum about "The Greatest," including his career highlights and controversial moments. Exhibits allow visitors to try their hand at training with the boxer and even reenacting his iconic photo.

» It's Derby Day year-round at the **Kentucky Derby Museum** (704 Central Ave., Louisville; derbymuseum.org; 502-637-1111) at Churchill Downs, which allows guests to learn about the "fastest two minutes in sports" without placing any bets. Admission includes a tour of the racetrack and exhibits on famous Derby winners.

» Statesman Henry Clay, known as the "Great Compromiser" lived at **Ashland** (120 Sycamore Rd., Lexington; henryclay.org; 859-266-8581), an 18-room mansion in Lexington. Tours are open to the grounds and the house, which has been restored to how it looked when the family lived there with original furnishings.

(clockwise) Louisville Slugger Museum and Factory, Ashland Mansion, Muhammad Ali Center, The Kentucky Derby

(left) Abraham Lincoln Birthplace National Historical Park, (right) Shaker Village of Pleasant Hill

» The **Shaker Village of Pleasant Hill** (3501 Lexington Rd., Harrodsburg; shakervillageky.org; 859-734-5411) in Harrodsburg was the settlement of a religious movement that believed in chastity and community cooperation. Buildings resemble how they would have looked during that time period with demonstrations on Shaker crafts, a restaurant, and activities such as horseback riding, hiking, and guided walks.

» Lexington's Smithsonian-affiliated **Kentucky Horse Park** (4089 Iron Works Pkwy., Lexington; kyhorsepark.com; 859-233-4303) teaches visitors about the area's long legacy of horse racing. The International Museum of the Horse has exhibits on horse racing traditions in America, China, and Arabia. Also within the park is the American Saddlebred Museum, which has the world's largest collection of Saddlebred artifacts such as photographs, tack, and trophies.

» Illinois may be the "land of Lincoln," but Kentucky has many ties to the president. The **Abraham Lincoln Birthplace National Historical Park** (2995 Lincoln Farm Rd., Hodgenville; nps.gov/abli/index.htm; 270-358-3137) contains a memorial as well as a replica of the cabin where he was born. His boyhood home at Knob Creek is also included within the park. If you haven't had enough Lincoln history, there's also the **Lincoln Museum** (66 Lincoln Sq., Hodgenville; lincolnmuseum-ky.org; 270-358-3163);

Lincoln Homestead State Park (5079 Lincoln Park Rd., Spring-field, parks.ky.gov/parks/recreationparks/lincoln-homestead; 859-336-7461), where his mother grew up; and the **Lincoln Legacy Museum** (111 E. Main St., Springfield; kentuckytourism.com/lincoln/lincoln-legacy-museum/12106; 859-336-5410).

» Visit the childhood home of his wife at the **Mary Todd Lincoln House** (578 W. Main St., Lexington; mtlhouse.org; 859-233-9999) in Lexington. The 1800s brick building opened to the public in 1977, making it the first museum devoted to a First Lady. It has items belonging to the Todds and Lincolns.

» **My Old Kentucky Home State Park** (501 E. Stephen Foster Ave., Bardstown; parks.ky.gov/parks/recreationparks/old-ky-home; 502-348-3502) in Bardstown includes the Federal-style house where Stephen Foster stayed that inspired the state song. You can tour the historic home and catch a performance of *The Stephen Foster Story*, the state's longest-running outdoor drama.

» The **Kentucky African-American Heritage Center** (1701 W. Muhammad Ali Blvd., Louisville; kcaah.org; 502-583-4100) in Louisville recognizes the contributions of African-Americans in the state through exhibits and performances.

» Known for his inventions such as the light bulb, Thomas Edison is celebrated at the inventor's former residence, now the **Thomas Edison House** (729 E. Washington St., Louisville; historichomes.org/thomas-edison-house; 502-585-5247), a Louisville museum devoted to his period as a Western Union telegraph operator. His room has been recreated to how it looked during those years.

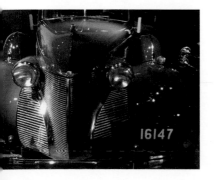

» The notable general is recognized at the **Patton Museum** (4554 Fayette Ave., Fort Knox, generalpatton.org; 502-624-3812); at Fort Knox south of Louisville. Exhibits focus on his life and career, but also include antique weaponry and other artifacts.

Patton Museum

» Perhaps the biggest reason people travel to Kentucky is for the **Bourbon Trail** (kybourbontrail.com). Established by the Kentucky Distillers Association in 1999, the official route contains only a few of the dozens of distilleries in this area. The official passport allows imbibers to earn a free t-shirt after visiting all ten, including **Angel's Envy**, **Bulleit**, **Evan Williams**, **Four Roses**, **Heaven Hill**, **Jim Beam**, **Maker's Mark**, **Town Branch**, **Wild Turkey**, and **Woodford Reserve**.

» New distilleries open frequently, but don't forget **Buffalo Trace Distillery** (113 Great Buffalo Trace, Frankfort; buffalotracedistillery.com; 502-696-5926) in Frankfort, which operated continuously through Prohibition creating "medicinal liquor." It's also popular for the cult-like following of Pappy Van Winkle.

(left) Buffalo Trace Bourbon Water Tower, (below) Horse Farm in Lexington

⬙ Off the Beaten Path

>> Horse farm tours are a highlight of visiting this part of Kentucky and you'll find dozens of companies and farms that offer them. But **Second Stride** (7204 Hwy 329, Crestwood; secondstride.org; 502-241-8440), **Our Mims** (2810 Millersburg Ruddles Mill Rd., Paris; ourmims.org; 859-227-6304), and **Old Friends Farm** (1841 Paynes Depot Rd., Georgetown; oldfriendsequine.org; 502-863-1775) house retired thoroughbred horses that need love too.

>> Learn about Kentucky's favorite liquor at the **Oscar Getz Museum of Whiskey History** (114 N. 5th St., Bardstown; whiskeymuseum.com; 502-348-2999) in Bardstown. Located on the main floor of Spalding Hall, the museum features rare artifacts such as antique moonshine stills and medicinal bottles.

>> Over 200 miniatures are in the **Great American Dollhouse Museum** (344 Swope Dr., Danville; thedollhousemuseum.com; 859-236-1883) in Danville that range from early American settlement to the present. The building itself is a Works Progress Administration structure.

>> The diverse collection in Louisville's **Frazier History Museum** (829 W. Main St., Louisville; fraziermuseum.org; 502-753-5663) has three floors of exhibits, including surprising finds from the UK Royal Armoury, Teddy Roosevelt's "Big Stick," and letters from Jesse James. A popular section covers Kentucky's bourbon history.

>> Louisville's most impressive art collection is found at the **Speed Art Museum** (2035 S. 3rd St., Louisville; speedmuseum.org; 502-634-2700), which boasts over 13,000 works that span 6,000 years. Highlights include Egyptian artifacts, contemporary

art, and early Kentucky-made furnishings. The nearby **Kentucky Museum of Art and Craft** (715 W. Main St., Louisville; kmacmuseum.org; 502-589-0102), which covers folk art and contemporary works, is also worth a visit.

» The **Thomas D. Clark Center for Kentucky History** (100 W. Broadway, Frankfort; history.ky.gov/visit/thomas-d-clark-center-kentucky-history; 502-564-1792) in Frankfort covers all aspects of the state's history, including Lincoln memorabilia, homemade quilts, and Kentucky-made products. The center also includes entry to the Old State Capitol and Kentucky Military History Museum.

» Founded in 1968 by jewelry designer George Headley and his wife Barbara Whitney, the **Headley-Whitney Museum** (4435 Old Frankfort Pike, Lexington; headley-whitney.org; 859-255-6653) in Lexington displays their eccentric collection of art, dollhouses, and rare jewels.

» Owned by a car dealership family from Elizabethtown, the **Swope's Cars of Yesteryear Museum** (1012 N. Dixie Ave., Elizabethtown; swopemuseum.com; 270-763-6175) features classic automobiles from the 1900s to the 1960s. The collection includes a 1914 Model T, a 1956 Thunderbird, and a 1936 Rolls Royce Phantom III.

» With multiple attractions in one, **Louisville Mega Cavern** (1841 Taylor Ave., Louisville; louisvillemegacavern.com; 877-614-6342) offers underground zip lining, tram rides through the cave, an underground mountain bike park, and a ropes course. The cave itself operated as a limestone quarry for 42 years before opening to the public.

» Built around 1792, the Georgian home known as **Locust Grove** (561 Blankenbaker Ln., Louisville; locustgrove.org; 502-897-9845) welcomed guests ranging from John James Audubon to Lewis and Clark to James Monroe. Tours of the house and grounds are offered.

» The **Museum of the American Printing House for the Blind** (1839 Frankfort Ave., Louisville; aph.org/museum; 502-895-2405) in Louisville recognizes the publishing house that produces books and Braille materials for the visually impaired. Visitors can see the factory where the "Talking Book" products are made.

» See the stunning landscapes of Central Kentucky through the windows of the **Bluegrass Scenic Railroad and Museum** (175 Beasley Rd., Versailles; bluegrassrailroad.com; 859-873-2476), which operates 90-minute rides from Versailles. Their museum has train memorabilia.

» The brave can visit the **Waverly Hills Sanatorium** (4400 Paralee Ln., Louisville; therealwaverlyhills.com; 502-933-2142) in Louisville, considered to be one of the most haunted places in America. The former tuberculosis hospital was left abandoned to decay for years, but now has guided tours during part of the year.

Tours for Every Interest

» **Horse Farm Tours** (horsefarmtours.com, 800-976-1034) operates out of Lexington and visits horse farms where thoroughbreds live and train, the Keeneland race course, and other area attractions over the course of three hours.

» Both public and private tours are offered by **Mint Julep Tours** (mintjuleptours.com, 502-583-1433), which focuses on the Louisville's breweries, the Bourbon Trail, and the best of the Derby City.

» Visit the spookiest sites in the city with **Louisville Ghost Tours** (louisvilleghosttours.com, 888-844-3999), which offers 90-minute excursions nightly.

» Passengers aboard the *Belle of Louisville* (belleoflouisville.org, 866-832-0011) can travel the way early visitors did: by steamboat. The two ships in the fleet run lunch and dinner sightseeing cruises.

Keeneland Horse Race

» **Food Guide Food Tours of Louisville** (foodguidefoodtours. com, 502-353-0308) visits both downtown and "NuLu" restaurants for tastings while also sprinkling in local history.

» See the city on two wheels with **Louisville Bicycle Tours** (louisvillebicycletours.com, 855-502-2453). Choose from the City Highlights or Waterfront tours as well as private options.

» Lace up your shoes for a tour with **My Old Kentucky Running Tours** (myoldkentuckyrunningtour.com, 502-373-1754), which operates in historic Bardstown. Their 5K running and walking tours cover 13 stops, but come with a t-shirt and donut!

» As the name implies, **Kentucky Bourbon Boys** (kentuckybourbonboys.com, 502-777-0761) focuses solely on tours of the state's finest distilleries in Louisville as well as the southern and eastern portions of the Bourbon Trail.

» Visit the grand Victorian neighborhoods with **Louisville Historic Tours** (louisvillehistorictours.com, 502-718-2764), which offers walking tours of the architectural gems and haunted landmarks.

Five Unique Sleeps in Central Kentucky

» The Brown Hotel may be one of Louisville's most well-known hotels, but the **Seelbach Hilton** (500 S. 4th St., Louisville; seelbachhilton.com; 502-585-3200) has hosted guests such as Al Capone, John F. Kennedy, and F. Scott Fitzgerald over the years. In fact, the hotel inspired *The Great Gatsby*. Public spaces retain their 1920s-style look, but guest rooms have modern conveniences.

» **The Inn Shaker Village** (3501 Lexington Rd., Harrodsburg; shakervillageky.org/the-inn; 859-734-5411) puts you in the heart of the attraction with rooms in the Trustees Office and other out-buildings, decorated in simple but functional Shaker style. Don't miss dinner in the Trustees Table restaurant.

» Sleep in a historic tavern once frequented by Jesse James and Daniel Boone at **Talbott Tavern** (101 W. Stephen Foster Ave., Bardstown; talbotts.com; 502-348-3494). Six guest rooms are furnished with period antiques and include breakfast.

» **Paris Landing** (Paris Landing, Kentucky; parislanding.us/glamping; 859-321-2293) is a glamping and camping resort near the thoroughbred farms. They rent cabins and safari-style tents that come fully furnished.

» In Lexington, stay at **The Campbell House** (1375 South Broadway Rd., Lexington; thecampbellhouse.com; 859-255-4281), a property that dates back to 1951 but has recently been renovated. Enjoy equestrian-inspired decor and their award-winning restaurant in the heart of Horse Country.

Western Kentucky

Native American tribes called this region home thousands of years before European arrival. Later, intrepid explorers wandered the passageways of Western Kentucky caves, never fully finding their ends. Above ground, towns such as Owensboro and Paducah have long been a stronghold for an old way of life, especially in terms of music and the arts. The Land Between the Lakes, named for the space between Lake Barkley and Kentucky Lake, offers recreation unrivaled in the state. The city of Bowling Green is equal parts city and town, home to the area's regional airport as well as impressive museums. Travelers might find it easier to fly into nearby Nashville and drive from there.

WHAT LIES BENEATH

Western Kentucky is unparalleled when it comes to number of underground caves and just how far they extend beneath our feet. The first human entered **Mammoth Cave** over 4,000 years ago, marveled by its beauty. It's been a tourist attraction from as far back as the 1800s. Native American remains, preserved like a mummy because of the constant temperature in the cave, were discovered by Civilian Conservation Corps members in 1935. The cave has even been used as a church. But it's not the only one around. **Cub Run Cave** north of Mammoth was discovered as recently as 1950, while **Diamond Caverns** dates back to 1859. **Frenchmen Knob Cave**, **Hidden River Cave**, **Lost River**, and **Mammoth Onyx Cave** are just a few of the others that are open for tours. You never know what new cave might be discovered before your next trip!

⊙ Can't-Miss Landmarks

» Made up of the world's longest cave system at over 400 miles, **Mammoth Cave National Park** (1 Mammoth Cave Parkway, Mammoth Cave; nps.gov/maca/index.htm; 270-758-2180) is the only national park in the state. In addition to the tours of the caves, explore the 52,800 acres of land.

» Gearheads will love the **National Corvette Museum** (350 Corvette Dr., Bowling Green; corvettemuseum.org; 270-781-7973) in Bowling Green, which documents the history of one of America's greatest classic cars. Admire the exhibits featuring 80 cars, including rare and prototype models. Adjoining NCM Motorsports Park also has a test track where you can take a lap in the cars.

» The **International Bluegrass Music Museum and Hall of Fame** (117 Daviess St., Owensboro; bluegrassmuseum.org; 270-926-7891) celebrates the style of music native to the South. Oral history projects and exhibits showcase the artists who created the signature sound with their instruments and memorabilia.

Mammoth Cave National Park

(above) National Corvette Museum, (below) International Bluegrass Music Museum and Hall of Fame

» Nearby is the **Bill Monroe Homeplace** (6210 US 62, Beaver Dam; ohiocounty.com/billmonroe; 270-274-3551), a museum devoted to the man known as the "Father of Bluegrass Music" in his childhood home. **Uncle Pen's Cabin** (Pen Lane, Rosine; visitohiocountyky.com/attractions/historic-sites/uncle-pens-cabin; 270-775-5420) is another must-see for Monroe fans, as it is where he lived with his Uncle Pendleton Vandiver, a well-known fiddle player. And if you want to see live music, catch the **Rosine Barn Jamboree** (8225 Hwy. 62 E., Rosine; kentuckytourism.com /rosine-barn-jamboree/2344; 270-363-9425), held seasonally.

» Operated by Western Kentucky University in Bowling Green, the **Kentucky Museum** (1400 Kentucky St., Bowling Green; wku.edu/kentuckymuseum; 270-745-2592) features six permanent exhibits as well as traveling ones, focusing on the slave trade, decorative arts, and Bowling Green native Duncan Hines. The **Downing Museum at Baker Arboretum** (4801 Morgantown Rd., Bowling Green; wku.edu/downingmuseum; 270-842-7415) is another campus museum, with works by alumnus Joe Downing alongside artists from around the world.

» The Pulitzer Prize–winning author is memorialized at the **Robert Penn Warren Birthplace** (122 Cherry St., Guthrie; robertpenn warren.com/birthpla.html; 270-483-1004) in Guthrie. The home features items related to Warren and sells his published works.

» **John James Audubon State Park** (3100 US 41, Henderson; parks.ky.gov/parks/recreationparks/john-james; 270-826-2247) is named for the naturalist who spent time in the state. The park's nature center honors his commitment to wildlife and the area is known for its birding. Don't miss the museum, which contains his original works.

» You don't have to go out West to see these majestic creatures. The **Elk and Bison Prairie** (Elk & Bison Prairie Rd., Golden Pond; landbetweenthelakes.us/seendo/attractions/elk-bison-prairie; 877-861-2457) in the Land Between the Lakes National Recreation Area is a 700-acre grassland enclosure where the animals can roam freely. Visitors can drive on the paved loop to see them from the safety of their vehicles.

Off the Beaten Path

» Harrodsburg isn't the only Kentucky town with Shaker roots. **Shaker Village at South Union** (850 Shaker Museum Rd., Auburn; southunionshakervillage.com; 270-542-4167) was the state's second settlement and remains as a living history museum with exhibits of artifacts and reconstructed buildings.

» The local arts community is best seen at the **Owensboro Museum of Fine Arts** (901 Frederica St., Owensboro; omfa.us; 270-685-3181), which contains a sculpture park and works of Asian, American, and European art. The museum is housed in a 1909 Carnegie Library and the John Hampden Smith House, a pre-Civil War mansion.

» Learn about the prehistoric Mississippian tribes of what is now Kentucky at the **Wickliffe Mounds State Historic Site** (94 Green St., Wickliffe; parks.ky.gov/parks/historicsites/wickliffe-mounds; 270-335-3681). Home to earthen mounds, the site features a museum of artifacts found here, a walking trail, and wildlife.

» The **Trail of Tears Commemorative Park** (1730 E. 9th St., Hopkinsville; trailoftears.org; 270-887-2300) is located on the site of a documented camp during the forced removal of Cherokee tribes. It contains the burial sites of two Cherokee chiefs who didn't survive the journey as well as a Heritage Center that informs visitors about the tragedy.

» The **National Quilt Museum** (215 Jefferson St., Paducah; quilt-museum.org; 270-442-8856) educates visitors on the art form that is both functional and creative. The collection has more than 500 pieces and the museum also welcomes traveling exhibits throughout the year.

» The city has surprising connections to notable African-Americans, which are documented at the **Hotel Metropolitan** (724 Oscar Cross Dr., Paducah; nps.gov/nr/feature/wom/2003/metropolitan.htm; 270-443-7918), a former hotel turned museum. It

Insert Image Paducah Quilt Museum near here

focuses on the Underground Railroad and performers, such as Tina Turner and Ella Fitzgerald, who visited the original hotel.

» Located at Hidden River Cave, the **American Cave Museum** (119 Main St., Horse Cave; hiddenrivercave.com/museum.html; 270-786-1466) features artifacts discovered in Kentucky caves and interprets the history of caving and mining.

▶ Tours for Every Interest

» There's more to Mammoth Cave than the namesake caverns. **Mammoth Cave Canoe and Kayak** (mammothcave-adventures. com/ck-home, 270-773-3366) visits the waterways in the park, offering excursions ranging from three hours to three days. **Mammoth Cave Adventures** (mammothcave-adventures.com,

270-773-6087) offers adventurous experiences like zip lining, rope swings, and horseback riding on the edge of the national park.

» Jesse James Riding Stables is just one element of **Kentucky Action Park** (kentuckyactionpark.com, 270-773-2560), as well as their alpine slide, zip line, bumper cars, and cave tours popular with families.

» **Unseen BG** (unseenbg.com, 270-977-3717) tours the haunted landmarks of downtown Bowling Green. The Downtown Haunted History Walking Tour is family-friendly, but the Histories, Mysteries, Scandals and Haunts is for adults only.

Trail at Mammoth Cave National Park

Five Unique Sleeps in Western Kentucky

>> The **Country Girl at Heart Farm Bed and Breakfast** (6230 Priceville Rd., Munfordville; bedandbreakfastkentucky.net; 270-531-5276) is the ideal getaway, set on a working 140-acre farm. It has five themed guest rooms with daily breakfast made of farm-fresh ingredients.

>> In a building that dates back to 1901, **The Meadows Hotel** (101 Commercial Ave., Fulton; meadowshotelfulton.com; 270-472-5555) was named for and built by a local businessman. After a fire destroyed much of the building, the remaining section was turned into a 14-room boutique hotel in 2016.

>> Bowling Green's finest property is the **Kentucky Grand Hotel and Spa** (635 College St., Bowling Green; kentuckygrand.com; 270-779-8988), offering luxurious suites, an in-house spa, and their Derby Bar. Each room is named for an aspect of state history, including the Man O'War and Bourbon suites.

>> Certainly the kitschiest accommodation in the region, **Wigwam Village Inn #2** (601 N. Dixie Hwy., Cave City; wigwam-village.com; 270-773-3381) in Cave City is reminiscent of the roadside motels of the 1950s. Inspired by those found out West, the wigwams offer "glamping" with fully furnished tents.

>> **Eddy Creek Marina Resort** (7612 KY 93, Eddyville; eddycreek.com; 270-388-2271) is a lakeside getaway with cozy cabins, an RV park, motel rooms, and a marina for your houseboat. There's an onsite restaurant with live music and countless nearby attractions.

New Orleans

Louisiana

Frequently associated with Mardi Gras and "bon temps," the state of Louisiana is much more diverse than many travelers realize. While French influences are still heavily felt, many of the traditions and flavors come from Spain, Africa, and the Caribbean. But the land was inhabited by Native American tribes before ships came from Europe, dating back as far as 2200 BCE at Poverty Point. Slavery was a large part of the plantation system starting in the 1700s to grow sugar cane. Some of these buildings are still standing in the southern portion of the state.

The state became a part of the US through the famous Louisiana Purchase, which included New Orleans and surrounding territory later explored by Lewis and Clark. The Civil War left its mark, and during Reconstruction, the iconic Supreme Court case Plessy vs. Ferguson took place in New Orleans, alleging that "separate but equal" was constitutional. Louisiana in modern times has been known for a number of things, but it was Hurricane Katrina in 2005 that brought it to the world stage. Some residents ended up staying in the places to which they were displaced, but if the success of the Saints football team is any indication, you can't keep Louisiana down.

15 Things to Taste in Louisiana

There's no way to limit the delicious dishes you'll eat around Louisiana to 15 items, but when traveling through the state, be sure to brake for these.

1. Boiled crawfish, **Kim's Seafood** (901 Benton Rd # E, Bossier City; 318-752-2425)

2. Muffaletta, **Fertitta's Delicatessen** (1124 Fairfield Ave., Shreveport; 318-424-5508)

3. Shrimp Buster, **Herby K's** (1833 Pierre Ave., Shreveport; herbyks.net; 318-424-2724)

4. Catfish DeSiard, **Waterfront Grill** (5201 Desiard St., Monroe; waterfrontgrill.com; 318-345-0064)

5. Chicken and sausage gumbo, **Bergeron's Boudin & Cajun Meats** (3933 Benton Rd., Bossier City; bergeronscajunmeats.com; 318-741-2243)

6. Natchitoches meat pie, **Lasyone's Meat Pie Kitchen** (622 2nd St., Natchitoches; lasyones.com; 318-352-3353)

7. Cracklins, **Quebedeaux's** (3710 S. MacArthur Dr., Alexandria; quebedeauxsboudin.com; 318-528-8788)

8. Zwolle tamales, **EB's Tamale Company** (1017 N. Main St., Zwolle; theoriginalzwolletamales.com; 318-645-9086)

9. Catfish Beaucoup, **Merci Beaucoup**, (127 Church St., Natchitoches; mercibeaucouprestaurant.com; 318-352-6634)

10. Alligator tail, **Cajun Landing** (2728 N. MacArthur Dr., Alexandria; cajunlanding.com; 318-487-4912)

11. Boudin, **Herbert's Boudin and Cracklins** (3213 Grand Point Hwy., Breaux Bridge; hebertsboudin.com; 337-667-8827)

12. Beignets, **Morning Call** (56 Dreyfous Dr., New Orleans; neworleanscitypark.com/in-the-park/morning-call; 504-300-1157)

13. Po boy, **Darrell's** (119 W. College St., Lake Charles; darrellspoboys.com; 337-474-3651)

14. Crawfish etouffee, **Randol's** (2320 Kaliste Saloom Rd., Lafayette; randols.com; 337-981-7080)

15. Oysters Rockefeller, **Antoine's** (713 St Louis St., New Orleans, antoines.com; 504-581-4422)

North Louisiana

The cities and towns of Northern Louisiana are often overlooked by travelers, but each has their own unique traditions, flavors, and history that are worth a trip. For example, Shreveport was where the famous phrase "Elvis has left the building" was uttered after Presley's performance at the Municipal Auditorium. The Red River runs through the top portion of the state, creating waterways and lakes Bistineau and Claiborne and earning the area the nickname "Sportsman's Paradise." And the town of Monroe has been caught on camera with the popular *Duck Dynasty* television show. Minden and Ruston have quaint downtowns lined with antiques stores and local businesses, also found in West Monroe's Antique Alley. Shreveport is also known as a gambling town, with casinos lining the river. It has a humble airport that services the region, but can easily be accessed from Texas to the west.

AN UNLIKELY HOME FOR THE ARTS

The northern Louisiana city of Shreveport sometimes gets a bad rap from those who prefer the more popular destinations farther south. But in the last few years, it's become a surprising home to the arts community. In 2016, artist Nick Cave brought his multimedia art piece *As Is* to the Municipal Auditorium, bringing acclaim from the international arts community. Previously known for his colorful "soundsuits," he also collaborated with local artists and supported area charities during his eight-month residency. Beyond Cave's work, visitors can see pieces by local artists at **Artspace** (708 Texas Street, artspaceshreveport.com), a downtown gallery, and **Agora Borealis** (421 Lake Street, theagoraborealis.com), an artisan marketplace that sells handcrafted jewelry, decor, and gifts and also teaches classes.

⊙ Can't-Miss Landmarks

» **Poverty Point National Monument** (6859 LA-577, Pioneer; nps.gov/popo/index.htm; 318-926-5492) in Pioneer tells of a culture that existed over 3,000 years ago in northern Louisiana. It contains some of the largest prehistoric earthworks in North America, engineered and built by the advanced native culture between 1700 and 1100 BCE.

» Shreveport's 1920s Art Deco **Municipal Auditorium** (705 Grand Ave., Shreveport; shreveportmunicipalauditorium.com; 318-841-4000) saw notable acts such as Elvis Presley, Johnny Cash, and Hank Williams through the Louisiana Hayride program. The venue still hosts performances today and has public tours. Snap your photo with the Elvis statue in front.

Biedenharn Museum and Gardens

>> Fans of the show *Duck Dynasty* can't miss the **Duck Commander Warehouse** (117 Kings Ln., West Monroe; duckcommander.com/visit-west-monroe-louisiana; 318-387-0588) in West Monroe where the Robertson family manufactures their duck calls and hunting gear. Browse the gift shop and see the exhibit about the show. You can also grab a map that highlights their favorite local hot spots.

>> Multiple museums in one, Monroe's **Biedenharn Museum and Gardens** (2006 Riverside Dr., Monroe; bmuseum.org; 318-387-5281) includes an art-filled home, a rare Bible museum, and a museum of Coca-Cola memorabilia. The namesake family was one of the first bottlers of the beverage. Don't forget about the stunning gardens.

◉ Off the Beaten Path

》 Shreveport has a surprising arts culture with multiple galleries and museums. **Meadows Museum of Art** (2911 Centenary Blvd., Shreveport; centenary.edu/campus-community/meadows-museum; 318-869-5040) at the Centenary College of Louisiana is free to visit and has galleries of works from Africa, Mexico, and Asia, as well as the US. The **Southern University Museum of Art** (610 Texas St., Suite 110, Shreveport; susla.edu/sumas; 318-670-6631) focuses on the work of the African diaspora. The **Marlene Yu Museum** (710 Travis St., Shreveport; marleneyumuseum.org; 318-717-9111) showcases the work of the namesake artist.

》 Created as a New Deal program, the **Louisiana State Exhibit Museum** (3015 Greenwood Rd., Shreveport; laexhibitmuseum. org; 318-632-2020) in Shreveport features dioramas on life in 1940s Louisiana, exhibits on natural history, original artwork, and panels on Native American traditions.

》 Roam the gardens at the **American Rose Society** (8877 Jefferson Paige Rd., Shreveport; rose.org/our-gardens /gardens-of-the-american-rose-center; 318-938-5402) in Shreveport, which offers tours of the grounds. Visit during the spring for peak blooming or in the winter for their holiday lights display.

》 In Monroe, the **Chennault Aviation and Military Museum** (701 Kansas Ln., Monroe; chennaultmuseum.org; 318-362-5540) honors the sacrifice of our military heroes and informs on the aircrafts they use. It's free to visit and is located on the site of an aviation navigation school.

》 Football fans will enjoy a trip to the **Eddie G Robinson Museum** (126 Jones St., Grambling; robinsonmuseum.com; 318-274-2210), which has interactive panels and memorabilia. It honors the contributions of the namesake man who was NCAA Division 1 football's all-time winningest coach with Grambling State University.

» See for yourself why they call northern Louisiana "Sportsman's Paradise" at **Black Bayou Lake** (480 Richland Place, Monroe; fws.gov/refuge/black_bayou_lake; 318-387-1114). The visitor center in a historic planter's house offers exhibits about the ecosystem of this part of the state as well as nature trails.

» **Louisiana Purchase Gardens and Zoo** (1405 Bernstein Park Rd., Monroe; monroezoo.org; 318-329-2400) welcomes more than 100,000 visitors annually for its diverse collection of species, 80 acres of gardens, and boat rides through the swamp.

» The **Mansfield Historic Site** (15149 LA 175, Mansfield; crt.state.la.us/louisiana-state-parks/historic-sites/mansfield-state-historic-site/index; 318-872-1474) recognizes the location of an important battle from the Civil War. The outnumbered Confederate troops overpowered the Union troops before they reached Shreveport. Today visitors can view re-enactments and living history demonstrations at the site.

▶ Tours for Every Interest

» Taste the unique flavors of North Louisiana with **Us Up North** (foodtourslouisiana.com), a company that showcases four local eateries, but also offers cooking demonstrations and classes led by Chef Hardette Harris. She worked to have the area's cuisine officially recognized by the state.

» Hop aboard the **Spirit of the Red River Cruise** (redrivercruise.com, 318-564-3560), an hour-long boat trip that showcases Shreveport and Bossier City's waterways. Bring your binoculars to spot birds and other local wildlife.

(above) Red River at Shreveport, (below) Fairfield Bed and Breakfast

Five Unique Sleeps in North Louisiana

Shreveport has a number of hotel options, especially its river-front casinos.

» **Fairfield Place Bed and Breakfast** (2221 Fairfield Ave., Shreveport; thefairfieldplace.com; 318-848-7776) is a quieter experience in a cozy 1870 home. Their breakfasts are beloved and include croissants that are baked fresh daily.

» Also in Shreveport, **Remington Suite Hotel and Spa** (220 Travis St., Shreveport; remingtonsuite.com; 318-425-5000) has top-notch amenities, from the indoor and outdoor saltwater pools to the social hours to the historic location.

» Located in Minden's historic district, **Grace Estate** (1114 Broadway St., Minden; graceestatemindenla.us; 318-639-9595) welcomes guests to the colonial revival mansion for stays in three elegantly furnished suites. The century-old Camellia gardens are ideal for an afternoon stroll and your breakfast can be enjoyed on the porch.

» In the historic Cotton Port district of West Monroe, the **Hamilton House Inn** (318 Trenton St., West Monroe; hamiltonhouseinn.com; 318-366-2412) has five guest suites with memory foam mattresses and claw foot tubs. Gourmet breakfast is also included with your stay.

» For something a bit more rustic, **Jimmie Davis State Park** (1209 State Park Rd., Chatham; crt.state.la.us/louisiana-state-parks/parks/jimmie-davis-state-park/index; 318-249-2595) in Chatham lets you stay near recreational activities such as freshwater fishing, watersports, and cycling. Both standard campsites and cabins are available.

Central Louisiana

Southern Louisiana certainly has its fair share of history but the city of Natchitoches (pronounced NACK-UH-TISH) dates back over 300 years. The area around the Cane River was first settled by the Caddo people, including the namesake Natchitoches tribe. French explorers arrived in 1701 and began trading with the people; archaeologists have uncovered artifacts from this time period. The Spanish also claimed territory nearby. Central Louisiana created an economy, similar to other parts of the region, based on plantations, specifically cotton, tobacco, and indigo. The Civil War's Red River Campaign tore through the region, burning cotton gins and storehouses as well as property. Reconstruction was a slow process, but the 20th century brought new structures and industry. The Cane River National Heritage Area was created, protecting the historic landmarks of the region. The town of Natchitoches is now known for its ties to the book and film *Steel Magnolias*, which filmed throughout the area. Alexandria has an airport that connects throughout central Louisiana.

NOT YOUR AVERAGE PIE

Tell someone you're visiting Louisiana and they'll no doubt provide you with a list as long as your arm of all the dishes you must try and where to have them. Natchitoches is known for one signature dish: the meat pie. Resembling an empanada or a meat pie you might find in England, the regional dish is made up of seasoned meat, generally beef or pork; seasoned peppers and onions; and a flaky crust. Everyone has their own take and you can find the dish at both white tablecloth restaurants and down-home eateries. The **Natchitoches Convention and Visitor's Bureau** (780 Front Street # 100, natchitoches.com) even has their own official recipe! You should pair your pies with a drive-through daiquiri, another quirky Louisiana tradition from **Maggio's** (230 South Drive). Just don't put the straw in your beverage until you get home!

Downtown Natchitoches

📍 Can't-Miss Landmarks

» The modern building that houses the **Louisiana Sports Hall of Fame and Northwest Louisiana History Museum** (800 Front St., Natchitoches; louisianastatemuseum.org/museums/louisiana-sports-hall-of-fame-northwest-louisiana-history-museum; 318-357-2492) seems out of place in historic downtown Natchitoches, but the dual museums are inspired by the motion of the nearby Cane River. Memorabilia from athletes like Shaquille O'Neal and Olympian Audrey "Mickey" Patterson are displayed, along with exhibits on local history from Native American times to the present.

» Learn about the 18th-century French colonial base at **Fort St. Jean Baptiste State Historic Site** (155 Jefferson St., Natchitoches; crt.state.la.us/louisiana-state-parks/historic-sites/fort-st-jean-baptiste-state-historic-site/index; 318-357-3101) in Natchitoches. Originally no more than crude huts, the fort was the first permanent European settlement in the land that became the Louisiana Purchase. The site features replica buildings and reenactors.

» A remaining example of French colonial architecture, the **Kent Plantation House** (3601 Bayou Rapides Rd., Alexandria; kent-house.org; 318-487-5998) is the oldest building in central Louisiana. Built by a French officer in 1796, the Creole homestead now serves as a historic site to educate visitors about what life was like in French Louisiana.

» Other plantations found nearby include **Melrose Plantation** (3533 LA-119, Melrose; melroseplantation.org; 318-379-0055), a home owned by free people of color, including world renowned primitive artist Clementine Hunter. **Magnolia Plantation** (5487 Hwy. 119, Derry; nps.gov/cari/learn/historyculture/magno-lia-plantation-history.htm; 318-352-0383 x316), located within Cane River Creole National Historical Park, retains outbuildings from the Creole cotton plantation, including the blacksmith shop, slave cabins, and overseer's house. **Oakland Plantation** (4386 LA-494, Natchez, nps.gov/cari/learn/historyculture/oak-land-plantation-history.htm; 318-352-0383 x316) is also managed within the park and is undergoing restoration. **Frogmore Cotton Plantation and Gins** (11656 U.S. 84, Ferriday; frogmoreplantation.com; 318-757-3333) tells the story of 1800s cotton plantations worked by slaves as well as modern mechanized production.

Off the Beaten Path

» Established to foster the arts community in Central Louisiana through exhibitions and classes, the **Alexandria Museum of Art** (933 2nd St., Alexandria; themuseum.org; 318-443-3458) also has a permanent collection of over 800 works, mostly from the 20th and 21st centuries.

» Learn about the tribes that allied with the French and Span-ish during colonial times at the **Adai Indian Nation Cultural Center** (4460 Hwy. 485, Robeline; adaicaddoindiannation.com/adai-caddo-cultural-center; 318-472-1007), which has exhibits on American Indian culture and history. For another take on Native

American culture in Louisiana, visit the **Tunica Biloxi Museum** (151 Melacon Rd., Marksville; tunicabiloxi.org/cerc/museum; 318-253-9767) in Marksville, home to the "Tunica Treasure" of artifacts.

» Central Louisiana boasts many historic sites and state parks. **Fort Jesup Historic Site** (32 Geoghagan Rd., Many; nps.gov/nr/travel/caneriver/for.htm; 318-256-4117) was built in 1822 and managed by then-commander Zachary Taylor. It was used as a staging ground for the Mexican-American War. **Los Adaes State Historic Site** (6354 LA-485, Robeline; nps.gov/nr/travel/caneriver/los.htm; 601-522-1900) was established as a Spanish mission and served as the capital of Spanish Texas.

» Started as the burial site of an unknown Civil War Soldier, the **Rebel State Historic Site** (1260 Louisiana 1221, Marthaville; crt.state.la.us/louisiana-state-parks/historic-sites/rebel-state-historic-site/index; 318-472-6255) in rural Marthasville is also home to the **Louisiana Country Music Museum**. It holds a collection of items related to the music genre and also hosts concerts.

» Small-town Winnfield has the **Louisiana Political Museum** (499 E. Main St., Winnfield; lapoliticalmuseum.com; 318-628-5928), which documents some of the state's notorious statesmen such as Huey Long and O.K. Allen. Set in a former railroad depot, the museum has items belonging to state politicians such as their cars and furniture, as well as a Politician Hall of Fame.

» The town of Angola is known for being home to one of the harshest prisons in the country, the Louisiana State Penitentiary. At the **Angola Museum** (Tunica Trace, Tunica; angolamuseum.org; 225-655-2592), exhibits document the dark past and preserves the historic landmark-listed structures. It's also the only prison museum to be located within an active prison.

» Mississippi isn't the only home to the blues. The **Delta Music Museum** (218 Louisiana Ave., Ferriday; deltamusicmuseum.com; 318-757-9999) documents the styles of music to come out of the state as well as the people, including Mickey Gilley, Jimmy Swaggart, and Jerry Lee Lewis. It's open for tours and live music.

» John James Audubon is known for his work with plants and animals and especially for the period he spent in New Orleans. But he later traveled upriver and stayed at the Oakley Plantation in St. Francisville. Now the **Audubon State Historic Site** (11788 Highway 965, St. Francisville; crt.state.la.us/louisiana-state-parks/historic-sites/audubon-state-historic-site; 225-635-3739). Travelers can tour the restored home.

» **Kisatchie National Forest** (229 Dogwood Park Rd., Provencal; fs.usda.gov/kisatchie; 318-472-1840) was used for lumber in the 19th century, but was set aside for preservation in 1930 thanks to the tireless work of Caroline Dormon. Within her namesake nature preserve, visitors can see the Briarwood educational center, walk the trails, and admire the waterfalls. Don't miss the Longleaf Trail Scenic Byway, which cuts through the forest.

» Connect with central Louisiana's natural landscapes at **North** (2907 N. Toledo Park Rd., Zwolle; crt.state.la.us/louisiana-state-parks/parks/north-toledo-bend-state-park; 318-645-4715) and **South Toledo Bend State Parks** (120 Bald Eagle, Anacoco; crt.state.la.us/louisiana-state-parks/parks/south-toledo-bend-state-park; 337-286-9075), located on each side of the Toledo Bend Reservoir bluffs. Both are popular spots for birding, fishing, cycling, and hiking.

▶ Tours for Every Interest

» **Tour Natchitoches with Barbara** (tournatchitocheswithbarbara.com, 318-663-5468) offers every type of tour you could want of the historic town, including plantations, architecture, history, colonial, and *Steel Magnolias*, all led by a native of the area.

💤 Five Unique Sleeps in Central Louisiana

» Fans of the classic film featuring Julia Roberts and Sally Fields can stay at the **Steel Magnolias House** (320 Jefferson St., Natchitoches; steelmagnoliahouse.net; 318-238-2585), an 1830s home filled with antiques. Enjoy your gourmet breakfast before exploring downtown Natchitoches.

» The **Cabins at Horseshoe Hills Ranch** (240 Bayou Pierre Cutoff Rd., Natchitoches; horseshoehillscabins.com; 318-352-2920) feel as if they could be tucked into the mountains, but are actually only a short drive to the city's attractions. The 40-acre property has six pine cabins, all outfitted with kitchens and cozy furnishings.

Hotel Bentley

» Originally built in 1908, **Hotel Bentley** (200 Desoto St., Alexandria; hotelbentleyandcondos.com; 318-442-22260) in Alexandria has been reopened and restored for a new generation of guests. The lavish lobby features chandeliers and murals and the Mirror Room Lounge retains its speakeasy feel.

» Located on scenic Toledo Bend, **Cypress Bend Resort** (2000 Cypress Bend Dr., Many; cypressbend.com; 318-590-1500) is a favorite of outdoors lovers in search of bass fishing, golf, or just relaxation. They have both rooms and suites and are pet-friendly!

» Stay amongst the cypress trees at **Chicot State Park** (3469 Chicot Park Rd., Ville Platte; crt.state.la.us/louisiana-state-parks/parks/chicot-state-park; 337-363-2403), south of Alexandria, which offers cabins and lodges as well as traditional campsites. You'll have easy access to the fishing pier and hiking trails.

South Louisiana

The places of South Louisiana are likely the reason you booked your trip to the state, with iconic locations such as Bourbon Street and Jackson Square in New Orleans. But there are still some lesser-known towns and attractions to add to your must-see list.

The Big Easy, better known as New Orleans, was settled in the 1700s by the French as a port connecting the Gulf of Mexico with the Mississippi River. Native tribes inhabited coastal areas long before European arrival, but the Spanish ruled the city as well. The entire region became a part of the US in 1803 with the Louisiana Purchase, which was actually a negotiation for the port of New Orleans. Battles during the War of 1812 and the Civil War were fought around the city. The area is a melting pot of cultures, including the Acadians from Nova Scotia, slaves from Africa and the Caribbean, the Spanish, and the French. Lafayette is known as the unofficial capital of Cajun country, while Baton Rouge is the state capital. Lake Charles has become a favorite hot spot for gambling and outdoors. Hurricanes have devastated the region since the very beginning of its founding, but none more than Hurricane Katrina in 2005, which affected the entire coast. New Orleans is home to the state's largest airport, making it a hub for travel to nearby destinations, but Baton Rouge also has an airport. New Orleans is also served by long distance trains and buses.

⊛ Can't-Miss Landmarks

» Even if you're not visiting during Carnival season, you can experience the fun of the celebration at **Blaine Kern's Mardi Gras World** (1380 Port of New Orleans Place, New Orleans; mardigrasworld.com; 504-361-7821). This studio builds the majority of the lavish floats used in the New Orleans festivities. Here, visitors can learn about the krewes, themes, and costumes that are just as important as the beads.

WHAT'S IN A NAME?

Cajun and Creole are two names frequently used when it comes to South Louisiana, especially in terms of food, but what's the difference? The term *Creole* was first applied to the colonists of European heritage that settled in Louisiana in the 1700s. This group mingled with the descendants of African slaves and Native Americans, creating their own language and independent culture, including Zydeco music. Dishes recognized as Creole have ties to Africa, especially gumbo, a stew of many ingredients, usually meat, vegetables, and rice. Oysters Bienville, crawfish etouffee, and beignets are other dishes recognized for their Creole influences that you can sample.

Cajun, on the other hand, is a shortened version of Acadian, a group of French Canadians who came to south Louisiana from Nova Scotia. They settled in rural areas, building what's known as Acadian houses, identified by their front porches and rooms surrounding a central hall. The Cajun language is still spoken in parts of Louisiana, even at universities, and their music is played in dance halls throughout the bayou region at community events called *fais-do-dos*. Cajun dishes are characterized by spice and heavy flavor and take advantage of the plentiful seafood of the region. Andouille sausage and boudin are two other food items that are classically Cajun, found at roadside meat markets and in restaurants.

» Give yourself at least three hours to visit the **National World War II Museum** (945 Magazine St., New Orleans; nationalww2museum.org; 504-528-1944). The facility includes exhibits on the role the area played in the war locally as well as nationwide, including the use of the Higgins Boat. Rotating exhibits, award-winning films, and a restaurant are also included within the museum.

» Don't miss the above-ground cemeteries of New Orleans, which were built to protect them from flooding. Each one has its own famous "residents" and spooky backstory. **St. Louis Cemetery No. 1** (425 Basin St., New Orleans) is reportedly the final resting place of Voodoo Queen Marie Laveau and visitors leave her offerings. Nicolas Cage also has his future crypt here. **St. Louis No. 2** (300 N. Claiborne Ave., New Orleans) is where pirate Jean Lafitte is buried. **Lafayette Cemetery** (1416-1498 Washington Ave., New Orleans), in the Garden District, was once part of a plantation.

» Live music is an essential part of any visit to New Orleans. Music fans can see the city's finest performers at the noted **Preservation Hall** (726 St. Peter St., New Orleans; preservationhall.com; 504-522-2841), which has been home to jazz since 1961. **One Eyed Jack's** (615 Toulouse St., New Orleans; oneeyedjacks.net; 504-569-8361), also in the French Quarter, has a more offbeat atmosphere with a diverse lineup of acts. In the Uptown neighborhood, **Maple Leaf Bar** (8316 Oak St., New Orleans; mapleleafbar.com; 504-866-9359) hosts local and national artists in just about every genre. And on Frenchmen Street, the younger, less touristy sister to Bourbon Street, the cozy spaces of **Snug Harbor** (626 Frenchmen St., New Orleans; snugjazz.com; 504-949-0696) and **Spotted Cat** (623 Frenchmen St., New Orleans; spottedcatmusicclub.com; 504-943-3887) are always full of jazz fans.

» Get outside of the city and head to Avery Island, known worldwide as the home of Tabasco hot sauces. The **Tabasco Factory Tour and Museum** (32 Wisteria Rd., Avery Island; tabasco.com/visit-avery-island; 337-373-6129) offers visitors a behind-the-scenes look at the brand and the McIlhenny Family who grows the peppers. They also have an onsite restaurant and offer cooking classes.

» The **Atchafalaya National Heritage Area** (nps.gov/attr/index.htm; 337-228-1094) actually extends from central Louisiana near Alexandria all the way to the south, but this region offers the most unique opportunities for wildlife spotting. Rent a kayak to paddle the waters or roam the nature trails at the state parks located within the heritage area.

(clockwise from above) Preservation Hall, beautiful architecture in the French Quarter, and lively Bourbon Street at night.

» The capital city of Baton Rouge has a strong lineup of museums, but the **Capitol Park Museum** (660 N. 4th St., Baton Rouge; louisianastatemuseum.org/museums/capitol-park-museum; 225-342-5428) serves as a primer on all things Louisiana. It has exhibits on the most notable towns, types of food, music, and festivals.

» The stunning **Old State Capitol** (100 North Blvd., Baton Rouge; louisianaoldstatecapitol.org; 225-342-0500) in downtown has seen its fair share of scandal over the 100 years it was in operation. The Gothic building is known for its stained-glass atrium. It became a museum in 1994 and has an interactive video narrated by one of the castle's ghosts.

» Visitors to South Louisiana often visit the famed plantation homes, especially those along the River Road. Most are located within a short drive from New Orleans and a few can be visited in a day. **Oak Alley** (3645 LA-18, Vacherie, oakalleyplantation.com; 225-265-2151) is one of the most famous, named for its iconic row of oak trees that line the entry. **Houmas House** (40136 LA-942, Darrow; houmashouse.com; 225-473-9380) is another, a restored Greek Revival mansion where one of the wealthiest sugar barons once lived. **Nottoway** (31025 LA-1, White Castle; nottoway.com; 225-545-2730) is the region's largest remaining

Capitol Park Museum

Nottoway Plantation

antebellum mansion and has been transformed into a resort. Considered to be the most haunted, **Myrtles** (7747 U.S. Highway 61, St. Francisville; myrtlesplantation.com; 225-635-6277) is built in the Creole cottage design.

 Off the Beaten Path

» New Orleans isn't the only one that celebrates the festival. Lake Charles has the **Mardi Gras Museum of Imperial Calcasieu** (809 Kirby St., Lake Charles; imperialcalcasieumuseum.org; 337-430-0043), set in a historic school. The small museum has rooms full of costumes worn in parades and lavish attire from the kings and queens of local krewes.

» Running in a circle south of Lake Charles, the **Creole Nature Trail** (1205 N. Lakeshore Dr., Lake Charles; visitlakecharles. org/creole-nature-trail; 337-436-9588) is a scenic byway where you'll find 28 species of mammals, over 400 types of birds, and plenty of amphibians, reptiles, and fish. The Creole Nature Trail

Adventure Point is the perfect jumping off point to learn about the area before visiting one of the walking trails and boardwalks.

» Climb to the top of Baton Rouge's most recognizable feature: the 450-foot-tall skyscraper known as the **Louisiana State Capitol** (900 N. 3rd St.; Baton Rouge; nps.gov/nr/travel/louisiana/cap.htm, 225-342-7317). Commissioned by Huey Long, the observation deck offers the best views of downtown. He was later assassinated here and buried on the grounds.

» The Burden Museum and Gardens in Baton Rouge includes the **LSU Rural Life Museum** (4560 Essen Ln., Baton Rouge; lsu.edu/rurallife; 225-765-2437), which shows visitors the significance of the agrarian lifestyle for early settlers in Louisiana as well as throughout the US with reconstructed cabins and other plantation buildings. The complex also contains the **LSU AgCenter Botanic Gardens** (101 Efferson Hall, Baton Rouge; lsuagcenter.com; 225-578-4161).

» Louisiana State University also has the **LSU Museum of Art** (100 Lafayette St., Baton Rouge; lsumoa.org; 225-389-7200), which has a permanent collection featuring works from China, America, and beyond. Traveling

(top left) Creole Nature Trail Lake Charles, (bottom left) Louisiana State Capitol

exhibits are also worth catching. Located at the Shaw Center for the Arts, it has over 13,000 square feet of exhibit space. Nearby, the **Louisiana Art and Sciences Museum** (100 S. River Rd., Baton Rouge; lasm.org; 225-344-5272) also showcases art, along with artifacts from ancient Egypt and even a planetarium.

» In New Orleans, see both the past and present of art at two of the region's finest museums. The **New Orleans Museum of Art** (1 Collins Diboll Circle, New Orleans; noma.org; 504-658-4100) first opened in 1911 with only nine pieces, but has expanded greatly, now showcasing art from France, the Americas, Africa, and Japan, as well as a sculpture garden. The **Ogden Museum of Southern Art** (925 Camp St., New Orleans, ogdenmuseum.org; 504-539-9650) holds the largest collection of works from the region, including works by Walter Anderson and Clementine Hunter.

» Louisiana State Museum has locations around the state, including the Capitol Park Museum in Baton Rouge and the Louisiana Sports Hall of Fame in Natchitoches. But many are set around New Orleans. The **New Orleans Jazz Museum at the US Mint** (401 Barracks St., New Orleans; louisianastatemuseum. org; 504-568-6993) focuses on the city's most well-known music export in a historic setting. House museums **Madame John's Legacy** (632 Dumaine St., New Orleans; louisianastatemuseum. org; 504-568-6968) and the **1850 House** (523 St. Ann St., New Orleans; louisianastatemuseum.org; 504-524-9118) discuss different times in local history, while the **Presbytere** (751 Chartres St., New Orleans; louisianastatemuseum.org; 504-568-6968) and the **Cabildo** (701 Chartres St., New Orleans; louisianastatemuseum.org; 504-568-6968) sit on both sides of St. Louis Cathedral as residences for Capuchin monks.

» It's more than just gumbo at the **Southern Food & Beverage Museum** (1609 Oretha C. Haley Blvd., New Orleans; natfab.org /southern-food-and-beverage, 504-267-7490). This complex covers all aspects of the companies and cuisines that make up the region, including exhibits on barbecue and Creole chefs. Also included with entry is the Museum of the American Cocktail and a gallery about absinthe.

New Orleans National Historic Voodoo Museum

» A frequently misunderstood religion, voodoo is more than poking dolls with pins. Visit the **New Orleans National Historic Voodoo Museum** (724 Dumaine St., New Orleans; voodoomuseum.com; 504-680-0128) to learn about the practices, which have their roots in the Caribbean. Hear stories about its priestesses and see artifacts such as "gris-gris" bags.

» The **Backstreet Cultural Museum** (1116 Henriette Delille St., New Orleans; backstreetmuseum.org; 504-577-6001) is one of the city's underrated attractions, educating on the city's contributions by the African-American community. Included are exhibits on music, Mardi Gras Indians, and second line parades.

» In Lafayette, the Acadian Cultural Center in **Jean Lafitte National Historical Park and Preserve** (Visitor's Center, 419 Decatur St., New Orleans; nps.gov/jela/index.htm; 504-589-3882) teaches visitors about the people who came from Nova Scotia and settled in south Louisiana. Exhibits, films, and ranger talks focus on their way of life and traditions. The park extends throughout the state with five other visitor centers.

» **Vermilionville Living History and Folk Life Park** (300 Fisher Rd., Lafayette; vermilionville.org; 337-233-4077) is another essential stop to understand the Acadians, as well as Creole and Native peoples during the 1700s. The facility has restored buildings, costumed interpreters, and demonstrations in crafts and music.

» The **Paul and Lulu Hilliard University Art Museum** (710 E. St Mary Blvd., Lafayette; hilliardmuseum.org; 337-482-0811) at the University of Louisiana at Lafayette has an extensive collection that includes Japanese prints, works from Louisiana artists, and folk art. The museum also hosts rotating exhibits.

» While you're on Avery Island learning about the world's most famous hot sauce, stop by **Jungle Gardens** (Louisiana 329 & Main Road, Avery Island; junglegardens.org; 337-369-6243), a natural garden of over 100 acres. Sculptures are set around the pathways and bird watchers can spot the species that call the bayou home.

» In addition to the well-known River Road plantations, there are many others worth a visit. **Laura** (2247 Louisiana 18, Vacherie; lauraplantation.com; 888-799-7690) interprets the history of a Creole family, including slaves and freed people. **Whitney** (5099 LA 18, Edgard; whitneyplantation.com; 225-265-3300) is the only plantation to focus solely on slavery and recently opened to the public after 260 years of private ownership. **Destrehan** (13034 River Rd., Destrehan; destrehan plantation.org; 985-764-9315) is the oldest plantation home in the lower Mississippi Valley. **Evergreen** (4677 LA 18, Edgard; evergreenplanta tion.org; 985-497-3837) is still a working plantation and was seen in the film *Django Unchained*.

» Most of these plantations grew rice, an important product during those times and even today. **Conrad Rice Mill** (307 Ann St., New Iberia; conradrice.com; 337-364-7242) in New Iberia is the oldest rice mill in America and operates tours for the public.

» **Bayou Teche Museum** (131 E. Main St., New Iberia; bayou techemuseum.org; 337-606-5977) details the legacy of the

Aligator

coastal parish, including the food, history, industries, and notable residents. Mardi Gras costumes, zydeco instruments, and Native American baskets are all on display.

» The **Center for Traditional Louisiana Boat Building** (202 Main St., Lockport; nicholls.edu/boat; 985-532-5106) is a surprising find in the small town of Lockport. It details the legacy of boat building, from the flat-bottomed boats used to navigate the bayous to the modern shrimping trawlers.

» The **River Road African-American Museum** (406 Charles St., Donaldsonville; africanamericanmuseum.org; 225-474-5553) provides a look into the African-Americans who lived in rural areas from slavery to the present. Exhibits include influences on cuisine, history of jazz, and black folk artists.

» Get outside of south Louisiana's cities to truly experience the region and visit the waterways that make it so unique. Paddle through the Spanish moss–draped Cypress swamps in **Bayou**

Teche (1725 Willow St., Franklin; fws.gov/refuge/bayou_teche; 337-828-0061) and **Bayou Sauvage National Wildlife Refuges** (61389 Hwy. 434, Lacombe; fws.gov/refuge/Bayou_Sauvage; 985-882-2000), where you'll see countless species of birds, alligators, and, if you're lucky, the Louisiana black bear. And if you can get to remote **Grand Isle State Park** (108 Admiral Craik Dr., Grand Isle; crt.state.la.us/louisiana-state-parks/parks/grand-isle-state-park/index; 985-787-2559), you won't soon forget the stunning beaches, deep sea fishing, and birding.

▶ Tours for Every Interest

» There are hundreds of tour operators in New Orleans, each focusing on an element of the city's culture, including haunted locations, voodoo, Civil War history, architecture, and food tours. Skip the bus and carriage tours, as the city is best seen from the ground level. **Free Tours by Foot** (freetoursbyfoot.com/new-orleans-tours; 504-222-2967) runs a number of tours based on tips around the French Quarter, Garden District, and more.

» **Kayak-iti-yak** (kayakitiyat.com, 985-778-5034) runs kayaking tours of Bayou St. John, one of the many bodies of water that surrounds the city. They also have tours that combine a day of kayaking with sightseeing downtown by bicycle.

» Skip the Hurricane Katrina bus tours, which focus on the still boarded up neighborhoods of the Ninth Ward and beyond. Instead, visit the **Musicians Village** (ellismarsaliscenter.org /musicians-village, 617-354-2736), a colorful housing project by Habitat for Humanity and native Harry Connick Jr. Stop by for one of their monthly concerts.

» Tour the nation's oldest African-American neighborhood with **Treme & Mardi Gras Indian Cultural Tours** (tremeindiantours .com, 504-975-2434). Led by locals to places such as Congo Square, the tour was featured on the HBO series *Treme*.

» Swamp tours are another popular attraction and many companies offer the chance to combine the outing with plantation tours. **Beyond the Bayou** (beyondthebayoutours.com, 504-264-2519) sets itself apart as an environment-friendly operator, as they don't feed the wildlife and they use a quiet boat to prevent noise pollution.

» South of New Orleans in Buras, **Cajun Fishing Adventures** (cajunfishingadventures.com, 985-785-9833) has been operating for over three decades, offering saltwater fishing charters, duck hunting outings, and wildlife tours. They also offer their own accommodations for guests.

» Taste all the capital city has to offer with **Baton Rouge Food Tours** (batonrougefoodtours.com, 800-662-3241). Their "C'est Si Bon" tour visits beloved local restaurants to try their signature dishes over the course of two and a half hours. You'll also learn about the history of the political center of the state.

» Lafayette has **Cajun Food Tours** (cajunfoodtours.com, 337-230-6169), which highlights notable local dishes such as boudin and gumbo as well as international influences. They also run walking tours of Breaux Bridge and another on Cajun art.

Classic Po Boy Sandwich

Five Unique Sleeps in South Louisiana

» Equal parts live music venue and guesthouse, **Blue Moon Saloon** (215 E. Convent St., Lafayette; bluemoonpresents.com; 337-234-2422) in Lafayette sums up the city's atmosphere. Located in a 1900s home, this location offers options from budget-friendly dorm rooms to private rooms to bungalows, which include Internet, morning coffee, and a drink ticket for the saloon.

» **Bayou Cabins Bed and Breakfast** (100 W. Mills Ave., Breaux Bridge; bayoucabins.com; 337-332-6158) offers vintage cabins on the Bayou Teche, each with daily breakfast, Internet, and rustic furnishings. There's also an unrestored 1869 house that serves as a museum as well as a cafe.

» North across Lake Pontchartrain from New Orleans, Covington's **Southern Hotel** (428 E. Boston St., Covington; southernhotel.com; 844-866-1907) is steeped in history but has been restored with modern amenities. Built in 1907, it originally drew in guests for the nearby mineral springs. Today, it has stylish rooms and suites and its banquet rooms display memorabilia of local Mardi Gras krewes.

» The **Old No. 77 Chandlery** (535 Tchoupitoulas St., New Orleans; old77hotel.com; 504-527-5271) is just one of many affordable boutique hotels to open in New Orleans in the past few years. Built as a warehouse to store goods being traded in the port, its guest rooms are covered in artwork from local students and its in-house restaurant brings in locals as well as visitors.

» The area's most beautiful plantation, **Oak Alley** (3645 LA-18, Vacherie; oakalleyplantation.com; 225-265-2151), offers overnight stays in their onsite cottages. They also have a restaurant that serves up Cajun and Creole dishes.

Mississippi River

Mississippi

Long before it joined the US in 1810, Mississippi's rolling plains were home to Native American tribes such as the Natchez, Chickasaw, and Choctaw. Members of these tribes were later removed to Oklahoma on the Trail of Tears. They are not forgotten, however, and some Native names still have a presence in the names of towns. Named for the mighty Mississippi River that runs in a zigzagging form nearly the entire length of the country, this area also saw Spanish and French explorers who passed through the state. The past was marked by slavery and the fall of the cotton industry as well as the Civil War. The Civil Rights Movement of the 1960s saw the admission of African-Americans equally into universities, jobs, and voting booths. The state's most notable contributions to American history wouldn't be possible without the slave songs and African spirituals that found their way into Blues music. Today, the state has a little bit of everything, from the bustling capital of Jackson to the college towns of Oxford and Starkville. Despite damage during Hurricane Katrina and the BP Oil Spill, the Mississippi Gulf Coast proudly showcases its seafood industry and beaches.

15 Things to Taste in Mississippi

There's no way to limit the delicious dishes you'll eat around Mississippi to 15 items, but when traveling through the state, be sure to brake for these.

1. Delta tamales, **Delta Fast Food** (701 S. Davis Ave., Cleveland; 662-846-8800)

2. Barbecue shrimp, **Delta Bistro** (222 Howard St., Greenwood; deltabistropub.com; 662-459-9345)

3. Fried Dill Pickles, **Hollywood Café** (1585 Old Commerce Rd., Robinsonville; thehollywoodcafe.com; 662-363-1225)

4. Braised brisket with Charboneau coffee rum, **Kings Tavern** (613 Jefferson St., Natchez; kingstavernnatchez.com; 601-446-5003)

5. Pig ear sandwich, **Big Apple Inn** (509 North Farish, Jackson; 601-354-9371)

6. Fried chicken with crawfish sauce, **Restaurant Tyler** (100 E. Main St., Starkville; eatlocalstarkville.com/wp; 662-324-1014)

7. Big Bad BLT, **Big Bad Breakfast** (719 N. Lamar Blvd., Oxford; citygroceryonline.com/big-bad-breakfast; 662-236-2666)

8. Fried catfish, **Taylor Grocery** (4 First St., Taylor; taylorgrocery .com; 662-236-1716)

9. Dough burger, **Johnnie's Drive In** (908 E. Main St., Tupelo; 662-842-6748)

10. Black bottom pie, **Weidmann's Restaurant** (210 22nd Ave., Meridian; weidmanns1870.com; 601-581-5770)

11. Shrimp po' boy, **Old Biloxi Schooner** (14391 MS 15, Biloxi; 228-207-2882)

12. Chili cheese bun, **Edd's Drive Inn** (3834 Market St., Pascagoula; eddsdrivein.com; 228-762-2177)

13. Katrina piece, **Tatonut Shop** (1114 Government St., Ocean Springs; 228-872-2076)

14. Fried oyster platter, **Blow Fly Inn** (1201 Washington Ave., Gulfport; blowflygulfport.com; 228-265-8225)

15. Mississippi Gumbo, **Cotton Blues** (6116 US 98, Hattiesburg; cottonblues.com; 601-450-0510)

Delta

The Mississippi Delta is a place unlike anywhere else in the world, named for the floodplains between the mighty Mississippi and Yazoo Rivers. As the famous quote from David Cohn goes, "The Mississippi Delta begins in the lobby of The Peabody Hotel in Memphis and ends on Catfish Row in Vicksburg." Along the way, stop for casino havens, small towns you can blink and miss, and quirky landmarks. Tunica was once the most impoverished part of the country, but has seen great success with the arrival of gaming. There's no rival for Clarksdale's music connections, as the small town hosts the Juke Joint Festival every year, showcasing the live music venues. History buffs visit Vicksburg for the Civil War connections and to tour its antebellum homes. And the capital city of Jackson is the ideal jumping off point for adventures throughout the state. Most travelers visiting this area will need to fly into Memphis or Jackson before renting a car.

DELTA BLUES

This region is the birthplace of modern American music, especially the blues. Familiar blue markers are found throughout the state, but especially along Highway 61. Visit the "juke joints" where names such as Memphis Minnie, BB King, and Robert Johnson got their start. Many grew up working on nearby farms but would play in any space they could find, including the makeshift cabins like **Po' Monkey's Lounge** (93 Poor Monkeys Road, Merigold). It closed after the death of its owner in 2016, the last of the remaining establishments where blacks could go to listen to music, drink, and dance in the segregated South. It stood as a reminder for generations about the power of music to connect people. It now has a blues trail marker to tell visitors about it. But you can still catch a blues act while traveling around the Delta. **Ground Zero Blues Club** (387 Delta Avenue, groundzerobluesclub.com) in Clarksdale is a notable one, owned in part by Morgan Freeman and covered in hand scrawled graffiti. **Red's Lounge** (398 Sunflower Ave., no website) and **Hambone Art and Music** (111 E. 2nd St.,

Sidebar continues on the next page

Ground Zero Blues Club

stanstreet.com/hambone-gallery.html) are others. **Dockery Farms** (229 MS 8, Cleveland, dockeryfarms.org) originated in 1895 as a cotton producer and a number of aspiring blues musicians, such as Charley Patton, worked there. Some still play here. And you can't miss "The Crossroads," the area of Clarksdale where Highways 61 and 49 intersect. It was here that blues are believed to have begun, starting with the tale of Robert Johnson selling his soul to the devil for guitar playing skills. Pick up an official **Mississippi Blues Trail** (msbluestrail.org) map to see where all of the historical markers are located in every corner of the state.

⊙ Can't-Miss Landmarks

» Start your journey through the Delta at the **Gateway to the Blues Museum** (13625 Highway 61 N., Tunica Resorts; tunica-travel.com/gttb_microsite/blues; 888-488-6422), an interpretive center set in a historic train depot in Tunica. It has exhibits on the history of blues music and its origins in the region. Interactive displays teach you how to write a blues song while others show-case iconic instruments such as BB King's "Lucille" guitar.

» And if you can't get enough of King, visit the **B.B. King Museum and Delta Interpretive Center** (400 2nd St., Indianola; bbkingmuseum.org; 662-887-9539) in his hometown of Indi-anola. It covers what life was like in Mississippi when he was growing up as a sharecropper and tractor driver and showcases some of his famous instruments and attire.

» The **Grammy Museum Mississippi** (800 W. Sunflower Rd., Cleveland; grammymuseumms.org; 662-441-0100) in Cleveland is a welcome addition to the region and is a sister museum to the one in Los Angeles. It honors the musical contributions that have come from the region with exhibits and events.

» The **Delta Blues Museum** (1 Blues Alley, Clarksdale; deltab-luesmuseum.org; 662-627-6820) educates visitors about the

town's blues history and the artists who came from or played in the Delta. The museum is located inside the town's historic freight depot.

Delta Blues Museum

» The **Museum of the Mississippi Delta** (1608 US 82, Greenwood; museumofthemississippidelta.com; 662-453-0925) also covers the region's history and environment, including exhibits on Native Americans, regional art, agriculture, and military history. It first opened in 1969, making it one of the area's oldest museums.

» Culinarians flock to small-town Greenwood, which is home to the Viking range of kitchen appliances as well as the **Viking Cooking School** (325 Howard St., Greenwood; thealluvian.com /cooking_school.php; 662-451-6750). Visitors can take classes to learn to cook dishes inspired by *The Help*, which was filmed in town. They also have a retail store where you can pick up kitchen essentials.

» Pay tribute to fallen soldiers at the **Vicksburg National Military Park** (3201 Clay St., Vicksburg; nps.gov/vick/index .htm; 601-636-0583), the site of a Civil War battle. Start with the introductory film to get the background on the conflict, which stemmed from desired control of the Mississippi River. The complex includes the **USS Cairo Gunboat and Museum** and the **Vicksburg National Cemetery.**

» At the southern end of the Mississippi sits the 300-year-old town of Natchez. One of the towns stunning antebellum mansions, **Longwood** (140 Lower Woodville Rd., Natchez, stanton-hall.com/longwood.php; 601-446-6631), sets itself apart as the only one to be designed in an octagonal shape and unfinished on the inside. Construction on Haller Nutt's "Oriental villa" was started before the Civil War, but was never completed. Tools and materials were simply left in place.

» Visit the **Medgar Evers Home** (2332 Margaret W. Alexander Dr., Jackson; tougaloo.edu/library/archives-special-collections; 601-977-7706), a memorial to the slain Civil Rights leader. The house itself has been kept in much of the same condition as it was during his time, but the furnishings are not original. They are from the film *Ghosts of Mississippi*, which used it for production. One room has been transformed into a museum. It's open for tours by appointment through Tougaloo College.

(top to bottom)
Longwood, Vicksburg
Monument, Medgar
Evers Home

» Also see the **Eudora Welty Home** (1119 Pinehurst St., Jackson; eudorawelty.org/the-house; 601-353-7762), where the Pulitzer Prize–winning author lived for more than 70 years. Inside, you'll find a collection of her original furnishings, items from her travels, a collection of over 5,000 books, and the desk and typewriter where she wrote her most notable titles. House tours are by reservation and the visitor center has a museum with permanent exhibits.

» The largest museum in the state is the **Mississippi Museum of Art** (380 S. Lamar St., Jackson; msmuseumart.org; 601-960-1515). It seeks to connect the state with the visual arts through the permanent collection and rotating exhibits, including 4,000 works from artists from Mississippi and beyond.

» The **International Museum of Muslim Cultures** (201 E. Pascagoula St., Jackson; muslimmuseum.org; 601-960-0440) is the first of its kind in the US, educating the public on the contributions of Islamic people, history, and culture. Two permanent exhibits document Africa's Islamic cultures and Spain's Moorish traditions.

» Sports fans can't miss the **Mississippi Sports Hall of Fame and Museum** (1152 Lakeland Dr., Jackson; msfame.com; 601-982-8264), named one of the country's best baseball museums. The state's notable athletes, including Jerry Rice, Brett Favre, and Dizzy Dean, are all honored here.

(top left) Eudora Welty Home,
(bottom left) Mississippi Museum of Art

⊘ Off the Beaten Path

» Learn about the state's diverse species at the **Mississippi Museum of Natural Science** (2148 Riverside Dr., Jackson; mdwfp.com/museum.aspx; 601-576-6000). Live alligators, fish, and snakes are all on display, along with fossils and other exhibits. The 2.5-mile hiking trail winds around the museum, allowing visitors to spot even more wildlife.

» Set on the same campus in downtown, the **Museum of Mississippi History** (222 North St., Jackson; mmh.mdah.ms.gov; 601-576-6800) and the **Mississippi Civil Rights Museum** (222 North St. #2205, Jackson; mcrm.mdah.ms.gov; 601-576-6800) document the state's past with interactive galleries. Highlights include the state's Native American history, its music, and its writers.

» The uniquely designed **Tunica County RiverPark** (1 Riverpark Dr., Robinsonville; tunicariverpark.com/home.html; 662-357-0050) is set on the wide banks of the Mississippi River. Inside, you'll find a museum devoted to the wildlife of the powerful body of water. Explore the walking trails that surround it to get even closer to the river.

» Founded in 1997 by revenue raised from gambling, the **Tunica Museum** (1 Museum Blvd., Tunica; 662-363-6631) documents the town's rise from Native American settlement to the present. It's free to visit.

» North of Jackson in Flora lies the **Mississippi Petrified Forest** (124 Forest Park Rd., Flora; mspetrifiedforest.com; 601-879-8189), a quirky landmark where a log jam 36 million years ago caused trees to become petrified. A local couple acquired the land in 1962, turning it into a popular tourist attraction.

» There are countless small music museums dotted around the Delta, depending on your interests. Located in an old hotel in Leland, the **Highway 61 Blues Museum** (307 N. Broad St., Leland; highway61blues.com; 662-686-7646) highlights the

Highway 61 Blues Museum

musical traditions of the area, as does the **Rock & Blues Museum** (113 E. 2nd St., Clarksdale: blues2rock.com; 662-524-5144). Learn about the legendary guitarist at the **Robert Johnson Museum** (218 E. Marion Ave., Crystal Springs; robertjohnsonbluesfounda tion.org/photos/museum; 601-647-1821) in Crystal Springs.

» If you enjoy offbeat roadside attractions, visit the **Glenwood Cemetery** (visityazoo.org/glenwood-cemetery) in Yazoo City and hear about the legend of the Witch of Yazoo.

» Did you know that Leland is home to the **Birthplace of Kermit the Frog Museum** (415 S. Deer Creek Dr. E., Leland; birthpla-ceofthefrog.org; 662-686-7383)? Puppeteer Jim Henson is a native of the Greenville area and the museum in his boyhood home showcases what inspired his most famous creation.

» The **Hazel & Jimmy Sanders Sculpture Garden** (Highway 8 West, Clevelandl thesculpturegardenms.com; 662-846-4625) on the campus of Delta State University has outdoor sculpture pieces set around the grounds.

» Vicksburg is home to the **Biedenharn Coca-Cola Museum** (1107 Washington St., Vicksburg; biedenharncoca-colamuseum. com; 601-638-6514), where the internationally recognized beverage was first bottled outside of its home state of Georgia in 1894. Coca-Cola memorabilia covers the walls of this building, operated by Joseph Biedenharn, a candy merchant and soda fountain operator.

» Greenville's Native American past is experienced at the **Winterville Mounds** (2415 MS 1, Greenville; mdah.ms.gov/new/visit/winterville-mounds; 662-334-4684), a 42-acre historic site with 12 prehistoric mounds dating back to 1000 AD. It also has an interpretive museum with items found during archaeological digs.

» The **Windsor Ruins** (Rodney Rd., Port Gibson) near Port Gibson is a stunning stop along the Natchez Trace Parkway. The 23 Neoclassical columns are all that remains of a mansion built in 1859 by Smith Daniell. It survived the Civil War, and was used as a Union hospital, before a lit cigar at a post-war house party caused it to burn to the ground.

» Natchez's **Museum of African-American History and Culture** (301 Main St., Natchez; visitnatchez.org/what-to-do-2/attractions/napac) is located in a former post office in front of the Natchez Burning Blues Trail marker, which documents the tragic story of a nightclub fire that killed more than 200 people. Inside, the museum details the city's settlement, the end of slavery, and modern times.

(left) Kermit the Frog Museum, (right) Windsor Ruins

» The area also has Native American history, best learned at **Grand Village of the Natchez** (400 Jeff Davis Blvd., Natchez; nps.gov/nr/travel/mounds/gra.htm; 601-446-6502). The 128-acre site has three ceremonial mounds and a museum that showcases items found during excavations.

▶ Tours for Every Interest

» See downtown Natchez via open air golf cart with **Open Air Tours** (openairtoursntz.com, 601-446-6345). Tours run four times per day and stop by the city's most stunning homes and historic landmarks.

» **Miss Lou Heritage Group** (misslouheritagegroup.com, 601-597-2112) highlights the Natchez's African-American history with tours on the Civil Rights Movement, the Blues, and St. Catherine Street, known as "Black Wall Street of Mississippi." Their heritage tour, however, is the most popular.

» **Everyday Adventure** (everydayadventure.net, 601-392-3079) offers guided tours of Natchez's waterways via kayak. Tours last two hours and include all the gear you might need.

» Stop by the spookiest locations around with **Haunted Vicksburg Tours** (hauntedvicksburg.com, 601-618-6031), which offers walking and nighttime ghost tours. Cemeteries and haunted homes are among the destinations visited.

» Learn about Greenwood's music history on the **Delta Blues Legend Tour** (hoovertours.homestead.com/home.html; 662-392-5370), a 3.5-hour jaunt that includes information on Robert Johnson and Eddie "Guitar Slim."

» With locations in Natchez, Clarksdale, and Helena, **Quapaw Canoe** (island63.com, 662-627-4070) is the best way to get on the water. The Natchez outpost offers day, overnight, and multi-day tours, but the rest mainly handle rentals.

» In addition to their popular Clarksdale guesthouse, **Delta Bohemian Tours** (deltabohemiantours.com, 662-701-5020) is run by a Delta native. Tours can be tailored to focus on Civil War history, music, literature, agriculture, and anything in between.

Five Unique Sleeps in the Mississippi Delta

» There's nowhere quite like Clarksdale's **Shack Up Inn** (1 Commissary Circle, Clarksdale; shackupinn.com; 662-624-8329), a grouping of restored sharecropper flats with its own restaurant and music venue. As their website says, "The Ritz we ain't."

» **The Alluvian** (318 Howard St., Greenwood; thealluvian.com; 662-451-1500) is a boutique hotel and spa with a rooftop restaurant across the street from the Viking Cooking School. Amenities include the in-house yoga studio and Giardina's, an old school Italian restaurant.

» Casinos aren't just for Vegas. **Gold Strike** (1010 Casino Center Dr., Robinsonville; goldstrike.com; 888-245-7829) is owned by MGM Resorts, so you can expect top-notch service, amenities, and, of course, gaming.

» The more than 300-year-old town of Natchez is full of historic homes. Guests of **Monmouth Historic Inn** (1358 John A Quitman Blvd., Natchez; monmouthhistoricinn.com; 601-442-5852) can sleep in one. The antebellum home sits on 26 acres and each room is decorated differently.

» When you reach the capital, enjoy your stay at the **Fairview Inn** (734 Fairview St., Jackson; fairviewinn.com; 601-948-3429), a historic-home-turned-boutique inn. Each room and suite is unique and the inn has its own spa and restaurant.

North Mississippi

The communities in the northeast part of the state run between the Delta to the west, Jackson to the south, Tennessee to the north, and Alabama to the west. The rolling hills of the Natchez Trace Parkway were a Native American trading route long before they became a national byway. Today, the college towns of Oxford and Starkville can give anyone team spirit, while literary legends such as William Faulkner, Tennessee Williams, and John Grisham all called this area home at some point. Music fans can tour the former homes of Elvis Presley and Jerry Lee Lewis or learn about Jimmie Rodgers and Howlin Wolf at their respective museums. Memphis and Jackson are the main access points for flying in and renting a car.

⦿ Can't-Miss Landmarks

» When in Oxford, you can't miss **Rowan Oak** (916 Old Taylor Rd., Oxford, rowanoak.com; 662-234-3284), the famous home of author William Faulkner. He purchased the tree-lined plantation in 1930 and lived here for most of his life, including when

Rowan Oak

SATURDAY IN THE SOUTH

College football exists around the US, but, like barbecue, it has an almost religious-quality in the South. Each school, especially in the Southeastern Conference ("SEC"), has traditions all their own. For Georgia, it's "the Hedges," the tall bushes that surround the football field. For Clemson, it's Howard's Rock, a rock at the top of the stadium that players rub for good luck. At Auburn, there's the traditional toilet papering of Toomer's Corner after a victory. Even Mississippi State in Starkville has their cowbells. But you haven't seen anything unless you've seen game day in Mississippi. The Grove is Ole Miss' tailgating area, a shaded grove of trees where families have had the same plot for generations. They walk through the Walk of Champions, an archway on one side of the Grove.

he wrote some of his most notable titles. The home is now a museum run by the University of Mississippi. While you're nearby, stop by **Faulkner's grave** at **Saint Peter's Cemetery** (Corner of Jefferson Ave. and N. 16th St., Oxford; visitoxfordms. com/attractions/saint-peters-cemetery), leaving a bottle of his favorite Jack Daniel's whiskey behind.

» The campus of the **University of Mississippi** (145 Martindale, Oxford; olemiss.edu; 662-915-7226), known as "Ole Miss," has a number of landmarks worth visiting. Start at the Civil Rights monument, which honors James Meredith, the school's first

African-American student. The **University Museum** (University Avenue and 5th St., Oxford; museum. olemiss.edu; 662-915-7073) has a number of collections,

(above) Ole Miss, (below) Statue of Elvis Presley

including the **Marie Buie Collection**, bequeathed by the artist's family. It includes decorative arts, Civil War relics, and historic costumes. The **J D Williams Library** (1 Library Loop, Oxford; libraries.olemiss.edu/j-d-williams-library; 662-915-5858) is home to the **Blues Archive**. **The Center for Study of Southern Culture** (southernstudies.olemiss.edu, 662-915-5993), located in the historic Barnard Observatory, one of the school's oldest buildings, hosts exhibits focused on the region.

» Set on the Mississippi State University campus in Starkville, the **Ulysses S. Grant Presidential Library** (449 Hardy Rd., Starkville; usgrantlibrary.org; 662-325-4552) has archives related to the president and Civil War legend.

» Elvis Presley, known as "The King," grew up in a humble shotgun home in Tupelo. A visit to the **Elvis Presley Birthplace** (306 Elvis Presley Dr., Tupelo' elvispresleybirthplace.com; 662-841-1245) is a must-visit for any music fan, and includes a museum on his life. And downtown is the famous Elvis statue and a small exhibit at **Tupelo Hardware** (114 Main St., Tupelo; tupelo-hardware.myshopify.com; 662-842-1637) where a young Presley purchased his first guitar.

» Located at the halfway point on the scenic drive, the **Natchez Trace Parkway Visitors Center** (2680 Natchez Trace Pkwy., Tupelo; nps.gov/natr/index.htm; 662-680-4027) in Tupelo has a short movie on the road as well as exhibits, brochures, and a gift shop.

» **Tennessee Williams Home and Welcome Center** (300 Main St., Columbus; 662-328-0222) in Columbus shares the history of the Pulitzer Prize–winning playwright. Born here in 1911, he lived his early years in the Victorian home that served as a church rectory with his grandfather, the reverend. It was moved to its current location in 1993, where it became a national landmark and the Columbus visitor center.

⊘ Off the Beaten Path

» The Greek Revival **L.Q.C. Lamar House** (616 N. 14th St., Oxford; lqclamarhouse.com; 662-513-6071) in Oxford was built in 1869 and tells of the life of the owner, a 19th-century states-man. It contains some of its original furnishings and was restored by the local historic preservation commission.

» Located in the Mitchell Library at Mississippi State University in Starkville, the **John Grisham Room** (395 Hardy Rd., Starkville; lib.msstate.edu/grisham; 662-325-6634) honors the legislator, author, and MSU alum. Exhibits showcase his novels and work in government.

» History buffs can stop by the **Oktibbeha County Heritage Museum** (206 Fellowship St., Starkville; oktibbehaheritagemu-seum.com; 662-323-0211), a community museum with Native American artifacts, exhibits on local beauty pageants, Civil War items, and early photographs.

» Get up close with nature at the **Sam D. Hamilton Noxubee National Wildlife Refuge** (13723 Bluff Lake Rd., Brooksville; fws.gov/refuge/noxubee; 662-323-5548), a 48,000-acre plot of land that spans three counties. A popular breeding ground for migra-tory birds, this is one of the best places in the state to spot the endangered red-cockaded woodpecker.

» Originally a private collection, the **Tupelo Automobile Museum** (1 Otis Blvd., Tupelo; tupeloautomuseum.com; 662-842-4242), boasts over 200 vehicles from the 1800s to the present. Owner Jane Spain continues her late husband's legacy caring for the cars, which include those owned by Elvis and BB King and a DeLorean.

» The **Bynum Mound and Village Site** (Milepost 232.4, Nat-chez Trace Parkway; nps.gov/nr/travel/mounds/byn.htm) is an important reminder of the state's Native American history. On this site, six burial mounds date between 100 B.C. and 100 A.D. Two have been restored and artifacts have been found inside.

» The **Tupelo Bald Cypress Swamp** (Milepost 122.0, Natchez Trace Parkway, Canton; nps.gov/experiences/cypress-swamp.htm) has a nearly one-mile boardwalk trail where you can see the creatures that live in the swamp, including birds and alligators. It's a short detour from the Natchez Trace Parkway.

» In historic Columbus, **Catfish Alley** (4th Street South, Columbus; msbluestrail.org/locations/catfish-alley-map) served as a hub for the African-American community from the late 19th to early 20th centuries. Catfish sandwiches were sold, giving the area its name, and locals would bring items to sell in the alley. Today, a Blues Trail marker honors the community's musical contributions.

» Near the site of the Battle of Corinth and the deadly Battle of Shiloh, the **Corinth Civil War Interpretive Center** (501 W. Linden St., Corinth; nps.gov/shil/learn/historyculture/corinth.htm; 731-689-5696) provides visitors with information on both sides of the conflict. Visit the **Corinth National Battlefield** and the **Contraband Camp** (800 N. Parkway St., Corinth;

Taylor Grocery Catfish

nps.gov/shil/planyourvisit/contrabandcamp.htm; 731-689-5696), where African-Americans lived in a tent city with Union soldiers, for the well-rounded experience.

» Located at the crossroads of the railroad, the **Crossroads Museum** (221 N. Fillmore St., Corinth; crossroadsmuseum.com; 662-287-3120) is set in Corinth's historic depot. This area was an important strategic point during the Civil War and has relics from battles as well as railroad displays, Coca-Cola memorabilia from the nearby bottling works, and even a cannon used in the Battle of Shiloh.

» Music fans can't miss the **Jimmie Rodgers Museum** (1725 Jimmie Rogers Dr., Meridian; jimmierodgers.com/museum.html; 601-485-1808) in Meridian. It is only open seasonally, but it showcases the artist's guitars, outfits, and records. In nearby West Point, pay tribute to a blues legend at the **Howlin' Wolf Museum** (307 E. Westbrook St., West Point; 662-605-0770). Opened in 2005, the museum celebrates the life of Chester Arthur Burnett, his given name, and his music that continues in popularity to this day. South of Memphis in Nesbit is the **Jerry Lee Lewis Ranch** (1595 Malone Rd., Nesbit; thelewisranch.com, 901-488-1823), which opened to the public in 2017. Highlights include the piano gates to his home and the instruments he played.

» Downtown **Meridian** (visitmeridian.com) has different trails for each interest with highlight points for the Civil War, Civil Rights, and music landmarks.

» The **Chahta Immi Cultural Center** (101 Industrial Rd., Choctaw; choctaw.org/culture/cicc.html; 601-650-1685) honors the Choctaw tribe of Mississippi through educational programming on their history and exhibits featuring artifacts and artwork. Events and performances are also held here.

⚑ Tours for Every Interest

» Inspired by the town's English namesake, the city offers seasonal **double decker bus tours** (visitoxfordms.com/historic-double- decker-bus-tours; 662-232-2477) to showcase Oxford's landmarks and describe the history of the college town. They're held on Fridays for $10 and reservations (which you can book at the downtown visitor center) are recommended.

Oxford double decker bus tours and downtown Oxford.

💤 Five Unique Sleeps in the Northern Mississippi

» Staying in a college town doesn't have to mean dorm rooms. At **Graduate Oxford** (400 N. Lamar Blvd., Oxford; graduate hotels.com/oxford; 662-234-3031), an outpost of the Graduate Hotels chain that specializes in their university-adjacent locations, the decor is tailored to the town, including an art piece of "The Grove" and furnishings in Ole Miss colors.

The Graduate Hotel

» Not far away is the rural **Taylor Inn** (736 Old Taylor Rd., Taylor; taylor-inn.com; 662-715-0799), a repurposed 1890 farmhouse with five rooms and the Chicken House, a "tiny house" cabin.

» The historic **Hotel Chester** (101 N. Jackson St., Starkville; historichotelchester.com; 662-323-5005) is an award-winning boutique property built in 1925. It has rooms and suites and a popular beer garden.

» **Moon Lake Farm Bed & Breakfast** (3130 Endville Rd., Belden; moonlakefarm.com; 662-420-1423) outside of Tupelo is another rural option, with 75 acres, three guest rooms, horseback riding, and daily breakfast.

» **French Camp Bed and Breakfast** (100 Robinson Dr., French Camp; frenchcamp.org/village-sites; 662-547-6835) is located near the Natchez Trace and is set inside three historic log cabins. The facility in the town of French Camp has a restaurant, historic village interpreting the Choctaw history, and gift shop.

Gulf Coast and Southern Mississippi

The small but mighty coast of Mississippi runs from the Louisiana to Alabama borders along the Gulf of Mexico and I-10, made up of small towns and inlets along the way. The area was originally settled by the French in the name of King Louis XIV, and Biloxi tribes already lived nearby. Barrier islands such as Horn, Deer, Ship, and Petit Bois boast untouched wildlife, while places such as Pass St. Christian seem straight out of a postcard. Hurricanes and oil spills weren't enough to keep the Mississippi Gulf Coast down. The beaches are back on top as well as the casinos that bring in poker fans. Indulge in the dive restaurants serving seafood caught that day, but without the frills of a white table-cloth establishment. Fly into Biloxi's international airport for the easiest travel logistics.

WHATEVER FLOATS YOUR BOAT

To those who have never been to a casino outside of Las Vegas, the ones found in Mississippi can be an interesting experience. While some form of gaming has been going on since the early days of the state, gambling was re-legalized in the state in 1994 starting with a band of Choctaw Indians. The Gulf Coast was able to start with riverboat casinos and those inland started with legal loopholes. Technically, all casinos in the state are considered boats and must have a licensed captain. Not all are on water, but all could reasonably one day be on water should the river flood. That's why you'll notice a hinge of sorts between hotel and casino portions. But you'll find all ranges of casino resorts in the state, including MGM-owned **Gold Strike** (1010 Casino Center Dr., goldstrike.com) in Tunica and **Beau Rivage** (875 Beach Blvd., beaurivage.com) in Biloxi. You don't need luck on your side to enjoy these properties' five-star hotel rooms, spas, and restaurants.

◉ Can't-Miss Landmarks

» Built in 1852, **Beauvoir** (2244 Beach Blvd., Biloxi; visitbeauvoir. org; 228-388-4400) is the antebellum home of Jefferson Davis, President of the Confederate States. The historic site features a Civil War Museum, Presidential Library, and Confederate Ceme- tery. Tours of the home are available and visitors can also wander the grounds.

» The Gulf Coast's most important industries are represented at the **Maritime and Seafood Industry Museum** (115 E. 1st St., Biloxi; maritimemuseum.org; 228-435-6320). Established in 1986, it has exhibits on early life on the coast, fishing traditions, and even hurricanes. They also have two replicas of the Biloxi Schooners.

◉ Off the Beaten Path

» Biloxi may seem an unlikely place for an arts scene, but the **Ohr-O'Keefe Museum of Art** (386 Beach Blvd., Biloxi; georgeohr. org; 228-374-5547) is named for master potter George Ohr and a local donor. The museum's original campus was destroyed in Hurricane Katrina, but it now sits inside a Frank Gehry–designed building. Folk art, pottery, and decorative arts are all displayed.

» Carnival celebrations aren't limited to the state of Louisiana. The **Mardi Gras Museum** (119 Rue Magnolia, Biloxi; gulfcoast. org/listings/mardi-gras-museum/5030; 228-435-6308) in Biloxi showcases the Gulf Coast's 300-year-old culture with exhib- its featuring costumes, photographs, and memorabilia. The museum itself is located inside the historic Magnolia Hotel.

» Lighthouses are becoming a rarity and the Mississippi Gulf Coast boasts three, including the remains of the Ship Island Lighthouse. The first **Biloxi Lighthouse** (1050 Beach Blvd., Biloxi; biloxi.ms.us/visitor-info/museums/lighthouse; 228-374-3105)

Biloxi Shrimp Boats

was built in 1848 of cast iron to protect ships coming into the harbor. A Fresnel lens was added and it was operated by civilians until 1939 when the Coast Guard took over. In the 1960s, the City of Biloxi opened it to tours, but Hurricane Katrina damaged it extensively. A complete restoration was done and it reopened in March 2010. In nearby Pascagoula, the **Round Island Lighthouse** (815 Cypress Ave., Pascagoula; cityofpascagoula.com/354/Round-Island-Lighthouse) dates back to 1859. It was saved from destruction in 2010 and is now open to visitors.

» The **Institute for Marine Mammal Studies** (10801 Dolphin Ln., Gulfport; imms.org; 228-896-9182, ext. 1750) was established in 1984 to educate the public and conserve species found along the coast. The facility includes an educational museum and veterinary hospital to treat the dolphins, sea turtles, and other creatures in the stages of rehabilitation.

» Originally started as a private collection, the **Busted Wrench Garage Museum** (2311 29th St., Gulfport; bustedwrench.com;

228-617-6660) in Gulfport features classic cars, motorcycles, gas pumps, and automotive memorabilia. Some of the cars date back to the 1940s, while others are rare models.

» The young and young at heart will appreciate the **Mississippi Coast Model Railroad Museum** (504 Pass Rd., Gulfport, mcmrcm.org; 228-284-5731), which has themed railroad tracks, including the largest LEGO Railroad display in the state. There's even a Thomas the Tank Engine track that kids can ride.

» Scenic Bay St. Louis is home to the **Alice Moseley Folk Art Museum** (1928 Depot Way, Bay St Louis; alicemoseley.com; 228-467-9223), a space devoted to the life of the local folk art painter. Set in the Bay St. Louis Railroad Depot, the museum features some of her notable works and is free to visit.

» Ocean Springs also has a connection with the arts. The **Mary C. O'Keefe Cultural Center for Arts** (1600 Government St., Ocean Springs; themaryc.org; 228-818-2878) is set inside a 1927 school building and includes exhibit spaces, performances, classes, and the Ocean Springs Museum of History. The nearby **Walter Anderson Museum of Art** (510 Washington Ave., Ocean Springs; walterandersonmuseum.org; 228-872-3164) opened in 1991 to honor its namesake artist. His works are showcased here, along with that of his brothers Peter, a potter, and James, a ceramist and painter.

» Spanning 160 miles from the Mississippi coast to Florida, the **Gulf Island National Seashore** (3500 Park Rd., Ocean Springs; nps.gov/guis/index.htm; 850-934-2600) provides endless opportunities to experience the biodiversity of the area. The state's section of the protected park includes hiking trails, a historic fort, and primitive camping.

» Inland from the Gulf Coast, Hattiesburg has a number of unique attractions. The **African-American Military History Museum** (305 E. 6th St., Hattiesburg; hattiesburguso.com; 601-450-1942) opened in the 1940s USO building, highlighting the important role of African-Americans in the US military. The

Walter Anderson Museum of Art

Mississippi Armed Forces Museum (Bldg. 850, 1001 Lee Ave. W., Hattiesburg; armedforcesmuseum.us; 601-558-2757) at Fort Shelby honors service members who have passed through the base over the past 100 years.

» William Carey University operates the **Sarah E. Gillespie Museum of Art** (498 Tuscan Ave., Hattiesburg; wmcarey.edu /page/sarah-gillespie-collection; 601-318-6148), dedicated to a local patron. Opened in 2009, it showcases the work of Mississippi artists such as Walter Anderson and Theora Hamblett.

» The **Longleaf Trace** (longleaftrace.org) stretches between Hattiesburg and Prentiss, offering more than 41 miles of paved pathways for running, biking, hiking, and horseback riding. The rails-to-trails project is a popular way to explore the area.

» Animal lovers should check out the **Hattiesburg Zoo** (107 S. 17th Ave., Hattiesburg; zoohattiesburg.com; 601-545-4576), which has educational animal encounters, a ropes course, and family-friendly programming.

⚑ Tours for Every Interest

Most of the Gulf Coast's tours are fishing excursions and day trips on kayaks, paddleboards, or boats.

» **Paddles Up** (paddlesupms.com, 228-334-5574) is one of the stand-up paddleboard and kayak outfitters in the area, located in Ocean Springs. They're only five minutes from the harbor, where you can enjoy a calm experience perfect for first timers. SUP Yoga and Paddlefit classes are also available. **Wut Sup Paddleboards** (wutsupboardshopms.com, 228-669-1802) in Gulfport rents kayaks, paddleboards, bikes, and even pontoon boats.

» Learn more about the Gulf Coast's sea creatures with the **Biloxi Shrimping Trip** (biloxishrimpingtrip.com, 228-392-8645). The 70-minute cruise teaches visitors about shrimps' journey from the sea to your plate. You might even spot other species such as flounder, blue crabs, and stingrays. Biloxi's **Fish Finder** (biloxicharterfishing.net, 228-860-0314) runs fishing charters, as does **Legends of the Lower Marsh** (legendsofthelowermarsh. com, 228-324-7612), which operates out of Pass Christian.

» Enjoy a day on the Gulf of Mexico with **North Star Sailing Charters** (northstarsailingcharters.com, 228-617-8057) in Gulfport or explore one of the coast's barrier islands with **Ship Island Excursions** (msshipisland.com, 228-864-1014), which has been operating ferries to the island since 1926.

💤 Five Unique Sleeps in the Gulf Coast

» Hundreds of chain hotels can be found in the Gulf Coast as well as casino properties for all budgets. What's harder to find is mid-range, locally owned businesses.

» **The Inn at Ocean Springs** (623 Washington Ave., Ocean Springs; oceanspringsinn.com, 228-875-4496) is a boutique property away from the bright lights of Biloxi. The area is

Ocean Springs

walkable, the rooms are immaculately designed, and the hospitality is unrivaled.

» The **Gulf Hills Hotel & Conference Center** (13701 Paso Rd., Ocean Springs; gulfhillshotel.com; 228-875-4211) is ideal for larger groups. Its waterfront location has views of Old Fort Bayou and its championship golf course.

» The **White House Hotel** (1230 Beach Blvd., Biloxi; whitehousebiloxi.com; 228-233-1230) is unlike anywhere else in town. The 1800s landmark has been updated with modern amenities, including ocean views and a rooftop terrace.

» If you want the full experience, MGM-owned **Beau Rivage Resort & Casino** (875 Beach Blvd., Biloxi; beaurivage.com; 888-567-6667) is by far the best hotel and casino around with luxurious suites, world-class entertainment, and top notch restaurants.

» **Paul B. Johnson State Park** (319 Geiger Lake Rd., Hattiesburg, mdwfp.com/parks-destinations/state-parks/paul-b-johnson; 601-582-7721) is an hour from the coast and 20 minutes from the University of Southern Mississippi campus. It's the perfect getaway into the iconic pine trees where you can "rough it" at traditional campsites or stay in one of their cabins.

Bodi Island Lighthouse

North Carolina

As one of the 13 original colonies, North Carolina was founded in 1709, but the Cherokee, Catawba, and other Native American tribes had already lived there for hundreds of years. The plantation system was established, similar to those in other Southern states, but the main crops were cotton and tobacco, the latter of which remains a staple today. The state made history in 1903 when the Wright Brothers succeeded in the first flight, which lasted 12 seconds, at Kitty Hawk. North Carolina has a long military history, establishing Fort Bragg in 1918. It still has one of the nation's highest percentages of active duty military members.

15 Things to Taste in North Carolina

There's no way to limit the delicious dishes you'll eat around North Carolina to 15 items, but when traveling through the state, be sure to brake for these.

1. Apple pie, Famous **Louise's Rock House Restaurant** (23175 Linville Falls Hwy; Linville Falls; 828-765-2702)

2. Pork chop sandwich, **Snappy Lunch** (125 N. Main St., Mt. Airy; thesnappylunch.com; 336-786-4931)

3. Albondigas, **Cúrate** (13 Biltmore Ave., Asheville; heirloomhg.com/curate; 828-239-2946)

4. Brisket, **Haywood Smokehouse** (403 Haywood Rd., Dillsboro; haywoodsmokehouse.com; 828-631-9797)

5. Country ham with redeye gravy, **Dan'l Boone Inn** (130 Hardin St., Boone; danlbooneinn.com; 828-264-8657)

6. Moravian cookie, **Mrs. Hanes Hand-Made Moravian Cookies** (4643 Friedberg Church Rd., Clemmons; hanescookies.com; 336-764-1402)

7. Livermush, **Mack's Liver Mush & Meat Co.** (6126 Mckee Rd., Shelby; 704-434-6188)

8. Macaroni au gratin, **Poole's Diner** (426 S. McDowell St., Raleigh; ac-restaurants.com/pooles; 919-832-4477)

9. Sausage biscuit, **Sunrise Biscuit Kitchen** (1305 E. Franklin St., Chapel Hill; sunrisebiscuits.com; 919-933-1324)

10. Chopped pork, **Lexington Barbecue** (100 Smokehouse Ln., Lexington; lexbbq.com; 336-249-9814)

11. Catch of the Day, **Waterfront Seafood Shack** (9945 Nance St., Calabash; calabashfishingfleet.com/calabash-seafood-restaurant; 910-575-0017)

12. Blueberry Donut with Powdered Sugar, **Duck Donuts** (1190 Duck Rd., Duck; duckdonuts.com; 252-480-3304)

13. Steam pot, **The Pilot House** (2 Ann St., Wilmington; pilothouserest.com; 910-343-0200)

14. Apple Ugly, **Orange Blossom Bakery** (47206 NC-12, Buxton; orangeblossombakery.com; 252-995-4109)

15. Whole hog BBQ tray, **Skylight Inn** (4618 S. Lee St., Ayden; skylightinnbbq.com; 252-746-4113)

The Mountains

The mountainous region of western North Carolina is made up of three distinct territories: the foothills around Asheville, the High Country farther east, and the Smokies, which run into Tennessee. This land was home to Native American tribes who were later removed on the Trail of Tears, but in the town of Cherokee, the tribal lands were reclaimed through a reservation in 1878. The city of Asheville was a favorite vacation spot during the Jazz Age, welcoming the Vanderbilts, Thomas Edison, and F. Scott Fitzgerald. Boone, a college town, was named for Daniel Boone, who passed through in his travels in the 1800s. The construction of the Blue Ridge Parkway transformed the region, putting locals to work through the Works Progress Administration and the Civilian Conservation Corps. The scenic drive that connects to Virginia was finally completed in 1987. Today, the region is a popular weekend getaway, especially during leaf and ski seasons. Asheville has a small airport and Charlotte handles larger volume flights.

GIVE ME THAT OLD TIME MUSIC

Somewhere between country and bluegrass, the music of western North Carolina dates back to the early days of Appalachian settlement. Used as a way to tell stories such as in ballads like those of Tom Dooley, songs were similar to those of Ireland and Scotland, from which many early residents came. Fiddles, banjos, and guitars are the main instruments used in this style, often called "Old Time Music." The tradition of artists such as Doc Watson and Earl Scruggs continue today through festivals such as the annual **Merlefest** (merlefest.org), named for Watson's late son and held in Wilkesboro. It brings together both artists playing the traditional music of this region as well as those influenced by it. Recent artists to take the stage include The Avett Brothers, Jason Isbell, Old Crow Medicine Show, and Brandi Carlile. Add in a visit to the **Earl Scruggs Center** (earlscruggscenter.org) in Shelby for more background.

⊙ Can't-Miss Landmarks

» Known as the largest private home in the US, **Biltmore Estate** (1 Lodge St., Asheville; biltmore.com; 800-411-3812) is the region's top attraction. The sprawling former home of the Vanderbilt family is a reminder of the Gilded Age, with its gardens, rooms with original furnishings, and even a basement bowling alley. Take the tour to see it all, but don't miss the temporary exhibits or a stop at the **Biltmore Winery**, which offers a free tasting with your ticket.

» **Breweries** (exploreasheville.com/foodtopia/beer-scene) are a large part of any visit to Asheville, which is why the mountain town has earned the nickname "Beer City USA." In downtown alone, you'll find **Wicked Weed**, **Lexington Avenue Brewing**, and **Green Man**. **Wedge**, **Pisgah**, and **Highland** are farther afield, as is **New Belgium**'s first East Coast operation.

» Named for a crag that resembles the face of an old man, **Grandfather Mountain** (2050 Blowing Rock Highway, Linville; grandfather.com; 800-468-7325) in Banner Elk also appeared in one of the running scenes in *Forrest Gump*. The park has a self-guided driving tour, hiking trails, and a nature preserve. The swinging bridge is another highlight.

» Like its namesake railroad that traveled through the region, **Tweetsie Railroad** (300 Tweetsie Railroad Lane, Blowing Rock; tweetsie.com; 828-264-9061) is a theme park that dates to the 1950s. It has a train track that runs throughout, and is transformed for their Halloween Ghost Train rides, as well as a ropes course, live shows, rides, and animal habitats.

» Far more than just a souvenir shop, the original **Mast General Store** (3565 NC-194, Sugar Grove; mastgeneralstore.com; 828-963-6511) in Valle Crucis still serves as the town's post office. It also sells old-school candies and toys as well as outdoor gear and clothing.

(from top to bottom)
The Biltmore Estate,
Grandfather Mountain
Winery, View from
Grandfather Mountain

(above) Lake Lure—Dirty Dancing Festival Life in Water, (bottom left) Chimney Rock Fall Color, (bottom right) Andy Griffith Statue

» There is nowhere better than the **Museum of the Cherokee Indian** (589 Tsali Blvd., Cherokee; cherokeemuseum.org; 828-497-3481) to learn about the original people who inhabited this area. Native tribes inhabited the land now called Cherokee starting as far back as 11,000 BC. The museum details their history with special effects and animation, artwork, and artifacts.

» Ride the rails with the **Great Smoky Mountains Railroad** (45 Mitchell St., Bryson City; gsmr.com; 800-872-4681), which starts in Bryson City. See leftover set pieces from *The Fugitive*, which filmed here. The train trips showcase the area's best scenery and they conduct themed rides such as the beloved Polar Express for holidays.

» Another spot with film connections, the town of **Lake Lure** (townoflakelure.com) is best known for being the backdrop of *Dirty Dancing*. The famous lake lift scene took place on the lake's shores and every year the **Dirty Dancing Festival** celebrates the iconic movie.

» **Chimney Rock State Park** (431 Main St., Chimney Rock; chimneyrockpark.com; 828-625-9611) is one of the state's most iconic natural landmarks, as seen in *The Last of the Mohicans*. The large rock outcropping was first purchased in 1890 and opened to the public in the early 1900s. The park has a number of trails of varying difficulty, an animal experience, and rock climbing.

» Set in the acting legend's hometown of Mt. Airy, the **Andy Griffith Museum** (218 Rockford St., Mt Airy; andygriffithmuseum.com; 336-786-1604) honors the most famous native son. See what drew inspiration for Mayberry on *The Andy Griffith Show* and admire memorabilia from his other hits such as *Matlock*.

» The town of **Highlands** (highlandschamber.org) is surrounded by waterfalls, which are best seen after a heavy rain. **Dry Falls** and **Bridal Veil Falls** are both easily accessible by car and on foot with paved paths, as is **Cullasaja Falls.**

Dry Falls Highlands

 Off the Beaten Path

» **Asheville Art Museum** (175 Biltmore Ave., ashevilleart.org; 828-253-3227) has a collection of works that includes American paintings, sculpture, and frequent exhibitions. To learn about what's happening in the local arts scene, visit the **River Arts District** (riverartsdistrict.com), a former industrial neighborhood that has been transformed into a space for shops, galleries, restaurants, and breweries along the French Broad River. More than 165 artists create here. The **Southern Highland Craft Guild Folk Art Center** (Milepost 382, Blue Ridge Parkway, Asheville; southernhighlandguild.org/folk-art-center; 828-298-7928) has a free museum with contemporary crafts of the Appalachians.

» Part museum and part arcade, the **Asheville Pinball Museum** (1 Battle Square #1b, Asheville; ashevillepinball.com; 828-776-5671) makes you feel like a kid again. Admission includes access to more than 75 pinball machines you can play. If you find one you can't live without, they also sell machines!

» The **North Carolina Arboretum** (100 Frederick Law Olmsted Way, Asheville; ncarboretum.org; 828-665-2492) showcases the state's finest natural scenery and native plants over more than 400 acres. Take advantage of the walking and biking paths with artwork placed throughout.

» **Oconaluftee Indian Village** (218 Drama Rd., Cherokee; visitcherokeenc.com/play/attractions/oconaluftee-indian-village; 800-438-1601) is another important stop during a visit to Cherokee. Open seasonally, the interpretive park transports visitors to the 1760s when local tribes first interacted with European settlers. While you're there, don't miss *Unto These Hills*, a large-scale outdoor drama that is the state's third largest. It tells of the Cherokee's history until their removal.

» The **Hickory Ridge Living History Museum** (591 Horn in the W. Dr., Boone; hickoryridgemuseum.com; 828-264-2120) interprets life from the 1700s with reconstructed cabins and period costumes. The park is home to *Horn in the West*, another outdoor drama, that tells of Daniel Boone and the state's fight for independence.

Horn in the West

» The mountains of North Carolina are one of the few places in the South where you can go skiing during the winter. Near Boone, resorts such as **Beech Mountain** (1007 Beech Mountain Pkwy., Beech Mountain; beechmountainresort.com; 800-438-2093), **Sugar Mountain** (1009 Sugar Mountain Dr., Sugar Mountain; skisugar.com; 828-898-4521), and **Appalachian Ski Mountain** (940 Ski Mountain Rd., Blowing Rock; appskimtn.com; 800-322-2373) are open to the public. Farther into the Smokies is **Cataloochee** (1080 Ski Lodge Rd., Maggie Valley; cataloochee.com; 828-926-0285), another ski resort.

» The **Southern Appalachian Radio Museum** (315 Elm Building, A B Tech College, Victoria Rd., Asheville; avlradiomuseum.org) is the region's largest teaching collection of amateur and vintage radios, educating generations about the early days of radio. Free and open to the public, their programming focuses on STEM applications.

» Set in historic Grovewood Village in Asheville, the **Antique Car Museum** (111 Grovewood Rd., Asheville; grovewood.com/antique-car-museum; 828-253-7651) started as a private collection of a local dealer. It holds rare automobiles such as horse-drawn vehicles and a 1957 Cadillac Eldorado Brougham.

» **Thomas Wolfe Memorial State Historic Site** (52 N. Market St., Asheville; wolfememorial.com; 828-253-8304) in Asheville honors one of literature's greats, set in the boarding house where the family lived which was featured in his books. Tours of the home are held throughout the day.

» While you're visiting the town in search of Andy Griffith, stop by the **Mount Airy Museum of Regional History** (301 N. Main St., Mt Airy; northcarolinamuseum.org; 336-786-4478), which has more than 35,000 square feet of exhibits. In addition to celebrating Mayberry's favorite citizen, the museum includes panels on Siamese twins Chang and Eng, the world's largest open face granite quarry, and Old Time music.

» Franklin's **Scottish Tartans Museum** (86 E. Main St., Franklin; scottishtartans.org; 828-524-7472) honors the people who immigrated to North Carolina from the Scottish Highlands. It has a register of all known tartan patterns and exhibits on early examples of kilts and Scottish dress.

Tours for Every Interest

» In the quirky city of Asheville, you really can take a tour on just about any topic. One of the most popular is **LaZoom** (lazoomtours.com, 828-225-6932), an offbeat bus tour that combines live comedy and a crazy cast of local actors. Tours can be themed, including general city, kid-friendly, haunted, and beer-centric.

» Safely visit the area's best breweries with **Asheville Brews Cruise** (ashevillebrewscruise.com, 828-545-5181), the city's original beer tour. Each tour visits a different set of breweries and transports you between them. Knowledgeable guides give you Intel on each one's must-sample brews.

» **Navitat Canopy Adventures** (navitat.com/asheville-nc, 828-626-3700) in Barnardsville, just outside of Asheville, offers the best zip lining around, focusing on the ecology of the North Carolina mountains. Visitors soar through the trees on one of two experiences. The company also offers guided RTV excursions.

» Foodies can't miss the food tours that run in Asheville. **Eating Asheville** (eatingasheville.com, 828-489-3266) visits some of the city's top eateries, offering samples along the way. **Alan Muskat & Co.'s No Taste Like Home Wild Food Adventures** (notastelikehome.org, 828-209-8599) goes even further, introducing guests to foraging and what it means to be truly "farm to table." Just outside of the city in Black Mountain, **Creative Mountain Food Tours** (creativemountainfoodtours. com, 828-298-0398) offers their Ultimate Foodie Tours, Pub and Grub Crawl, and Dessert Tours.

» Get outdoors to really appreciate the region, no matter your fitness level. **Wai Mauna SUP Tours** (waimaunaashevillesup-tours.com, 828-808-9038) bring travelers on four- to seven-mile paddles through the River Arts District or to Biltmore Estate. **Venture Birding Tours** (birdventures.com, 828-253-4247) brings nature lovers into the forest for day trips and longer excursions. **Electro Electric Bike Tours** (electrobiketours.com, 828-450-8686) visits the city's top attractions, including the Basilica of St. Lawrence and Grove Park Inn, all accessible via greenways and paved paths.

» Led by a local historian, **History @ Hand Walking Tours** (history-at-hand.com, 828-777-1014) showcase different aspects of Asheville's past. Similarly, **Asheville by Foot** (ashevillebyfoot-tours.com, 828-407-0435) visits downtown, Biltmore Village, and historic Montford. **Hood Huggers International Hood Tours** (hoodhuggers.com/hood-tours, 828-275-5305) focuses on the African-American history of Asheville and western North Carolina, led by a local artist and poet.

» Learn about Asheville's dark side with **Dark Ride Tours** (darkridetours.com, 828-747-9280), a ghost tour company that transports you in a former hearse.

» **Hunger Games Unofficial Fan Tours** (hungergamesunofficial fantours.com, 855-668-4332) in Brevard visits some of the filming locations used in the first movie, including DuPont State Forest. Hike the same trails that Katniss did in her effort to stay alive.

» See the setting for *Dirty Dancing* with **Lake Lure Tours** (lakeluretours.com, 828-625-1373), which offers guided boat tours and rentals. They also offer sunset and dinner cruises.

» Fly fishing is a popular activity in this region and **Rivers Edge Outfitters** (wncfishing.com, 828-497-9300) in Cherokee can get you set up with an excursion and all the gear you'll need.

Squad Car Tours

» **Nantahala Outdoor Center** (noc.com, 828-785-4844) in Bryson City is one of the area's top companies for whitewater rafting on the Nantahala, Pigeon, and French Broad Rivers. They also have zip lining and accommodations.

» Andy Griffith fans will love the one-and-only **Squad Car Tours** (tourmayberry.com, 336-789-6743), which drive visitors through Mount Airy in a vintage police car to the actor's favorite home-town spots.

💤 Five Unique Sleeps in the Western North Carolina

» The **Omni Grove Park Inn** (290 Macon Ave., Asheville; omnihotels.com/hotels/asheville-grove-park; 800-438-5800) in Asheville has a storied past, hosting legends such as William Jennings Bryan, Dwight Eisenhower, and F. Scott Fitzgerald since opening in 1913. Although it's been completely modernized, some rooms are in the historic wing.

Omni Grove Park Inn

» **Asheville Glamping** (ashevilleglamping.com, 828-450-9745) offers another unique experience with vintage trailers, glamping tents, tipis, domes, and yurts in West Asheville. Sites also have fire pits and nearby restrooms.

» **Sky Ridge Yurts** (200 Sky Ridge Dr., Bryson City; skyridge yurts.com; 704-701-5696) also offers "glamping" in the form of cozy Mongolian tents furnished with full beds, kitchens, bathrooms, televisions, and even WiFi. Views overlook the Nantahala Gorge, allowing you to appreciate the surroundings in comfort.

» Set in the stunning Valle Crucis, **Mast Farm Inn** (2543 Broadstone Rd., Banner Elk; themastfarminn.com; 828-963-5857) has welcomed guests since the 1800s. In addition to the rooms in the original farmhouse, the property has eight cottages and cabins, with some dating back to the 1790s, but furnished with modern amenities.

» **The Swag** (2300 Swag Rd., Waynesville, theswag.com; 828-926-0430) is an all-inclusive resort featuring luxurious accommodations, fine dining, and an unparalleled setting in the North Carolina Smokies. Lodge rooms and independent cabins are available for the perfect fall getaway.

The Piedmont

Central North Carolina, known as the Piedmont, was settled in the 1700s by the Moravian church, specifically in what is now Winston-Salem, two towns that were combined into one city in 1913. In the following century, tobacco became the main industry, led by companies such as R.J. Reynolds. The neighboring Yadkin Valley is a popular wine region. The capital city of Raleigh was established in 1792. Nearby Greensboro was settled by immigrants from Ireland, Scotland, and Germany and later played an important role in the Civil Rights Movement. The Research Triangle Park opened in 1959, bringing technology industries to Raleigh, Durham, and Chapel Hill. In Hickory and High Point, travelers can shop for home furnishings in the capital of the industry at countless outlets. Farther east, Pinehurst is known as the "Golf Capital of the World," built by renowned architect Frederick Law Olmsted. And the "Queen City" of Charlotte may not be the capital, but is the undisputed capital of industry, especially for banking giants such as Bank of America. It has the area's largest airport, but the Greensboro/Winston-Salem area also has one.

WHAT'S IN A NAME?

Triad, Triangle, what's the difference? The Triangle is considered to be Raleigh, Durham, and Chapel Hill. The Triad, on the other hand, is Greensboro, Winston-Salem, and High Point. Some of the nation's best universities are located in this part of the state, including Duke University, the University of North Carolina, and Wake Forest. North Carolina Central University, North Carolina State University, Shaw University, and dozens of smaller colleges are also here. UNC is one of the nation's most prestigious universities and has a basketball program that counts Michael Jordan as an alumni.

◉ Can't-Miss Landmarks

》 The **NASCAR Hall of Fame** (400 E. M.L.K. Jr Blvd., Charlotte; nascarhall.com; 704-654-4400) is appropriately placed in Charlotte, home to one of the sport's top raceways. The interactive experience gives visitors a card that tracks driving simulations and other activities. Exhibits of the cars, trophies, and other memorabilia are also included.

》 Beginners and pros are welcome at the **US National Whitewater Rafting Center** (5000 Whitewater Center Pkwy., Charlotte; usnwc.org; 704-391-3900), a 700-acre facility created by three-time Olympian Scott Shipley. The artificial river is made with pumps to create a whitewater slalom course, but there's also a ropes course if you'd rather stay dry.

》 Charlotte's **Mint Museum** is so sprawling that it has two campuses, **Uptown** (500 S. Tryon St., Charlotte; mintmuseum.org/visit/mint-museum-uptown; 704-337-2000) and **Randolph** (2730 Randolph Rd., Charlotte; mintmuseum.org/visit/mint-museum-randolph; 704-337-2000). Named for its latter location in a former US Mint, the collection includes European and American art from the 1700s to the present as well as African collections. The neighboring **Bechtler Museum of Modern Art** (420 S. Tryon St., Charlotte; bechtler.org; 704-353-9200) has even more galleries if you haven't gotten your culture fix.

》 To learn about the culture and history of the region, start at the **Levine Museum of the New South** (200 E. 7th St., Charlotte; museumofthenewsouth.org; 704-333-1887) in Charlotte. Exhibits cover the agricultural roots of the region, the Civil Rights Movement, and modern life in the South.

》 See where the city began at **Old Salem Museum & Gardens** (924 S. Main St., Winston-Salem; oldsalem.org; 336-723-7876), a living history museum with interactive exhibits and demonstrations. Don't miss the still-functioning tavern that George Washington once visited and the **Museum of Early Southern**

(clockwise) NASCAR Hall of Fame, Levine Museum of the New South Mint, Museum Interior

Old Salem

Decorative Arts (924 S. Main St., Winston-Salem; mesda.org; 336-721-7360), both located within the park.

» Also in Winston-Salem is the **Reynolda House Museum of American Art** (2250 Reynolda Rd., Winston-Salem; reynolda-house.org; 336-758-5150), set in the former home of tobacco magnate RJ Reynolds. Highlights of the permanent collection include works by Mary Cassatt, Georgia O'Keefe, and Albert Bierstadt.

» Established in the former Woolworth's building where a Civil Rights Movement sit-in took place, Greensboro's **International Civil Rights Center and Museum** (134 S. Elm St., Greensboro; sitinmovement.org; 336-274-9199) educates visitors about the Greensboro Four through film reenactments. The lunch counter has also been reconstructed.

» The **North Carolina Museum of Art** (2110 Blue Ridge Rd., Raleigh; ncartmuseum.org; 919-839-6262) in Raleigh has a collection of European and American works as well as highlights including works by Wyeth, Monet, and Rubens. In addition to

Civil Rights Center and Museum

traditional art, they also have Egyptian artifacts, Judaic art, and a complete set of Audubon's *The Birds of America*.

» The **North Carolina Museum of Natural Sciences** (11 W. Jones St., Raleigh; naturalsciences.org; 919-707-9800) is just one of Raleigh's excellent museums and is the largest of its kind in the region. The museum has exhibits on the state's natural resources and ecosystems, fossils of prehistoric creatures, and wildlife enclosures featuring snakes, turtles, and even a two-toed sloth.

» Another Capital City favorite is the **North Carolina Museum of History** (5 E. Edenton St., Raleigh; ncmuseumofhistory.org; 919-807-7900), which tells of the state's important legacy, including the First Flight, the first gold rush in the US, and famous residents from Dolley Madison to Michael Jordan.

» Famously featured in the film *Bull Durham*, the Durham Bulls minor-league baseball have played at the **Historic Durham Athletic Park** (500 W. Corporation St., Durham; milb.com; 919-687-6503) for more than 50 years. Visit for a game if they're in season.

(top) Durham Bulls, (bottom) Old well, University of NC Chapel Hill

» **Duke University** (2138 Campus Drive, Durham; duke.edu; 919-684-3214) dates back to 1838, making it one of the nation's oldest. Explore the campus and its facilities, including the Nasher Museum of Art, the Duke Chapel, and the Sarah P. Duke Gardens. There's also the Duke Lemur Center, Duke Forest, and even the Duke Basketball Museum.

» The **University of North Carolina** (250 E. Franklin St., Chapel Hill; unc.edu; 919-962-2211) campus in Chapel Hill is also worth exploring. Like its rival Duke, the school has the Carolina Basketball Museum as well as the Ackland Art Museum, Gimghoul Castle, and Coker Arboretum.

» Wine lovers should head to the **Yadkin Valley** (yadkinvalley-winecountry.com) for a taste of the region's wines. **Sanders Ridge Winery** (sandersridge.com) in Boonville, **Black Rock Winery** (blackrockvineyard.com) in Carthage, and **Adagio Vineyards** (adagiovineyards.com) in Elkin are just a few of the state's wineries.

🅞 Off the Beaten Path

» Set in the small town of Seagrove, the **North Carolina Pottery Center** (233 East Ave., Seagrove; ncpotterycenter.org; 336-873-8430) represents the tradition of handmade pottery from the Native Americans to the present day. Exhibits include functional pottery from early Appalachia to modern decorative pieces.

» Raised in Johnston County, the Hollywood legend is honored at the **Ava Gardner Museum** (325 E. Market St., Smithfield; ava-gardner.org; 919-934-5830), a 5,000-square-foot space in Smithfield. It features exhibits on the actress and her work, including her costumes, personal items, and posters from her films.

» Many of the NASCAR racing groups are based in Mooresville and have facilities open to the public. Dale Earnhardt Inc. and Richard Petty Motorsports both welcome visitors. **Memory Lane Motorsports and Historic Automotive Museum** (769 River Hwy., Mooresville; memorylaneautomuseum.com; 704-662-3673) boasts one of the largest private collections of retired NASCAR vehicles. The **North Carolina Auto Racing Hall of Fame** (119 Knob Hill Rd., Mooresville; ncarhof.com; 704-663-5331) has exhibits and notable cars.

» Pineville is the location of **President James Polk State Historic Site** (12031 Lancaster Hwy., Pineville; nchistoricsites.org/polk; 704-889-7145). Polk was born in Pineville and the facility documents his life and upbringing, including his service in the Mexican-American War and role in politics. The buildings have been reconstructed to how they would have been when he lived here.

» Beyond the larger art museums, there are smaller institutions dotted around the Piedmont that focus on different elements of art history. **CAM Raleigh** (409 W. Martin St., Raleigh; camraleigh. org; 919-261-5920) and the **Southeastern Center for Contemporary Art** (750 Marguerite Dr., Winston-Salem; secca.org; 336-725-1904) feature contemporary works through installations, video, and non-traditional paintings.

» **Weatherspoon Art Museum** (500 Tate St., Greensboro; weatherspoon.uncg.edu; 336-334-5770) has one of the region's leading collections of 20th- and 21st-century American Art, including pieces by Willem de Kooning and Henri Matisse.

» **North Carolina Central University** (1801 Fayetteville St., Durham; nccu.edu/artmuseum; 919-530-6211) and **North Carolina A&T University** (1601 E. Market St., Greensboro; www.ncat. edu/cahss/departments/vpa/visual-arts/university%20galleries. html; 336-334-3209) both have notable galleries featuring art of the African Diaspora.

» The **21C Museum Hotel Durham** (111 Corcoran St., Durham, 21cmuseumhotels.com/durham; 919-956-6700) showcases thought-provoking contemporary exhibits in its lobby spaces, which are always free and open to the public.

» You won't find anything as unique as the **Presidential Culinary Museum** (301 Cleveland Ave., Grover; theinnofthepatriots.com/ museum/presidential-culinary-museum.htm; 704-937-2940) in Grover, which details the history of the role of executive chef at the White House. Collections include china from the First Ladies, the tradition of the Easter Egg Roll, and the people who keep the famous residence running behind the scenes.

» To see what life in the Piedmont was like centuries ago, visit the **Duke Homestead State Historic Site and Tobacco Museum** (2828 Duke Homestead Rd., Durham; dukehomestead.org; 919-627-6990), where the Duke family lived from 1852 to 1854 and where their tobacco business started. Similarly, the **Tobacco Farm Life Museum** (709 N. Church St., Kenly, tobaccofarmlife-museum.org; 919-284-3431) interprets the culture on this turn-of-the-century homestead with exhibits and artifacts.

▶ Tours for Every Interest

» **Taste Carolina Food Tours** (tastecarolina.net, 919-237-2254) operates food tours through much of the Piedmont and the state, including Charlotte, Raleigh, Durham, Chapel Hill and Carrboro, Asheville, Hillsborough, Greensboro, Winston-Salem, and Wilmington. Each tour visits locally owned restaurants.

» Like its counterparts in other cities, **Charlotte Brews Cruise** (brewscruisecharlotte.com, 704-550-2005) stops by the Queen City's best breweries, including the hop-heavy NoDa neighborhood. Weekly tours take you behind the scenes at the establishments and introduce you to their brews. **Tap Hopper** (taphoppertours.com, 336-850-1477) runs brew tours in Greensboro with tastings and transportation, while **Beltline Brew Tours** (beltlinebrewtours.com, 919-285-1228) offers three tours in Raleigh and one in Durham.

» Scare yourself silly with **Carolina History and Haunts** (carolinahistoryandhaunts.com, 704-699-7959), which runs spooky tours of Charlotte, Winston-Salem, and Greensboro. Infamous locations are visited by lantern light for those brave enough.

» **Triad ECO Adventures** (triadecoadventures.com, 336-722-7777) operates out of Winston-Salem and offers Segway, paddleboarding, and electric bike excursions as well as rentals. They visit the city's top landmarks, including Old Salem, Washington Park, and downtown.

» Learn about the Triangle's past with **Tobacco Road Tours** (tobaccoroadtours.com, 919-371-2653), which offers tours in Raleigh and Durham including pub crawls, sightseeing tours, and haunted walks. **Preservation Durham** (preservationdurham. org, 919-682-3036) also offers free walking and biking tours that focus on the city's history and architecture.

💤 Five Unique Sleeps in The Piedmont

Use your time in the North Carolina Piedmont to splurge on one of the boutique hotel offerings.

» **Durham Hotel** (315 E. Chapel Hill St., Durham, thedurham. com; 919-768-8830) is a short walk from the Durham Bulls Athletic Park and is a mid-century modern lover's dream. Embrace your inner *Mad Men* character with a cocktail on the rooftop bar or dine in the restaurant on creations from James Beard award–winning chef Andrea Reusing.

» **Proximity Hotel** (704 Green Valley Rd., Greensboro; proximityhotel.com; 336-379-8200) is the first hotel in America to receive the LEED Platinum certification from the US Green Building Council and a AAA Four Diamond winner. Rooms are decorated with locally made furnishings and artwork from their artist-in-residence.

» **The Kimpton Cardinal Hotel** (401 N. Main St., Winston-Salem; thecardinalhotel.com; 877-216-3448) in Winston-Salem is a boutique property in the former R.J. Reynolds building, which has the same Art Deco features as the Empire State Building. Unique amenities include an in-house bowling alley, basketball court, and winding slide.

» Visitors to Chapel Hill should stay at **Carolina Inn** (211 Pittsboro St., Chapel Hill; carolinainn.com; 919-933-2001), the go-to accommodation since its opening in 1924. The design was inspired by George Washington's home at Mount Vernon and a portion of all stays benefit the university's library.

» If you'd rather spend time communing with nature, opt for the **Inn at Celebrity Dairy** (144 Celebrity Dairy Way, Siler City; celebritydairy.com; 919-742-5176), a working goat dairy in rural Siler City that crafts goat cheese and soaps. Guest rooms are furnished with cozy quilts and antique beds.

The Coast

The first English colony in America landed on the North Carolina coast, the same place where the Wright Brothers made their famous "First Flight." The land has been trolled by pirates and battered by hurricanes. The unusual coastline, which includes the Outer Banks, has also claimed its fair share of ill-prepared ships, making it a unique spot to scuba dive. We can thank the area for the creation of Pepsi, one of the most well-known beverages in the world, and some of our favorite movies. Before Georgia claimed most of the region's tax credits, Wilmington was known as "Hollywood of the South" with a massive studio and locations for *Dawson's Creek, One Tree Hill, A Walk to Remember, The Secret Life of Bees*, and many more. The Outer Banks are a famous getaway for families, but there's plenty of grown-up fun as well.

THE LOST COLONY

It's more than just a franchise of *American Horror Story*. Roanoke Island was the colony settled by Sir Walter Raleigh in 1585, made up of more than 100 men, women, and children. Virginia Dare was the first child to be born of English parents in the "New World." Her father John White, governor of the colony, returned to England shortly after their arrival, but was unable to return until 1590. When he arrived back on the island, the place was in disarray and no one was around. The word "CROATOAN" had been spelled out on a tree. The settlers were never found and no explanation for their disappearance has ever been proven. But in 1941, *The Lost Colony* outdoor play launched at Fort Raleigh National Historic Site to tell the story that has intrigued historians and visitors for generations.

⊛ Can't-Miss Landmarks

» The "First Flight" is recognized at the **Wright Brothers National Memorial** (1000 N. Croatan Hwy., Kill Devil Hills; nps. gov/wrbr/index.htm; 252-473-2111) in Kitty Hawk, denoted with a white hilltop obelisk and the flight path they took. Reconstructed buildings from their stay in 1903 interpret the time period and a sculpture of their glider is placed nearby.

» The **North Carolina Maritime Museum** (ncmaritimemuseums. com) is a must-see to learn about the coast's traditions and history. Exhibits focus on local lighthouses and lifesaving stations, the pirates that once inhabited the area, the thriving seafood industry, and artifacts salvaged from shipwrecks. The museum's collection spans across three locations in Beaufort, Hatteras, and Southport.

Wright Brother's National Memorial at Dusk

» Similarly, the **North Carolina Aquarium** (ncaquariums.com) has three facilities, including Roanoke Island, Pine Knoll Shores, and Fort Fisher. Conservation is emphasized over entertainment and visitors are educated on the native species such as sea turtles, sharks, and river otters.

» The **lighthouses** (visitnc.com/story/coastal-lighthouses) of coastal North Carolina are some of the nation's best examples of the structures built to protect incoming ships. **Bodie Island** is one of only a few brick tower lighthouses remaining in the US, located in Nags Head, with its iconic black and white stripes. It's still functional and is open for tours. **Cape Hatteras Light Station** in Buxton is designed with the same colors, but in an almost Candy Cane pattern. The **Currituck Beach Lighthouse** in Corolla is also open seasonally for climbs. **Old Baldy** on Bald Head Island is North Carolina's oldest standing lighthouse and has an

Bodie Island Lighthouse and Visitor Center

interpretive museum. Cape Lookout, Oak Island, and Ocracoke also have lighthouses open to tours, but the latter is no longer open to climbs.

» Similar to those in western North Carolina, nationally protected lands in the coastal region are the best places to interact with nature. **Cape Hatteras National Seashore** (US 64 and NC 12, Nags Head; nps.gov/caha/index.htm; 252-473-2111) was the first of its kind in the country, followed by **Cape Lookout** (Cape Lookout Road, Harkers Island, nps.gov/calo/index.htm; 252-728-2250). **Alligator River National Wildlife Refuge** (100 Conservation Way, Manteo; fws.gov/refuge/alligator_river, 252-473-1131) boasts over 150,000 acres of wetland habitats home to alligators and black bears. **Croatan National Forest** (US 70, New Bern; fs.usda.gov/recarea/nfsnc/recarea/?recid=48466; 828-257-4200) is the east's only true coastal forest and is where you can see the carnivorous Venus Flytrap in the wild. **Pea Island National Wildlife Refuge** (14500 NC-12, Rodanthe; fws.gov/refuge/pea_island; 252-473-1131) is a must-see for birders.

» Named for the many shipwrecks that have taken place along the coast, the **Graveyard of the Atlantic Museum** (59200 Museum Dr., Hatteras; graveyardoftheatlantic.com; 252-986-2995) interprets the 1,000 known shipwrecks. Exhibits describe the conditions that cause them to happen and the artifacts found in recovery efforts. It's one of the North Carolina Maritime Museums facilities.

» Explore the tallest active sand dune on the East Coast at **Jockey's Ridge State Park** (300 W. Carolista, Nags Head; jockeysridgestatepark.com; 252-441-7132) in Nags Head, which climbs to over 100 feet. The park has a visitor center and museum and is a popular location for hang-gliding and sand boarding.

» See the "banker ponies" that have inhabited the islands for 400 years at **Shackleford Banks** (nps.gov/calo/learn/nature/horses.htm; 252-728-2250), accessible only by ferry to the southernmost barrier island on Cape Lookout. Brochures provided by the

Shackleford Horses

park can tell you the best places to photograph the horses and watch their movement.

» The **Birthplace of Pepsi** (256 Middle St., New Bern; pepsistore. com; 252-636-5898) documents the brand's rise from pharmacy beverage called "Brad's Drink" to internationally distributed Pepsi-Cola. The attraction includes a recreated soda fountain, tastings, and Pepsi-centric souvenirs and gifts.

» Also in New Bern, **Tryon Palace** (529 S. Front St., New Bern; tryonpalace.org; 800-767-1560) is a replica of the 1700s mansion that belonged to the Royal Governor of the Province of North Carolina. The original burned shortly after the state's capital moved to Raleigh, but the current version serves as a museum on statehood. There are also 16 acres of gardens.

» The *USS North Carolina* **Battleship Memorial** (1 Battleship Rd NE, Wilmington; battleshipnc.com; 910-399-9100) was first built in 1937 in New York and served in World War II before being per-manently docked in 1962 to honor the servicemen and -women of the state. It holds a number of historic vessels.

Deck of WWII Battleship the USS North Carolina

» Originally land given by a grant from King George II, **Airlie Gardens** (300 Airlie Rd., Wilmington; airliegardens.org; 910-798-7700) was first designed by a local woman named Sarah Jones, but it was the Corbett family who opened it to the public, especially during azalea blooming season. The gardens also contain the work of folk artist Minnie Evans, who was the gatekeeper for many years.

» Located where the first English colonists arrived, **Fort Raleigh National Historic Site** (1500 Fort Raleigh Rd., Manteo; nps.gov /fora/index.htm; 252-473-2111) on Roanoke Island highlights the Native American, European American, and African-American people who lived here. Performances of *The Lost Colony* take place within the park.

» See a version of the early days of North Carolina's third-oldest town at **Beaufort Historic Site** (130 Turner St., Beaufort; beauforthistoricsite.org; 252-728-5225). Over 150 restored buildings are located within the site, including homes dating back to the 1700s, the old jail, and the local apothecary.

Off the Beaten Path

» The adventurous types can set sail for the lesser-known barrier islands that are accessible only by boat or single roads. **Cedar Island** (fws.gov/refuge/cedar_island), **Bald Head Island** (baldheadisland.com), and **Harkers Island** (nps.gov/calo/index.htm) all have miles of sandy beaches and nature reserves.

» The **British Graveyard** (British Cemetery Rd., Ocracoke; visitnc.com/listing/british-cemetery; 252-928-6711) in Ocracoke tells the nearly unheard story of the crew of the *HMS Bedfordshire*, who perished when a German U-boat hit the ship with a torpedo. Combined with another cemetery in Cape Hatteras, these plots are maintained by the National Parks Service, but the Union Jack flies above them as a reminder.

» Just as the name implies, the **Museum of the Bizarre** (201 S. Water St., Wilmington; museumbizarre.com; 910-399-2641) in Wilmington has an unusual collection of pieces such as a shrunken head, a crystal skull, Alexander Hamilton's hair, and props from the many movies filmed in town. Be prepared to embrace the kitsch.

» **Moores Creek National Battlefield** (40 Patriots Hall Dr., Currie; nps.gov/mocr/index.htm; 910-283-5591), north of Wilmington in Currie, was the site of one of the first Revolutionary War battles in the South. It was also the site of the first Patriot victory against the British. See the namesake creek and search for birds since the site is included in the North Carolina Birding Trail.

» Set at Fort Bragg, the **Airborne and Special Operations Museum** (100 Bragg Blvd., Fayetteville; asomf.org; 910-643-2778) in Jacksonville honors the soldiers from the early days of the Parachute Test Platoon to the modern day. The museum has simulator rides and exhibits on modern conflicts.

» Built in 1886, the **Roanoke River Lighthouse** (West Water Street, Plymouth; roanokeriverlighthouse.com, 252-217-2204) in Edenton brought ships from the Albemarle Sound into the namesake river. It was decommissioned in 1941 and relocated to its present site. Now fully restored, it's the only remaining screw-pile lighthouse in the state.

» The **History House Museum** (321 Community Center Rd., Tillery; cct78.org/history-house.html; 252-826-3017) in Tillery tells the untold story of African-Americans in the area, starting as slaves before becoming sharecroppers after the Civil War. During the New Deal Resettlement Program, they were given the opportunity to buy the land.

» The small town of Little Washington is home to the **North Carolina Estuarium** (223 E. Water St., Washington; 252-948-0000), the world's first facility devoted to estuaries and coastal rivers. Over 200 exhibits showcase crabs, alligators, and other sea creatures.

▶ Tours for Every Interest

» **Haunted Wilmington** (hauntedwilmington.com, 910-794-1866) is far more than the name implies. While they do offer a ghost walk and haunted pub crawl that visit the city's more sinister locations, their Hollywood Locations tour is also a favorite for fans of *Dawson's Creek*, *One Tree Hill*, and countless Nicholas Sparks films. **Beaufort Ghost Walk** (beaufortghostwalk.com, 252-772-9925) and **Ghosts of New Bern** (ghostsofnewbern.com, 252-571-4766) tell the eerie stories of other coastal towns.

» Cruise the waterway around Cape Fear with **Wilmington Water Tours** (wilmingtonwatertours.net, 910-338-3134). Their fully accessible catamaran can hold 49 passengers for daily narrated cruises and private charters. Excursions scout for wildlife and showcase the beauty of the Cape Fear River. They also offer an acoustic sunset cruise. **Crystal Coast Lady Cruises** (crystal-coastlady.com, 252-728-8687) runs sightseeing cruises from Beaufort's harbor.

» Navigate the area by kayak with **Mahanaim Adventures** (mahanaimadventures.com, 910-547-8252), which offers guided excursions from Wilmington to Eagle Island, Shark Tooth Island, and other destinations along the Cape Fear River for day trips or overnight.

» Sample some of Wilmington's best craft beers with **Port City Brew Bus** (portcitybrewbus.com, 910-679-6586). Their tours include transportation between venues, tastings, and a behind-the-scenes look at the facilities that make the tasty brews.

» **Feel Good Fishing Charters & Adventures** (feelgoodfishing. com, 910-431-7777) also operates trips to the open water from Wilmington and its surrounding beaches. Enjoy fishing charters that include all the necessary gear or scenic tours.

» Scuba dive the Crystal Coast's wrecks with **Aquatic Safaris SCUBA** (aquaticsafaris.com, 910-392-4386), which offers charters throughout the year. They book walk-ons for those without a diving buddy and the company has been operating since 1988.

» Learn about the town of Beaufort with **Hungry Town Tours** (hungrytowntours.com, 252-648-1011), which incorporates stories of the city with historic walking tours and culinary bike tours.

» **Surf City Surf School** (surfcitysurfschool.com, 910-616-2280) in the town of Surf City north of Wilmington offers surf lessons for beginners as well as rentals of paddleboards and surfboards. Rent kayaks and paddleboards or go on guided tours with **Outer Banks Kayak Adventures** (obxadventure.com, 252-489-8146) in Nags Head.

» See the famous wild horses of Corolla on safari with **Wild Horse Adventure Tours** (wildhorsetour.com, 252-489-2020), which brings guests in open air Hummers. The company also collects trash on local beaches and keeps their carbon footprint as low as possible.

Five Unique Sleeps on the North Carolina Coast

» If you're willing to "rough it," there's no better location than **Carolina Beach State Park** (1010 State Park Rd., Carolina Beach; ncparks.gov/carolina-beach-state-park; 910-458-8206), which has rustic cabins and campsites. Amenities include a bathhouse, boat ramp, laundry facilities, kayak rentals, and trails through the park.

» **Harborlight Guest House** (332 Live Oak Drive, Cape Carteret; harborlightnc.com; 252-393-6868) in Swansboro overlooks the scenic Bogue Sound and has welcomed visitors since it opened as a restaurant and bar in 1963. After a period of closure, it reopened as an inn, with six suites named for different elements of North Carolina history.

» Set in downtown Wilmington, **The Wilmingtonian** (101 S. 2nd St., Wilmington; thewilmingtonian.com, 910-343-1800) has been a longtime favorite of the film industry, hosting cast and crew during shoots. The all-suite hotel is made up of three restored buildings, each fitting a different theme.

» **Sanderling Resort** (1461 Duck Rd., Duck; sanderling-resort.com, 855-412-7866) in Duck sits at the opposite end of the spectrum, offering luxurious oceanfront accommodations. The full-service spa, onsite restaurant, and pools keep vacationers returning year after year.

» **The Cedars Inn** (305 Front St., Beaufort; cedarsinn.com, 800-548-2961) is a 1768 home-turned-inn that overlooks the historic port. They offer rooms, suites, and even a detached cottage.

Carolina Beach State Park

Magnolia Plantation and Garden

South Carolina

The state of South Carolina has more than 180 miles of coastline extending from the mountains and piedmont, making the state diverse in landscapes, including the second-most acreage of swamps in the country. Founded in 1670, much of the state ran on agriculture, especially rice, indigo, and cotton. Plantations relied on the labor of slaves, brought into the port of Charleston and dispersed through-out the barrier islands and inland. Few states have as an iconic flag as South Carolina's, with the moon and palmetto tree set among the blue background. You'll see it on shirts, stickers, and everywhere in between during your travels around the state.

15 Things to Taste in South Carolina

There's no way to limit the delicious dishes you'll eat around South Carolina to 15 items, but when traveling through the state, be sure to brake for these.

1. Frogmore Stew, **Bowen's Island Restaurant** (1870 Bowens Island Rd., Charleston; bowensisland.com; 843-795-2757)

2. Big Nasty, **Hominy Grill** (207 Rutledge Ave., Charleston; hominygrill.com; 843-937-0930)

3. She Crab Soup, **82 Queen** (82 Queen St., Charleston; 82queen.com; 843-723-7591)

4. Shrimp and Grits, **Lucky Rooster** (841 William Hilton Pkwy. Unit A, Hilton Head; luckyroosterhhi.com; 843-681-3474)

5. Croissant Eggs Benedict, **Croissants** (3751 Robert M Grissom Pkwy., Myrtle Beach; croissants.net; 843-448-2253)

6. Pulled pork, **Scott's Barbecue** (2734 Hemingway Hwy., Hemingway; 843-558-0134)

7. Buttermilk fried quail, **Motor Supply** (920 Gervais St., Columbia; motorsupplycobistro.com; 803-256-6687)

8. Southern Belly Dipper Sandwich, **Southern Belly** (819 Harden St., Columbia; southernbellybbq.com; 803-764-3512)

9. North Carolina Flounder, **The Bradley** (231 The Alley, Aiken; 803-226-0567)

10. Meat and three, **Crossroads Cafe** (1738 Sand Bar Ferry Rd., Beech Island; 803-827-1429)

11. Chili cheeseburger, **Beacon Drive In** (255 John B White Sr. Blvd., Spartanburg; beacondrivein.com; 864-585-9387)

12. Royal Red Shrimp Scampi, **The Anchorage** (586 Perry Ave., Greenville; theanchoragerestaurant.com; 864-219-3082)

13. Sausage potato crepe, **Tandem Creperie** (2 S. Main St., Travelers Rest; tandemcc.com; 864-610-2245)

14. Pulled pork, **Mike & Jeff's BBQ** (2401 Old Buncombe Rd., Greenville; mikeandjeffsbbq.com; 864-271-5225)

15. Surf and turf, **Rick Erwin's** (127 Market St., Clemson; rickerwins.com/clemson; 864-654-9466)

The Lowcountry

Founded in 1670 as Charles Towne in honor of King Charles II, the port city of Charleston was settled by French Huguenots escaping religious persecution, traders from Barbados, and later the Spanish, although Kiawah Indians had long lived here. Pirates such as Blackbeard made their name here and the city was an entry point for the Middle Passage from Africa, bringing slaves to the nearby plantations. It was also the site of a few Revolutionary War battles before the "shot heard 'round the world" at Fort Sumter, signaling the start of the Civil War. Gershwin based his popular opera *Porgy and Bess* on life in Charleston and the city has inspired musicians, artists, and writers ever since. Today it's known as the "Holy City" for its abundance of churches and synagogues and has become highly regarded for its restaurant scene. Food items only found here have seen a resurgence, namely the Benne seed and Carolina Gold rice.

Hilton Head was first claimed by English sea captain William Hilton for England in 1663, but he didn't stay long at his namesake land. Cotton planters later settled in 1800, establishing 15 plantations, one of which was later developed into a golf course now known as Sea Pines Plantation. Today, the communities around Hilton Head Island, including Beaufort, Daufuskie Island, and Bluffton, are favorite places for nature lovers and still have ties to the Gullah community. Beaufort was featured in a number of films, but perhaps the most notable is *The Big Chill*, which set up production in the town in 1983.

The area now known as the Grand Strand officially runs from the historic port of Georgetown to the North Carolina border, including Myrtle Beach, Pawleys Island, Murrells Inlet, and dozens of smaller coastal communities. The beaches around Myrtle Beach have long been a popular place for tourists dating back to the 1940s. Few of the locations from the Golden Age of Grand Strand tourism exist today, replaced with condo skyscrapers, chain restaurants and tourist-focused stores. But there's no shortage of family-friendly things to do.

SLAVE TRADE

It's important to know about South Carolina's history with the slave trade before visiting. Slaves were first brought over from mostly Senegal and Sierra Leone in the 1600s but increased into the 1700s. Charleston was a major point of entry for slaves and a number of markets were set up around the present-day City Market. During this time, an estimated 40 percent of all African slaves transported to North America came through the city. Rice was the main crop, accounting for much of the country's supply, as well as the sought-after Sea Island cotton.

During this time, the creole language of the Gullahs was developed between Beaufort, Charleston, and Georgetown, which is still spoken today. But in 1739, the state's first major slave uprising took place at the Stono River. A group led an armed march bound for Spanish Florida, but were intercepted by the local militia. At the end of the conflict, 44 slaves and 42 white soldiers were killed and six plantations were burned, making it the bloodiest slave revolt in colonial America. A law was passed to limit the slaves' rights to assemble and another put a decade-long moratorium on importing more slaves.

But in 1822, a freed slave named Denmark Vesey, was arrested for plotting a slave uprising of over 9,000 people. Despite defending himself at his trial, he was hanged for his crimes. Thirty-five of those said to be involved were also hanged and another 35 sold to plantations in the Caribbean.

Less than 40 years later, South Carolina seceded from the union and slavery was officially abolished in January of 1865 with the passage of the 13th amendment to the US Constitution. Change didn't take place overnight and scars from our country's dark history will always be present. Touring plantations is one of the Lowcountry's most popular activities for tourists, but keep in mind the conditions that people were kept in at these lavish estates, no matter the guide's stories of "slaves treated like family."

⊙ Can't-Miss Landmarks

» The iconic **Charleston City Market** (188 Meeting St., Charleston; thecharlestoncitymarket.com) is one of the most visited places in the city and has been selling everything from produce to gifts since the 1800s. It's been renovated in the last few years and now sells prepared foods and local items such as sweet grass baskets as well as souvenirs.

» Another recognizable location is **Rainbow Row** (East Bay Street), a strip of homes painted in pastel hues. They're among the oldest in the city and signal the start of The Battery, the area at the southernmost point on the peninsula that boasts the most elaborate homes. At the end is White Point Gardens, a shady space with Civil War cannons. It was here that Stede Bonnet, better known as the "Gentleman Pirate," was hung for his crimes.

» And speaking of pirates, Bonnet was held at the **Old Exchange Building & Provost Dungeon** (122 E. Bay St., Charleston; oldexchange.org; 843-727-2165), now a historic landmark. A popular stop on ghost tours, this building is also where George

(left) Charleston City Market, (right) Rainbow Row

(clockwise from top)
Old Exchange Building,
Old Slave Mart Museum,
South Carolina Aquarium,
Hunley Graves Magnolia
Cemetery

Washington greeted South Carolinians during a visit. The Declaration of Independence was read aloud to the locals and slaves were sold at the site.

» The *Hunley* (1250 Supply St., North Charleston; hunley.org; 843-743-4865) was a Civil War submarine that sunk three different times, but in 1864 it became the first successful combat submarine when it sank the *USS Housatonic*. In 2000, with help from writer Clive Cussler, the *Hunley* was brought up from the sea floor, restored, and displayed at the North Charleston museum. Also inside are artifacts found on board and information about the men who perished onboard.

» The **Old Slave Mart Museum** (6 Chalmers St., Charleston; nps.gov/nr/travel/charleston/osm.htm; 843-958-6467) is one of the only slave auction buildings still standing in the city, located on one of the last remaining cobblestone streets. It later became an apartment building, but in 1938 was purchased, becoming a museum devoted to African-American history and the slave trade.

» Younger visitors love the **South Carolina Aquarium** (100 Aquarium Wharf, Charleston; scaquarium.org; 843-577-3474), a modest facility that showcases the local ocean life as well as native species to the state. The Association of Zoos and Aquariums–certified attraction puts an emphasis on education and has the area's only sea turtle hospital.

» Civil War buffs tend to add **Fort Sumter** (340 Concord St., Charleston; nps.gov/fosu/index.htm; 843-883-3123) to their "must-visit" list since the conflict started here. Boats leave frequently for the island fort, where park rangers discuss what led up to the war and what made this fort so unique. If time allows, head to **Fort Moultrie** (1214 Middle St., Sullivan's Island; nps.gov /fosu/learn/historyculture/fort_moultrie.htm; 843-883-3123) on Sullivan's Island, a fort originally built of palmetto logs and sand. It protected Charleston from British capture during the Civil War, but eventually fell. It was used again during the Civil War.

(above) Fort Moultrie, (left) Charleston Museum

» Get your dose of culture on Charleston's Museum Mile, a strip of attractions on Meeting Street. Start at the **Charleston Museum** (360 Meeting St., Charleston; charlestonmuseum.org; 843-722-2996), the country's oldest, which has exhibits on the Lowcountry and beyond. Highlights include a giant whale skeleton, items belonging to the city's founding families, and homemade quilts. The **Children's Museum of the Lowcountry** (25 Ann St., Charleston; explorecml.org; 843-853-8962) has nine interactive spaces dedicated to the arts, sciences, and humanities. The **Gibbes Museum of Art** (135 Meeting St., Charleston; gibbesmuseum. org; 843-722-2706) has one of the oldest museum buildings in the region, first opened in the 1900s. The collection was started by a local philanthropist and all pieces have connections to the city and the South.

» Touring plantations and historic homes is a popular activity in Charleston. Most of the plantations are located along the scenic Ashley River Road. Most of them did have slaves and some gloss over the topic while others discuss the past truthfully. **Middleton**

Place (4300 Ashley River Rd., Charleston; middletonplace.org; 843-556-6020), dating back to 1705, is known for its gardens, where you might see an alligator sunning itself. They have an onsite inn and restaurant and have tours of the home. **Magnolia Plantation and Gardens** (3550 Ashley River Rd., Charleston; magnoliaplantation.com; 843-571-1266) also has stunning gardens, especially when the camellias are blooming. In addition to the house, they have nature trails and the Audubon Swamp Garden. **Boone Hall Plantation** (1235 Long Point Rd., Mt Pleasant; boonehallplantation.com; 843-884-4371) was featured in *The Notebook* and holds frequent events such as their annual oyster festival. **Drayton Hall** (3380 Ashley River Rd., Charleston; draytonhall.org; 843-769-2600) is unique because it is unrestored and

(clockwise from top left) Middleton Place, Drayton Hall, Boone Hall Plantation, Magnolia Plantation

has been left free of "period furnishings." It also has nature trails of the surrounding swamp. Closer to Georgetown lie **Hopsewee Plantation** (494 Hopsewee Rd., Georgetown; hopsewee.com; 843-546-7891) and **Hampton Plantation** (1950 Rutledge Rd., McClellanville; southcarolinaparks.com/hampton; 843-546-9361), both open to the public.

» There are only four historic homes open for tours year-round, but others open seasonally, especially around Christmas. The **Aiken-Rhett House** (48 Elizabeth St., Charleston; historiccharleston.org/house-museums/aiken-rhett-house; 843-723-1159) is located on upper King Street and was built in 1820. The bright yellow home stayed in the family until it opened as a museum in 1975.

» The **Edmondston-Alston House** (21 E. Battery, Charleston; edmondstonalston.com; 843-722-7171) is the only one on the Battery open for tours, built in 1825. General P.T. Beauregard watched the attack on Fort Sumter from the balcony and a few months later Robert E. Lee stayed the night.

» Now operated by the Charleston Museum, the **Heyward-Washington House** (87 Church St., Charleston; charlestonmuseum.org/historic-houses/heyward-washington-house; 843-722-0354)

Joseph Manigault House

was built in 1772 in the Georgian style. It was the home of Thomas Heyward, Jr., one of the signers of the Declaration of Independence. George Washington also stayed here.

» The **Joseph Manigault House** (350 Meeting St., Charleston; charlestonmuseum.org/historic-houses/joseph-manigault-house; 843-723-2926), also run by the museum, was built in 1803. The family who lived here were Huguenots escaping persecution in France, but found wealth as rice planters and merchants.

» The **Harbour Town Lighthouse** (149 Lighthouse Rd., Hilton Head Island; harbourtownlighthouse.com; 866-305-9814) is Hilton Head Island's most iconic structure, with its signature red and white stripes. Built in 1970, it has always welcomed visitors to climb to the top. From here, you can see the harbor and popular golf courses.

» The 68-acre **Coastal Discovery Museum** (70 Honey Horn Dr., Hilton Head Island; coastaldiscovery.org; 843-689-6767) has plenty of non-beach fun to keep the little ones occupied, including nature trails, gardens, and a butterfly enclosure. The Smithsonian affiliate is a popular attraction for its events and programming.

» Originally a private garden, **Brookgreen Gardens** (1931 Brookgreen Garden Dr., Murrells Inlet; brookgreen. org; 843-235-6000) is now one of the Grand Strand's most beloved attractions, open for 85 years. In addition to the acres of landscaped gardens, unique sculptures are placed throughout. There's even a wildlife section. Their seasonal events are worth a visit, especially the Nights of a Thousand Candles.

Brookgreen Gardens

(clockwise from the top)
Myrtle Beach Boardwalk
and SkyWheel in the
distance, Charleston Tea
Plantation, Magnolia
Cemetery, Firefly Distillery

» And the **Myrtle Beach Boardwalk** (myrtlebeachdowntown.
com) can't be missed. As the oldest part of the beach, the
boardwalk offers classic eateries, an arcade, and newer attractions such as Ripley's Believe It or Not and a zip line course. **Fun
Plaza Arcade** (902 N. Ocean Blvd., Myrtle Beach; facebook.com
/Fun-Plaza-Arcade-120892377940140) has all the games of your
childhood, including Skee-Ball.

» You can't visit the boardwalk without seeing the **Myrtle Beach
SkyWheel** (1110 N. Ocean Blvd., Myrtle Beach; skywheel.com;
843-839-9200), a modern Ferris wheel that provides views of the
Grand Strand. Rides last around 10 minutes and the glass pods
provide 360-degree views. They run at night and VIP upgrades
are available.

 Off the Beaten Path

» The original sweet tea vodka was created by **Firefly Distillery** (6775 Bears Bluff Rd., Wadmalaw Island; fireflyspirits.com;
843-557-1405) on Wadmalaw Island, less than an hour from
downtown Charleston. Sample their varieties of flavored sweet
tea vodkas as well as those sold only here. The **Deep Water
Vineyard** (6775 Bears Bluff Rd., Wadmalaw Island; deepwater-
vineyard.com; 843-559-6867) is located on the same property,
so you can continue your outing with locally made wine. And
while you're on the island, visit **Charleston Tea Plantation** (6617
Maybank Hwy., Wadmalaw Island; charlestonteaplantation.com;
843-559-0383), the nation's only tea plantation that has been in
operation since 1799.

» As Meeting Street turns into North Charleston, **Magnolia Cemetery** (70 Cunnington Ave., Charleston; magnoliacemetery.net;
843-722-8638) is right on the water that holds the tomb of the
Hunley crew. It is also home to centuries of Charleston elite such
as the Manigaults, Aikens, and Draytons.

» Despite its imposing Greek Revival building and downtown location, **Karpeles Manuscript Library** (68 Spring St., Charleston; rain.org/~karpeles/chainfo.html; 843-853-4651) is not known by many visitors. Originally a Methodist church, the space was used as a medical storehouse during the Civil War. Today it houses a permanent collection and rotating exhibit of rare manuscripts, books, and letters.

» Check out the next generation of regional artists at the **Halsey Institute of Contemporary Art** (161 Calhoun St., Charleston; halsey.cofc.edu; 843-953-4422), located on the College of Charleston campus. The non-collecting museum focuses on visual arts from around the world.

» An unlikely home to Trappist monks, **Mepkin Abbey** (1098 Mepkin Abbey Rd., Moncks Corner; mepkinabbey.org/word-press; 843-761-8509) in Moncks Corner, outside of Charleston, grows its own mushrooms and serves as a spiritual retreat center. Visitors can explore their gardens.

Angel Oak

» **Charles Towne Landing** (1500 Old Towne Rd., Charleston; southcarolinaparks.com/charles-towne-landing; 843-852-4200) is located near the original British settlement outside of downtown Charleston. Today the park has replicas of the settlement and the ships that brought people over as well as a small zoo.

» **Angel Oak** (3688 Angel Oak Rd., Johns Island; 843-559-3496) is the oldest living thing east of the Mississippi, a massive oak tree estimated to be over 400 years old on Johns Island, one of Charleston's barrier islands. Its limbs sag under the weight, now held up with metal supports. The park that surrounds it is free to visit.

» **Colonial Dorchester State Historic Site** (300 State Park Rd., Summerville; southcarolinaparks.com/colonial-dorchester; 843-873-1740) honors the area's colonial history, first settled in the 1600s. All that remains today of the trading town are ruins, built mostly out of oyster shells, as well as the St. George's Bell Tower.

» The Military College of South Carolina, known better as The Citadel, is one of the nation's most prestigious military academies. The school is open to the public for weekly parades and also has **The Citadel Museum** (171 Moultrie St., Charleston; library.citadel.edu/museum; 843-953-2569), which interprets the institution's history from its founding in 1842 to the present.

» **Francis Marion National Forest** (2967 Steed Creek Rd., Huger; fs.usda.gov/scnfs; 843-336-2200) is named for the Revolutionary War hero who defeated the British troops in these swamps, giving him the nickname "Swamp Fox." Popular with hikers, boaters, and outdoors enthusiasts, it's also a stop along the Palmetto Trail, a statewide hiking path.

» Reptile fans should visit the **Edisto Serpentarium** (1374 SC-174, Edisto Island; edistoserpentarium.com; 843-869-1171). Here you'll get up close with turtles, snakes, and lizards that call this area home as well as species from around the world.

Old Sheldon Church Ruins

» Originally built in the 1700s, the church now known as the **Old Sheldon Church Ruins** (Old Sheldon Church Rd., Yemassee) outside of Beaufort was first burned during the Revolutionary War. It was rebuilt in 1826, but locals took it apart to rebuild their homes after Sherman's troops destroyed them. The original parish graves still exist here.

» **The Rice Museum** (633 Front St., Georgetown; ricemuseum. org; 843-546-7423) is devoted to the state's most important crop. It's made up of historic buildings such as the Old Market Building and the Kaminski Hardware Building. Exhibits discuss the origin of the crop and the town's maritime history. The nearby **Kaminski House Museum** (1003 Front St., Georgetown; kaminskimuseum.org; 843-546-7706) and **Gullah Museum** (123 King St., Unit 7; Georgetown; gullahmuseumsc.com; 843 527 1851) are worth a visit if you have time.

» Hilton Head Island is known for its diverse ecosystems. Wildlife enthusiasts should visit the **Pinckney Island Wildlife Refuge** (US 278 W., Hilton Head Island; fws.gov/refuge/pinckney_island; 843-784-2468), which is only accessible by the 14 miles of bike and foot paths. Facilities are bare bones, but there's nowhere better to spot alligators, herons, and deer.

» Near Hilton Head is Parris Island, home to the US Marine Corps. Visitors can learn about the island and corps' history at the **Parris Island Museum** (111 Panama St., Beaufort; parrisislandmuseum. com; 843-228-2951). The island is also open for parades.

» **Hobcaw Barony** (22 Hobcaw Rd., Georgetown; hobcawbarony.org; 843-546-4623) near Georgetown is equal parts historic home and nature preserve. Philanthropist Bernard M. Baruch purchased the property in 1905 and it was a family retreat for generations. It eventually passed to his daughter Belle. Here she entertained people such as Winston Churchill and Franklin D. Roosevelt. There is a small interpretive center that focuses on the barony's wildlife.

» Located within Huntington Beach State Park in Myrtle Beach, **Atalaya** (Atalaya Rd., Murrells Inlet; southcarolinaparks.com /huntington-beach; 843-237-4440) is the Moorish-style building that served as the former summer home of the wealthy Huntington family. The home is now a museum and is open to guided tours, and the state park has beach access and nature trails for exploring.

» Myrtle Beach seems an unlikely place for an art museum, but the **Franklin G. Burroughs-Simeon B. Chapin Art Museum** (3100 S. Ocean Blvd., Myrtle Beach; myrtlebeachartmuseum.org; 843-238-2510) excels in exhibiting regional paintings, textiles, sculpture, photography, ceramics, and more. Open since 1997, the best part about the museum is that it's free to visit.

» Inland in Conway, a short drive from Myrtle Beach, is the charming **Horry County Museum** (805 Main St., Conway; horrycountymuseum.org; 843-915-5320), which details the history of the Grand Strand. Located in a 1905 school building, exhibits include local artifacts, an aquarium featured on Animal Planet's *Tanked*, and a living history farm.

► Tours for Every Interest

》 If you're worried where to start when it comes to eating in Charleston, **Culinary Tours of Charleston** (bulldogtours.com/food-tours, 843-722-8687) can help. Their walking tours introduce visitors to the history of the city including its British, Native American, French, Spanish, and African influences.

》 Take to the water with **Charleston Harbor Tours** (charlestonharbortours.com, 843-722-1112) for the best views of the Holy City. The company offers the *Carolina Belle* tour, which showcases Fort Sumter, the Battery, and the Ravenel Bridge on an open-deck boat. They also have frequent events such as jazz brunch cruises.

》 You can also kayak Charleston's waterways with **Nature Adventure Outfitters** (natureadventureoutfitters.com, 843-568-3222), an outfitter that leaves from the Shem Creek area of Mount Pleasant, across the Charleston harbor. Tours visit the shrimping area for fishermen as well as the Crab Bank Island bird reserve. Outfitters are also set up in the Myrtle Beach and Hilton Head areas.

》 Many Charleston tour companies talk about the city's history, but **Gullah Tours** (gullahtours.com, 843-763-7551) is the only one that puts an emphasis on the contributions of Black Charlestonians. Sites visited include "Catfish Row" from *Porgy and Bess*, the Old Slave Market, and the blacksmith shop of renowned gate maker Philip Simmons.

》 The best way to experience Charleston is on foot. **Lowcountry Walking Tours** (lowcountrywalkingtours.com, 843-410-9688) runs three tours of downtown, focusing on the winding alleys and passages, the historic district, and downtown's most iconic landmarks.

》 To learn about Daufuskie Island's history, it's best to go with a guide. **Tour Daufuskie** (tourdaufuskie.com, 843-842-9449) offers guided and self-guided excursions, including kayaking tours, eco-tours, and tours led by a native Gullah.

💤 Five Unique Sleeps in the Lowcountry and Grand Strand

In Charleston alone, you'll find hundreds of hotels, inns, and properties, all with top-notch service and awards to prove it.

» The pink facade of the **Mills House Hotel** (115 Meeting St., Charleston; millshouse.com; 843-577-2400) has hosted well-known guests such as Theodore Roosevelt since opening in 1853. Rumored to be haunted, the hotel has all the modern amenities and is within walking distance from downtown attractions.

» Get fully off the beaten path with an excursion to Bulls Island, an uninhabited barrier island outside of Charleston. **Coastal Expeditions** runs trips to the 4,000-acre wildlife refuge, including a stay at the **Dominick House** (Bulls Island; coastalexpeditions.com/dominick-house-expedition; 843-884-7684), a 1920s manor house.

» In Beaufort, stay at the AAA-four-diamond-rated **Rhett House Inn** (1009 Craven St., Beaufort; rhetthouseinn.com; 843-524-9030), featured in *The Big Chill*, *Forrest Gump*, and *Prince of Tides*. You can even stay in the rooms where your favorite celebrities have slept and enjoy complimentary champagne, breakfast, and homemade desserts.

» One of the country's top-rated resorts is in the small town of Bluffton. The **Inn at Palmetto Bluff** (19 Village Park Sq., Bluffton; palmettobluff.com/stay; 866-706-6565) is set on the ruins of an antebellum mansion and has sprawling grounds to explore, multiple dining options, and wellness activities.

» Those traveling by RV or those who would rather camp than stay in a resort will enjoy **Myrtle Beach Travel Park** (10108 Kings Rd., Myrtle Beach; myrtlebeachtravelpark.com; 843-449-3714), a 125-acre oceanfront campground featuring WiFi, a water park, and fitness classes. Guests can choose from RV campsites as well as cabins and travel trailers for rent.

Midlands

Columbia is the geographic heart of the state, first settled as the capital in 1786 as a compromise between factions in the upstate and lowcountry. For many years, legislators came into the city only during session, spending as little time there as possible. But the University of South Carolina opened in 1801, bringing with it more residents. Much of the city was damaged during the Civil War thanks to Sherman's troops, so the architecture isn't as old as that of Charleston. But it's in a unique location, surrounded by the Saluda and Broad Rivers as well as Lake Murray.

To the west is Aiken, which served as a retreat for the Vanderbilts, Astors, and Mellons, who called it the "Newport of the South" from the 1880s to 1940s. The climate agreed with them so they built luxury hotels, started polo matches, and settled into country homes. Like in Camden, to the east, Aiken still holds annual horse races that are a favorite local tradition. Some of the towns nearby include North Augusta and Beech Island.

Newberry and Orangeburg are destinations with fewer traditional attractions to visit, but each has a unique history within the state. Orangeburg was settled by German immigrants in the 1730s and is now the state's largest cotton producer. It's also home to South Carolina State University, the state's top historically black college. Newberry is a charming town with a performing arts community that dates back to the 1800s.

⊚ Can't-Miss Landmarks

》 Local families love the **Riverbanks Zoo** (500 Wildlife Pkwy., Columbia; riverbanks.org; 803-779-8717), a West Columbia complex that includes an AZA-accredited zoo, zip lining courses that go over the river and animal enclosures, and a sprawling botanical garden. Visitors of all ages can enjoy the wildlife feedings and educational lectures.

BBQ DEBATE

If you're looking to start an argument with someone in the South, mention football or barbecue. Many parts of the region claim a barbecue culture, especially North Carolina, but South Carolina has four different styles of sauces found throughout. The state even claims to have "invented" barbecue and defines it specifically as barbecued pork. The four types of sauces are mustard, vinegar and pepper, light tomato, and heavy tomato. Mustard is the native style, first crafted by German immigrants in the 1700s. Vinegar and pepper, popular along the coast, is the most traditional method. And tomato sauces, with light or heavy tomato bases, are what people from outside the region know as "barbecue sauce." But you haven't had it until you've had barbecue in South Carolina! To see the state's best pork-tastic eateries, visit SCBBQTrail.com or pick up a map at their visitor centers.

» **Congaree National Park** (100 National Park Rd., Hopkins; nps.gov/cong/index.htm; 803-776-4396) is the state's only national park, as well as the newest, located about 45 minutes from downtown Columbia. Locals saved the 20,000 acres of bald cypresses and pushed for it to become nationally protected. Today visitors can kayak the floodplain or hike on the miles of boardwalks and trails.

Congaree National Park

» As the name implies, the **South Carolina State Museum** (301 Gervais St., Columbia; scmuseum.org; 803-898-4921) documents the history of the state, including its art, history, science, and technology. Highlights include their observatory and planetarium.

» Bring your little ones to the **EdVenture Children's Museum** (211 Gervais St., Columbia; edventure.org; 803-779-3100), an attraction that includes the world's largest statue of a child. Interactive exhibits show them what it's like to be a vet and other educational encounters.

» Built in 1871, the **Woodrow Wilson Family Home** (1705 Hampton St., Columbia; historiccolumbia.org/woodrow-wilson-family-home; 803-252-7742) tells of the family's life during Reconstruction where "Tommy" Wilson lived at age 14 until they moved three years later for his father's job. The home was extensively restored in 2014.

» The **Robert Mills House** (1616 Blanding St., Columbia; historiccolumbia.org/robert-mills-house-and-gardens; 803-252-1770) pays tribute to the state's native son, the architect behind the Washington Monument, the Treasury building, and this home. Designed for wealthy merchants in 1823, the National Historic Landmark is known for its ornamental gardens.

» The **South Carolina State House** (1100 Gervais St., Columbia; southcarolinaparks.com/education-and-history/state-house; 803-734-2430), first built and then destroyed in the 1800s, is at the center of the city's grid system with a dome viewable throughout the city. Even when legislature isn't in session, you can go on a self-guided tour of the building's highlights, including the African-American monument.

» North of Columbia lies the quaint town of Newberry. The **Newberry Opera House** (1201 McKibben St., Newberry; newberryoperahouse.com; 803-276-6264) was first built in 1881 and also served as a stable and fire station over the years. Now it's a theater that hosts touring acts and local troupes.

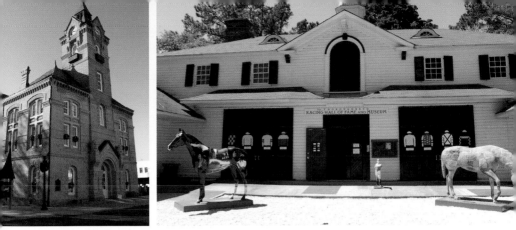

(left) Newberry Opera House, (right) Aiken Thoroughbred Museum

» History takes on new life at North Augusta's **Living History Park** (218 W. Spring Grove Ave., North Augusta; colonialtimes. us; 803-279-7560), near Aiken, which was created in 1991 to document the area's colonial past. Interpretive structures have been set up, including a tavern, apothecary, and mercantile.

» Learn about the city's horse racing history at the **Aiken Thoroughbred Racing Hall of Fame and Museum** (135 Dupree Place, Aiken; aikenracinghalloffame.com; 803-642-7631), a humble museum that displays jockey jerseys, trophies, and other memorabilia related to the steeplechase and other races. The museum is located within **Hopeland Gardens** (135 Dupree Place, Aiken; visitaikensc.com/whattodo/detail/hopelands_gardens; 803-642-

7650), a 14-acre estate donated to the city in 1969. The 100-year old oaks and walking paths make it a favorite of locals and visitors.

Hopeland Gardens

Off the Beaten Path

» Get a dose of culture at the award-winning **Columbia Museum of Art** (1515 Main St., Columbia, columbiamuseum.org; 803-799-2810), located on the University of South Carolina campus. The collection features American, Asian, and European artists as well as regularly changing exhibits. The Kress and Vogel collections were donated by benefactors.

» The state has a long military tradition and the **South Carolina Military Museum** (1 National Guard Rd., Columbia; scmilitary-museum.net; 803-299-4440) is one of the largest National Guard museums in the country. Exhibits chronicle the state's citizen soldiers from 1670 to the present.

» Founded in 1970, the **Lexington County Museum** (231 Fox St., Lexington; lexingtoncountymuseum.org; 803-359-8369) documents the history of the area around Columbia from 1770 to the present, including early quilts, the original county post office, and other historic structures.

» **701 Center for Contemporary Art** (701 Whaley St., Columbia; 701cca.org; 803-319-9949) showcases what's happening now in the art world, combining education and exhibits from up-and-coming artists from the state, the region, and the world.

» Another USC-affiliated museum is the **McKissick Museum** (816 Bull St., Columbia; artsandsciences.sc.edu/mckissickmu-seum; 803-777-7251), a Works Progress building from the 1930s that holds treasures from the South. Minerals, folk art, and political memorabilia make up the permanent collection.

» Columbia and its surrounding communities are at the heart of state parks and nature. **Lake Murray** (dnr.sc.gov/lakes /murray/description.html) is a short drive from downtown, offering boating, swimming, and fishing. **Poinsett State Park** (6660 Poinsett Park Rd., Wedgefield; southcarolinaparks.com /poinsett; 803-494-8177), **Dreher Island State Park** (19 Park Marina Dr., Prosperity; southcarolinaparks.com/dreher-island;

803-734-0156), and **Sesquicentennial State Park** (9564 Two Notch Rd., Columbia; southcarolinaparks.com/sesqui; 803-788-2706) all have miles of hiking trails and accommodations. **Harbison State Forest** (5600 Broad River Rd., Columbia, state.sc.us /forest/refharb.htm; 803-896-8890) and **Three Rivers Greenway** (Alexandria Road, Columbia; riveralliance.org; 803-765-2200) are also nearby green spaces.

» In Beech Island, an area near the Georgia border, **Redcliffe Plantation** (181 Redcliffe Rd., Beech Island; southcarolinaparks. com/redcliffe; 803-827-1473) sits as an 1859 antebellum mansion with its original furnishings. But the story is a unique one. Owner John Henry Hammond fought to keep slavery, treated women like they were lesser, molested his nieces, and had a slave mistress. But diaries were kept that later exposed him, which makes up much of the tour. It's an honest look into that time period. It was restored in the 1940s by his descendants, who turned it over to the state parks system.

» Located in the former Banksia estate, the **Aiken County Historical Museum** (433 Newberry St SW, Aiken; aikenmuseum. us; 803-642-2015) details the history of the area known as the

Redcliffe Plantation

Aiken County Museum

"Winter Colony." Exhibits cover the county's history and the family who lived here, and contain historic structures including an 1800s log cabin.

» The area of South Carolina along the Savannah River is known for its unique pottery, especially that of the town of **Edgefield** (exploreedgefield.com). The thick deposits of clay have been used for pottery since 2500 BC. In the 1800s, potters moved here to create pottery to sell for kitchen necessities, but few of these tradesmen exist today. The "face vessels" are now collectors' items, but some are sold in town.

» **Edisto Memorial Gardens** (200 Riverside Dr. SW, Orangeburg; orangeburg.sc.us/gardens; 803-533-6020) honors the six hundred Confederate soldiers who stalled the advancement of the Union army near this site in 1865. In the 1920s, five acres of azaleas were planted, followed by a playground, greenhouse, and, later, roses were added as well as a bronze marker for the soldiers.

» Located in the small town of Blackville between Aiken and Orangeburg, **God's Acre Healing Springs** (Springs Court, Black-ville; sciway.net/sc-photos/barnwell-county/healing-springs.

html; 803-284-2444) is one of the state's more unusual attractions. Legend of the water's healing properties began with the Native Americans and was picked up by Revolutionary War soldiers. Today, the mineral spring is located behind a church and is free to visit.

▶ Tours for Every Interest

» Visit Columbia's best restaurants and explore the Vista neighborhood with **Two Gals and a Fork** (twogalsfoodtours.com, 803-260-7992), a walking food tour company. Portions are large enough to make up an entire meal and drinks are optional.

» Check out the city's thriving craft beer scene with **Columbia Brew Bus** (columbiabrewbus.com, 757-871-8150). Founded by three friends from college, tours visit three breweries with tastings and transportation. Tours are held every weekend.

💤 Five Unique Sleeps in the Midlands

» **The Willcox Hotel** (100 Colleton Ave. SW, Aiken; thewillcox. com; 803-648-1898) has hosted countless celebrities over the years, including Winston Churchill, Franklin D Roosevelt, John Barrymore, and Fred Astaire, but was saved by locals after being closed for 40 years. Now it's back to its former glory with a luxurious spa and beloved brunch.

» Nearby, the **Rosemary Inn Bed and Breakfast** (804 Carolina Ave., North Augusta; rosemaryinnbb.com; 803-426-1546) is just one of a handful of antebellum-style properties overlooking the river. Built in 1902, the home was owned by the same family until the 1980s but is now a comfortable inn with daily breakfast and chic furnishings.

Wilcox Hotel

» The **Camden House Bed & Breakfast** (1502 Broad St., Camden; camdenhouse.us; 803-713-1013) has the same type of charm, located in an 1832 mansion. Rooms have high ceilings, private baths, and king or queen beds.

» Make the **Inn at USC-Wyndham Garden** (1619 Pendleton St., Columbia; innatusc.com; 803-779-7779) your base. Don't let the chain name fool you, as this hotel on the college campus contains part of the 1910 Black House. Now incorporated into the lobby design, rooms include complimentary breakfast and comfortable rooms.

» Staying at **Dreher Island State Park** (19 Park Marina Dr., Prosperity; southcarolinaparks.com/dreher-island; 803-734-0156), north of Columbia, doesn't mean you have to "rough it." The park has multi-room villas with WiFi, fireplaces, and small cooking spaces.

Upstate South Carolina

Referred to as the "Upcountry" or "Upstate," northern South Carolina borders the Blue Ridge Mountains, making it better suited for outdoor exploration and providing a comfortable climate year-round. The many lakes, mountain vistas, and waterfalls frequently draw in curious travelers and fishermen, especially to Lake Hartwell. Sassafras Mountain, the state's highest peak, is located in this part of the state along the North Carolina border. It contains large cities such as Greenville and smaller towns such as Pendleton, Travelers Rest, and Anderson. Originally settled by the Scots-Irish in hopes of turning it into an agricultural area, this part of the state was better suited to manufacturing and milling textiles. Native Americans lived here long before European arrival and their legacy is still found in the Cherokee names of towns and lakes such as Tamassee and Keowee.

EASY BEING GREEN

The city of Greenville has gone from being an overlooked Southern city to a highly acclaimed example of restoration. It's always been a great destination for outdoors lovers, especially for its proximity to a number of lakes and mountains. But even city dwellers can appreciate the city's green spaces with ease. **Falls Park on the Reedy** is a 32-acre park that straddles the Reedy River downtown. Restaurants and art galleries have set up alongside it and the **Peace Center** (peacecenter.org) hosts concerts and events overlooking it. The **Swamp Rabbit Trail** is another example, transforming a disused rail line into a paved biking and walking path that connects downtown Greenville to Travelers Rest, a town to the north that is home to **Furman University** (furman.edu). The city also has a bike share program, making it easy to be green.

⊙ Can't-Miss Landmarks

» The famous German car company opened their American headquarters, and the **BMW Zentrum** (1400 SC-101, Greer; bmwusfactory.com/zentrum; 864-802-5300) in Spartanburg. The one-of-a-kind visitor center and museum has exhibits on the company as well as some of their finest cars. It's free and open to the public.

BMW Zentrum

» **Falls Park on the Reedy** (601 S. Main St., Greenville; fallspark. com; 864-467-4350) is a 32-acre park in the heart of downtown Greenville. The Liberty Bridge spans the waterfalls and the park also includes art pieces, bike paths, and landscaped gardens.

» Located in Heritage Green, the **Greenville County Museum of Art** (420 College St., Greenville; gcma.org; 864-271-7570) has exhibits focused on the region and is free to visit. Next door, the kids can play at the **Children's Museum of the Upstate** (300 College St., Greenville; tcmupstate.org; 864-233-7755), which has a Michelin-sponsored playground.

» Cycle or walk between Greenville and Travelers Rest on the **Swamp Rabbit Trail** (Greenville and Travelers Rest; greenvillerec. com/ghs-swamp-rabbit-trail), a nearly 20-mile rail trail named for the former railroad that honored a native species. Along the way are restroom facilities as well as restaurants and breweries.

Greenville County Museum of Art

» The Pickens County native and baseball legend is honored at the **Shoeless Joe Jackson Museum** (356 Field St., Greenville; shoeless-joejackson.org; 864-346-4867), which is the home in which he lived and died. It opened as a museum in 2008 near Greenville's minor league baseball park with many of his belongings inside.

» Operated by Furman University, the **Upcountry History Museum** (540 Buncombe St., Greenville; upcountryhistory.org; 864-467-3100) in downtown Greenville hosts exhibits on the culture of the northern region of South Carolina. Some changing exhibits are targeted to kids, while others discuss themes from the state's past.

Off the Beaten Path

» If you've biked the entire Swamp Rabbit Trail, your next challenge should be the **Palmetto Trail** (palmettoconservation.org/palmetto-trail), a trail that spans the entire state and starts in Walhalla, near the state line with Georgia. You'll pass through a number of state parks as well as ecosystems.

» Many think about the state's connection to the Civil War, but this region was actually home to four national historic site–listed Revolutionary War battlefields. **Cowpens National Battlefield** (4001 Chesnee Hwy., Gaffney; nps.gov/cowp/index.htm; 864-461-2828) in Gaffney tells of an American victory over the British.

» The Greenville area is also home to historic bridges. **Campbell's Bridge** (171 Campbell Covered Bridge Rd., Landrum; greenvillerec.com/parks/campbells-covered-bridge) is the state's last remaining covered bridge, painted in an iconic shade of red. Nearby in Travelers Rest is the **Poinsett Bridge** (Callahan Mountain Rd., Landrum; greenvillerec.com/parks/poinsett-bridge), a stone spanning bridge that is believed to be the oldest remaining in the state.

» Tucked into the mountains in the small town of Cleveland is the Fred W. Symmes Chapel at YMCA Camp Greenville, better known as **Pretty Place** (100 YMCA Camp Rd., Cleveland; campgreenville. org/pretty-place; 864-836-3291) for its unmatched views. Originally built in 1914, a simple cross sits in front of the overlook.

▶ Tours for Every Interest

» Find out why the city has been recognized for its food scene with a food tour by **Greenville Tours** (greenvillehistorytours. com, 864-567-3940). The three tours they offer highlight breakfast eateries, barbecue joints, and chefs tables around town. The company also has history tours that visit the city's historic neighborhoods.

» Tour the city on Segway or bike with **Greenville Glides** (greenvillesegwaytours.com, 864-214-0119), a company that explores neighborhoods such as the West End. They have haunted tours and rent bikes for the nearby Swamp Rabbit Trail.

» Sip your way around the Upcountry with **The Brewery Experience's** (thebreweryexperience.com, 828-216-1343) Greenville Brewery Tour. It visits Quest, Thomas Creek, Swamp Rabbit, and other taprooms for samples and snacks. Transportation is included.

Five Unique Sleeps in the Upstate

>> There's no place like home at Greenville's **Swamp Rabbit Inn** (1 Logan St., Greenville; swamprabbitinn.com; 864-345-7990), a cozy self-catering bed and breakfast with Ikea furnishings and Danish pastries daily. The West End property is accessible to downtown and has many types of rooms.

>> **Hotel Domestique** (10 Road of Vines, Travelers Rest; hoteldomestique.com; 864-516-1715) in Travelers Rest is a world away from the city with unimpaired views of the mountains and a culinary program that will make you never want to leave. The rolling hills surrounding the resort are also a destination for cyclists.

>> Just because you're in a college town doesn't mean you have to sleep like one. **The Abernathy Hotel** (157 Old Greenville Hwy., Clemson; theabernathy.com; 864-654-5299) in Clemson is named for the town's mayor and has a prime location near campus, large guest rooms, and touches of the university's colors.

>> Listed on the National Register of Historic Places, the **Belmont Inn** (104 E. Pickens St., Abbeville; belmontinn.net; 864-459-9625) Abbeville is over 100 years old. Today, it has 25 remodeled rooms and a restaurant, located right on the town square.

>> You can connect with nature at **Sunrise Farm Bed & Breakfast** (325 Sunrise Dr., Salem; sunrisefarmbb.com; 864-944-0121) near Lake Keowee. The 1800s farm in the foothills of the Blue Ridge Mountains offers daily breakfast of farm-fresh ingredients. Get to know the animals roaming the property, including a llama and miniature horses.

Nashville

Tennessee

Founded in 1796, the land now known as Tennessee was originally inhabited by Chickasaw and Cherokee tribes. In fact, in later years, Tennessee native Andrew Jackson, then president, was responsible for their removal in the Trail of Tears. The Tennessee Valley Authority, developed in 1933, is responsible for much of the state's growth, especially its lakes and hydroelectric dams. The landlocked state may not have beaches, but there are a hundred other reasons to explore it. Music lovers can visit the places where their favorite performers, whether country, blues, or rock, lived, recorded, and performed. Its scenic byways such as the Natchez Trace Parkway and preserved land such as the Great Smoky Mountains combine with both big cities and rural areas. It's also full of history, from homesteaders of the 1800s to pre–Civil War plantations to the modern Civil Rights movement.

15 Things to Taste in Tennessee

There's no way to limit the delicious dishes you'll eat around Tennessee to 15 items, but when traveling through the state, be sure to brake for these.

1. Country Fried Steak, **The Old Mill Restaurant** (164 Old Mill Ave., Pigeon Forge; old-mill.com; 865-429-3463)

2. Pesto and sundried tomato pizza, **The Tomato Head** (12 Market Square, Knoxville; thetomatohead.com; 865-637-406)

3. The Fancy breakfast sandwich, **Niedlov's Breadworks** (215 E. Main St., Chattanooga; niedlovs.com; 423-756-0303)

4. DIY Donuts, **Courthouse Donuts** (160 Court Ave., Sevierville; courthousedonuts.com; 865-286-9073)

5. Tiramisu, **La Cucina** (6811 TN 67, Mountain City, W.; 423-727-0205)

6. Pancakes, **Pancake Pantry** (628 Parkway, Gatlinburg; pancakepantry.com; 865-436-4724)

7. Goo goo clusters, **Goo Goo Shop** (116 3rd Ave. S., Nashville; googoo.com/find/downtown-nashville; 615-490-6685)

8. Biscuits, **Loveless Cafe** (8400 TN 100, Nashville; lovelesscafe.com; 615-646-9700)

9. Hot chicken, **Prince's Hot Chicken** (123 Ewing Dr., Nashville; princeshotchicken.com; 615-226-9442)

10. Mojo burger, **Puckett's Grocery** (120 4th Ave. S., Franklin; puckettsgro.com; 615-794-5527)

11. Fried chicken, **Mary Bobo's Boarding House** (295 Main St.; Lynchburg; 931-759-7394)

12. Slawburger, **Honey's Restaurant** (109 Market St. E., Fayetteville; 931-433-1181)

13. Lemon pepper catfish, **Hagy's Catfish Hotel** (1140 Hagy Ln., Shiloh; catfishhotel.com; 731-689-3327)

14. Dry Rub Ribs, **Central BBQ** (2249 Central Ave., Memphis; cbqmemphis.com; 901-272-9377)

15. Soul Burger, **Earnestine & Hazel's** (531 S. Main St., Memphis; earnestineandhazelsjukejoint.com; 901-523-9754)

East Tennessee

East Tennessee sits in the hills of the Blue Ridge and Great Smoky Mountains, part of greater Appalachia. It is full of winding roads and backcountry towns as well as larger cities. Its isolation for many years is what has preserved many of its traditions, namely the music and arts. Chattanooga is recognized as one of the country's best towns for outdoors lovers, especially for rock climbing and bouldering. It even holds an annual Ironman competition. Knoxville is home to the University of Tennessee, which is why you'll see shades of orange all over town. But it's becoming popular with the postgraduate crowd, especially those starting businesses such as breweries and shops selling home-made crafts. The towns of the Tennessee Smokies have bounced back after a devastating fire in 2016, which destroyed thousands of acres and resulted in 14 fatalities, hundreds of injuries, and thousands of properties damaged. The Tri-Cities of Bristol, Johnson City, and Kingsport showcase their ties to music and stock car racing. This part of the state is accessible via airports in Knoxville, Chattanooga, and nearby Greenville, South Carolina. Smaller airports exist in Asheville and Hickory, North Carolina, and in the Tri-Cities.

MAKERS GONNA MAKE

There's no shortage of places to shop for locally made goods in East Tennessee for the perfect souvenir. These local handicrafts highlight the traditions of the region dating back from its early settlements, including hand-carved furniture, spun tapestries, and pottery. Gatlinburg's **Arrowmont School of Arts and Crafts** (556 Pkwy., Gatlinburg; arrowmont.org) has fostered the next generation of artists since its founding in 1912. They still have classes and workshops as well as a gallery showcasing student work. The **5 Arts Studio** (150 Troll Mountain Way, Cosby; trolls.com) has been crafting quirky trolls inspired by Scandinavian folklore since 1959. Pottery is an important part of Pigeon Forge's history, which you can learn about at **The Old Mill** (175

Sidebar continues on next page

Old Mill Ave., Pigeon Forge; old-mill.com/info/pigeon-river-pottery). In this area, galleries showcase the plates, bowls, and other serving pieces and they're also used in the restaurants. You can grab a map of Gatlinburg's Arts and Crafts community at one of the Smoky Mountain visitor centers. In Knoxville, **Knox Makers** (116 Childress St. SW, Knoxville; knoxmakers.org) carries on traditions as a community and workshop for woodworking and metalsmithing. The city as a whole is taking steps to welcome makers.

 Can't-Miss Landmarks

» As one of the best aquariums in the region, the **Tennessee Aquarium** (1 Broad St., Chattanooga; tnaqua.org; 800-262-0695) focuses on conservation and education. More than 800 species are represented at the facility. Favorite exhibits include the river otters, jellyfish, and seahorses.

Tennessee Aquarium

» For generations, painted barns have advertised **Rock City** (1400 Patten Rd., Lookout Mountain, GA 30750; seerockcity. com; 706-820-2531), Tennessee's quirkiest landmark since 1932. While it has a Georgia address, it's considered part of the Chattanooga area and advertises the fact that you can see seven states from the viewpoint. Don't miss Lover's Leap and the Fairyland Caverns.

» America's largest and deepest waterfall open to the public, **Ruby Falls** (1720 South Scenic Hwy., Chattanooga; rubyfalls. com; 423-821-2544), sits 1,120 feet below ground and falls 145 feet. The limestone cave has been a favorite tourist attraction since the 1920s.

» View the steep grade of Lookout Mountain from Chattanooga's **Incline Railway** (3917 St Elmo Ave., Chattanooga; ridetheincline.com; 423-821-4224), which was first built in 1895. Glass windows provide uninterrupted views of the St. Elmo neighborhood. At the top is Point Park, part of the greater Chickamauga and Chattanooga National Military Park.

Incline Railway Viewpoint

» The best way to experience East Tennessee's music culture is at **Blue Plate Special** (wdvx.com/program/blue-plate-special), a local radio station's live performances held six days per week at the Knoxville visitor center. You never know what type of music you might hear, but it's free and open to the public.

» As Knoxville's most recognizable building on the skyline, the futuristic **Sunsphere** was first created for the 1982 World's Fair. Visitors can see the city from the observation deck or enjoy a cocktail at the full-service restaurant and bar. Also explore the **World's Fair Park Lawn** (810 Clinch Ave., Knoxville; worldsfairpark .org; 865-363-9538), which has playgrounds and walking paths.

» The state's best theme park is **Dollywood** (2700 Dollywood Parks Blvd., Pigeon Forge; dollywood.com; 800-365-5996), founded by country superstar and Sevierville native Dolly Parton. The family-friendly park is designed around its Smoky Mountain surroundings and has a number of thrilling roller coasters such as the wooden Lightning Rod. They also have a seasonal water park.

» **Ripley's Aquarium of the Smokies** (88 River Rd., Gatlinburg; ripleyaquariums.com/gatlinburg; 888-240-1358) is one of a dozen attractions run by Ripley's Believe It Or Not, but this aquarium is one of the best with sharks, eels, and stingrays among others. The touch tanks and the underwater tunnel at Shark Lagoon can't be missed.

» You also can't miss the replica ship that is **Titanic Pigeon Forge** (2134 Parkway, Pigeon Forge; titanicpigeonforge.com; 417-334-9500), an extensive museum on the world's largest ocean liner and its subsequent tragedy. It has artifacts found on the sunken ship and information on the people onboard.

» The **Great Smoky Mountains National Park** (107 Park Head-quarters Rd., Gatlinburg; nps.gov/grsm/index.htm; 865-436-1200) is the country's most visited park. You might spot elk and black bears on your hikes. Stop by the Cades Cove Visitor Center and Museum for background information about the park's early settlers and, if you have the chance, drive the Roaring Fork Motor Trail.

(above) Dolly Parton Statue Sevierville, (below) A view of the Smoky Mountains

⊘ Off the Beaten Path

» Just like the aquarium, the **Chattanooga Zoo** (301 N. Holtz-claw Ave., Chattanooga; chattzoo.org; 423-697-1322) has a diverse collection of creatures, including native species as well as more exotic ones, such as its red pandas, Komodo dragons, and jaguars. Its keeper chats and special events make it a favorite of locals as well.

» Set on a bluff overlooking the Tennessee River in Chattanooga, the **Hunter Museum of American Art** (10 Bluff View Ave., Chattanooga; huntermuseum.org; 423-267-0968) is set in the former Faxon-Hunter Mansion and has a purpose-built modern wing. It has a collection of 19th- and 20th-century American art and has changing exhibits that have previously showcased the work of Chuck Close and Norman Rockwell.

Hunter Museum of Art

Hunter Museum of Art Interior

» The **Tennessee Valley Railroad Museum** (4119 Cromwell Rd., Chattanooga; tvrail.com; 423-894-8028) documents the railroad industry's mark on the Chattanooga area with a collection of retired locomotives and passenger cars. They also run scenic railroad tours, which is the perfect addition to your day at the museum.

» Chattanooga also has ties with the Civil War, as the site of one of the war's bloodiest battles. **Chickamauga and Chattanooga National Military Park** (3370 Lafayette Rd., Fort Oglethorpe; nps.gov/chch/index.htm; 706-866-9241) includes the battlefields and visitor centers with interpretive exhibits.

» **Songbirds Guitar Museum** (35 Station St., Chattanooga; songbirdsguitars.com; 423-531-2473) at the Chattanooga Choo Choo started as a private collection but has now opened to the public. It includes rare Les Paul guitars and those formerly owned by well-known musicians.

» Named for the legendary blues singer and native, Chattanooga's **Bessie Smith Cultural Center** (200 E. M L King Blvd., Chattanooga; bessiesmithcc.org; 423-266-8658) honors the contributions of Smith and other African-Americans.

» East Tennessee is one of the region's best places to get underground, with caves dotted around the state in addition to Ruby Falls, discussed earlier. **Raccoon Mountain Caverns** (319 W. Hills Rd., Chattanooga; raccoonmountain.com; 800-823-2267) on Lookout Mountain has guided tours, the option to stay overnight, and grounds with mountain biking and camping. The **Lost Sea Adventure** (140 Lost Sea Rd., Sweetwater; thelostsea.com; 423-337-6616) brings guests to an underground lake full of albino fish. **Cumberland Caverns** (1437 Cumberland Caverns Rd., McMinnville; cumberlandcaverns.com; 931-668-4396) north of Chattanooga, hosts the unique Bluegrass Underground, live musical performances in a massive cavern with chandelier lighting.

» Knoxville's **Ijams Nature Center** (2915 Island Home Ave., Knoxville; ijams.org; 865-577-4717) is a former marble quarry that has become the city's best-kept secret. Miles of hiking trails, mountain biking paths, and a quarry lake are all essential activities. The Keyhole Trail has a scenic viewpoint where pieces of stone were strategically placed. Navitat also has a campus here, offering ropes courses, zip lines, and treehouses in which you can spend the night.

» Located on the University of Tennessee campus, the **Frank H. McClung Museum** (1327 Circle Park Dr., Knoxville; mcclungmuseum.utk.edu; 865-974-2144) is a natural history museum featuring Egyptian mummies, dinosaur fossils, prehistoric skeletons, and Native American artifacts.

» The Smokies have a number of quirky attractions and museums. Gatlinburg's **Guinness World Records Museum** (631 Parkway, Gatlinburg; ripleys.com/gatlinburg/guinness-world-records; 865-430-7800) highlights the organization's unusual titles with interactive exhibits. Nearby, **Ripley's Believe It or Not** (800 Parkway, Gatlinburg; ripleys.com/gatlinburg; 865-436-5096) embraces the weird. The **Salt & Pepper Shaker Museum** (461 Brookside Village Way, Gatlinburg; thesaltandpeppershakermuseum.com; 865-430-5515) is the only one of its kind in the world, with over 20,000 pairs of shakers from around the globe.

» Catch the region's best views from the **Great Smoky Mountain Wheel** (131 The Island Dr., Pigeon Forge; islandinpigeonforge. com/play/the-great-smoky-mountain-wheel; 865-286-0119), a Ferris wheel with enclosed glass gondolas that soar to over 200 feet, located at The Island. Downtown Gatlinburg's **Space Needle** (115 Historic Nature Trail, Gatlinburg; gatlinburgspaceneedle. com; 865-436-4629) was built in 1969 and was the second tallest tower in the state when completed. You can also take the gondolas to **Ober Gatlinburg** (1001 Parkway Suite 2, Gatlinburg; obergatlinburg.com; 865-436-5423), the area's only ski resort, at any time of year.

» Adventure isn't for the faint of heart. Inspired by those in Austria, the **Smoky Mountain Alpine Coaster** (867 Wears Valley Rd., Pigeon Forge; smokymountainalpinecoaster.com; 865-365-5000) is open seasonally for a thrilling ride down the hill on toboggans. Zip through the trees at the **Foxfire Mountain Adventure Park** (3757 Thomas Ln., Sevierville; foxfiremountain .com; 865-453-1998), which has zip lines, a swinging rope bridge, climbing walls, and a cider distillery. And like those in New Zealand, the **Outdoor Gravity Park** (203 Sugar Hollow Rd., Pigeon Forge; outdoorgravitypark.com; 865-366-2687) is one of the few places you can "zorb" in America. Take one of three courses down the hill in a plastic bubble any time of year.

» Located on the Tennessee side of Bristol, the **Mountain Music Museum** (626 State St., Bristol; appalachianculturalmusic.org; 423-573-2262) honors the traditions of old time, gospel, country, and bluegrass music of Appalachia.

» The only facility in the world of its kind, the **International Storytelling Center** (100 W. Main St., Jonesborough; storytelling center.net; 423-753-2171) in Jonesborough offers visitors a look into the work of storytellers with exhibits, events, and live daily storytelling for much of the year.

» An unlikely attraction is the Oak Ridge outpost of the **Manhattan Project National Historical Park** (300 S. Tulane, Oak Ridge; nps.gov/mapr/oakridge.htm; 865-482-1942). The military and administrative headquarters were located here, with facilities for uranium enrichment and plutonium production. Visits can be arranged through the American Museum of Science and Energy, but only US citizens can tour the facility.

» **Davy Crockett Birthplace State Park** (1245 Davy Crockett Park Rd., Limestone; tnstateparks.com/parks/about/david -crockett-birthplace; 423-257-2167), south of Johnson City, has a replica of the frontiersman's log cabin. There are also exhibits and historic markers about his life as well as fishing, camping, and hiking.

» The **Museum of Appalachia** (2819 Andersonville Hwy., Clinton; museumofappalachia.org; 865-494-7680) is a living history museum that brings visitors back to the state's pioneer days, complete with a reconstructed farm village. The Smithsonian affiliate includes 35 log cabins, 250,000 artifacts, farm animals, and special events on 65 acres.

▶ Tours for Every Interest

» Experience the flavors of Knoxville with food tours with **East TN Tours** (easttntours.com, 865-410-8687) or **Knoxville Food Tours** (knoxvillefoodtours.com; 865-201-7270), which visit downtown restaurants and go behind-the-scenes in their kitchens. Craft beer lovers can stop by multiple breweries with **Knox Brew Tours** (knoxbrewtours.com, 865-951-6883).

» To learn more about the city's history, try **Knoxville Walking Tours** (knoxvillewalkingtours.com; 865-309-4522), which tells about the "Scruffy City" and its notable residents with Civil War and literary ties. The city's spooky past is also showcased with **Haunted Knoxville Ghost Tours** (hauntedknoxville.net; 865-377-9677).

» The Tennessee River winds through the city of Knoxville, so take the opportunity to see the area from the water. **Volunteer**

Princess Cruises (volunteerprincess.com; 865-541-4556) runs themed yacht cruises, including brunch, tailgating, and sunset. For something more active, **Billy Lush Boards and Brew** (billylushboards.com; 865-332-5874) rents stand up paddleboards and offers classes.

» Similarly, Chattanooga has tours that focus on different themes. Kids love the **Chattanooga Ducks** (chattanoogaducks .com; 423-756-3825), which has a vehicle that goes from the road to the river.

» Foodies can check out the many tasty eateries on the Southside, Downtown, and North Shore with **Eat Sip Walk** (tasteand seethecity.com; 423-708-5328), a food tour company, or earn their calories with **Pints and Pedals** (pintsandpedalstn.com), a tour that involves pedaling from bar to bar.

» History buffs can learn about the city from the ground level with **Free Walk Chattanooga** (freewalkcha.com), a company that offers free tours of downtown. **Chattanooga Ghost Tours** (chattanoogaghosttours.com; 423-800-5998) teaches visitors about the dark side of the city and the places that have been the sites of hauntings.

» In the Tri-Cities, scare yourself silly with a tour of Johnson City with **Appalachian GhostWalks** (appalachianghostwalks.com; 423-743-9255), which also runs tours throughout the region. Or for a calmer afternoon, Bristol's **South Holston River Fly Shop** (southholstonriverflyshop.com; 423-878-2822) offers guided fly fishing expeditions.

» There's no shortage of things to do in the Smokies. **A Walk in the Woods** (awalkinthewoods.com; 865-436-8283) has guided hikes and tours of the Great Smoky Mountains as well as birding treks. **Smoky Mountain Guides** (smokymountainguides.com; 865-654-4545) also has guided hikes, but has driving tours for the less outdoorsy. And for even more spookiness, **Ghost and Haunt Tours of Gatlinburg** (ghostandhaunt.com; 865-661-1980) runs walking tours through downtown.

Five Unique Sleeps
in the Tennessee Mountains

There's nowhere quite like East Tennessee for unique places to stay. The Smokies have thousands of hotel rooms, ranging from well-known chain hotels to offbeat options targeted toward families as well as camping facilities.

» **French Broad Outpost Ranch** (461 Old River Rd., Del Rio; frenchbroadduderanch.com; 800-995-7678) is the area's only dude ranch and offers horseback riding, rustic lodging, and communal meals.

» **The Crash Pad** (29 Johnson St., Chattanooga; crashpadchattanooga.com; 423-648-8393) is not your average hostel, but an LEED property targeted to the rock climbers who frequently visit. They have both dorms and private rooms as well as a sister restaurant, daily breakfast, and a convenient Southside location.

» Located on Knoxville's Market Square, the **Oliver Hotel** (407 Union Ave., Knoxville; theoliverhotel.com; 865-351-0987) is located in one of the city's historic buildings. Stylish rooms are one of the highlights, along with the trendy in-house bar and proximity to local restaurants.

» **The Carnegie Hotel** (1216 W. State of Franklin Rd., Johnson City; carnegiehotel.com; 423-979-6400) is a AAA Four Diamond hotel with a restaurant, spa, and luxurious rooms furnished with antiques.

» Get away from it all at Kingsport's **MeadowView Conference Resort and Convention Center** (1901 Meadowview Pkwy., Kingsport; marriott.com/hotels/travel/tricc-meadowview-conference-resort-and-convention-center; 423-578-6600), a Marriott property. Guest rooms have private balconies overlooking the Blue Ridge Mountains and visitors can enjoy the onsite winery and golf course.

Nashville and Surrounds

The state capital of Tennessee is, to put it mildly, having a moment. Praised in countless travel publications, Nashville has become a hot spot for country music fans, bachelorette weekends, and family fun. After the area was passed through by early explorers and fur traders, the city of Nashville was established in 1843. Much of the city was affected by the Civil War, especially the Battle of Nashville. Its ties with music, which it's best known for in modern times, began in 1941 when the first FM radio station was founded. This allowed the Grand Ole Opry show to thrive and, with it, record labels and music publishing companies. But don't overlook the towns outside of and near Nashville. There are great antiques shops in Franklin, the whiskey history of Lynchburg, and the town of Manchester, which swells well past its population for the yearly Bonnaroo Music and Arts Festival.

A LITTLE BIT COUNTRY, A LITTLE BIT ROCK AND ROLL

Visitors and locals alike seek out Nashville's live music scene, but you don't have to go far to experience it. Walk down Broadway on any given night and you'll see someone playing on a street corner, earning tips and selling their self-recorded albums. These days, it's more than just country music, as you can find plenty of bluegrass, rock, and indie artists as well. There's nowhere finer to see a performance than the **Ryman Auditorium**, known as the "Mother Church of Country Music." The Grand Ole Opry show was hosted here for many years, but now has a new home. Classic Nashville venues include Tootsie's Orchid Lounge, Robert's Western World, The Stage, and The Bluebird Cafe, which you might have seen on the television show **Nashville**. But there are also newer venues such as Exit/Inn, Station Inn, Mercy Lounge, and Listening Room Cafe. Keep in mind that some venues are bars and are only for those ages 21 and older.

📍 Can't-Miss Landmarks

» Start at the top, the most important musical landmark in the city: **Ryman Auditorium** (116 5th Ave. N, Nashville; ryman.com; 615-889-3060). Originally built as a church for evangelist Sam Jones, the stage here has seen countless stars, from Johnny Cash to Charlie Chaplin, Kings of Leon to Patsy Cline. Even if you can't catch a show at the famous theatre, take a behind-the-scenes tour to learn about its history and stories of the people who played here.

Ryman Auditorium

» Visitors can also see the current home of the **Grand Ole Opry** (2804 Opryland Dr., Nashville; opry.com; 615-871-6779), a weekly radio show, which moved to its present location in 1974. They still have frequent performances showcasing notable names in country as well as behind-the-scenes tours.

» Even if you're not a fan of country music, don't miss the **Country Music Hall of Fame** (222 5th Ave. S, Nashville; countrymusic halloffame.org; 615-416-2001), which interprets and preserves the history of the artists and songs of the genre. Exhibits detail how the style of music developed, Nashville's early country music acts, and the hall of fame itself. Nearby, the famed **RCA Studio B** (1611 Roy Acuff Place, Nashville; studiob.org; 615-416-2001), the city's oldest recording studio, and **Hatch Show Print** (224 5th Ave. S, Nashville; hatchshowprint.com; 615-256-2805), a letterpress company that created concert posters, are open for tours.

» Nashville is a surprisingly green city, with city parks located around the metropolis. One such space is Centennial Park, home to the **Parthenon** (2500 West End Ave., Nashville; nashville.gov/Parks-and-Recreation/Parthenon.aspx;

Parthenon Athena Statue

615-862-8431). This replica of the Greek original was created for the 1897 Centennial Exposition. Inside is the gold Athena statue, which disappeared from the original temple, as well as an exhibit about the exposition. Bicentennial Mall and Cumberland Park are also favorite parks.

» Tennessee native and President Andrew Jackson's home, known as **The Hermitage** (4580 Rachel's Lane, Nashville; the-hermitage.com; 615-889-2941), welcomes visitors to Nashville. The mansion served as his office, living quarters, and gathering hall and much of the original belongings are still inside. Don't miss the sprawling gardens and grounds as well as the Jackson Family tomb. Give yourself at least two hours here to explore.

» Easily one of the most recognizable brands in American whiskey, all of the **Jack Daniel's Tennessee Whiskey** (280 Lynchburg Hwy., Lynchburg; jackdaniels.com/en-us/visit-us; 931-759-6357) found in the world comes from the distillery in the small town of Lynchburg in a notoriously dry county. Visitors can tour the facility, including the barrel-making area, Jack's former office, and the stills.

◙ Off the Beaten Path

» The Country Music Hall of Fame isn't the only music-centric museum in town. Notable names also have their own attractions: there's the **Johnny Cash Museum** (119 3rd Ave. S, Nashville; johnnycashmuseum.com; 615-256-1777); the **George Jones Museum** (128 2nd Ave. N, Nashville; georgejones.com; 615-818-0128); and the **Willie Nelson and Friends Museum** (2613 McGavock Pike, Nashville; willienelsongeneralstore.com; 615-885-1515), all worth a visit. The **Musicians Hall of Fame** (401 Gay St., Nashville; musicianshalloffame.com; 615-244-3263), which celebrates the people who made your favorite songs happen with their backing performance, including Jimi Hendrix and other lesser-known artists, is also worth a stop.

» Scenic **Belle Meade Plantation** (5025 Harding Pike, Nashville; bellemeadeplantation.com; 615-356-0501 ext. 125) was built in 1807 outside of Nashville by John Harding and includes a thoroughbred horse farm and a stunning Greek Revival Mansion. The plantation still holds events and tours, which you can purchase in combination with other attractions.

» The former home of country singer Barbara Mandrell, **Fontanel Mansion** (4125 Whites Creek Pike, Whites Creek; fontanel.com; 615-724-1600) is open for visitor tours. But now the

Jack Daniels Statue

property has more to entertain guests, including walking trails, a distillery, a winery, zip lining, restaurants, and shopping. There's also an onsite inn and multiple stages for live music events.

» The **Frist Center for the Visual Arts** (919 Broadway, Nashville; fristcenter.org; 615-244-3340) showcases an impressive collection devoted to the artists of the state and region as well as changing exhibitions. Enter via the Art Deco–style grand lobby in downtown Nashville.

» Equal parts historic home and botanical gardens, **Chee-kwood Estate and Gardens** (1200 Forrest Park Dr., Nashville; cheekwood.org; 615-353-6984) includes the 1920s home of the Cheek family. The home hosts exhibits such as one on the fashion of *Downton Abbey*, while the grounds feature Japanese gardens and other places to sit and reflect.

» The **Tennessee State Museum** (505 Deaderick St., Nashville; tnmuseum.org; 615-741-2692) started its collection with a large-scale portrait of Andrew Jackson, which is still included today. In 1937, the museum grew with items from World War I and expanded into its current building in 1981 with more than 12,000 square feet of exhibits.

» Visit Sewanee, a small town that's home to the **University of the South** (735 University Ave., Sewanee; sewanee.edu; 931-598-1000). This stunning college campus has sprawling grounds on the Cumberland Plateau and a stone chapel popular for photo shoots and weddings.

» Founded by candy bar magnate Frank Mars in the 1930s, **Milky Way Farm** (520 Milky Way Rd., Pulaski; milkywayfarm.org; 931-808-2281) has over 1,000 acres of land that is home to deer and wild turkey. Today, the farm south of Nashville offers tours and trail rides.

» The **Polk Presidential Hall Museum** (301 W. 7th St., Columbia; jameskpolk.com; 931-388-2354) in Columbia is one of the state's presidential landmarks. It honors the nation's 11th president, a Tennessee native. Guests can visit his former home on a guided tour and also explore the grounds and exhibition center.

» Franklin also has historic landmarks to visit, including the **Carnton Plantation** (1345 Eastern Flank Circle, Franklin; boft.org/carnton; 615-794-0903) and the **Carter House** (1140 Columbia Ave., Franklin; boft.org/the-carter-house; 615-786-1864). Both played a role in the Civil War and the Battle of Franklin. Built as a home for the former Nashville mayor, Canton was one of the largest Confederate field hospitals. The Carter House was taken over as headquarters for General Jacob D. Cox.

► Tours for Every Interest

» Fans of whiskey should venture out beyond Lynchburg onto the **Tennessee Whiskey Trail** (tnwhiskeytrail.com, 629-888-2951). Stop by Tullahoma's George Dickel, Nashville's Nelson Greenbrier, and Leiper's Fork Distillery to get your passport stamped. You can also check out the Tennessee wineries, including Arrington Vineyards, owned by country star Kix Brooks.

» Led by two raucous sisters in a bright pink school bus, **Nash-Trash Tours** (nashtrash.com, 615-226-7300) are equal parts history and comedy. The Original Tour has some risque humor, while the Music Row Confidential tour tells stories about the city's musicians that might surprise you.

» **Music City Rollin Jamboree** (musiccityrollinjamboree.com, 615-430-3109) is the city's first sightseeing sing-along city tour, so audience participation is encouraged! The tour stops by important musical landmarks, including the Country Music Hall of Fame.

» Visit some of the Music City's most beloved local eateries with **Walk Eat Nashville** (walkeatnashville.com, 615-587-6138), a food walking tour. Three tours visit different neighborhoods, speak with chefs, and offer samples of the best dishes.

» To learn about the iconic names who first made their careers in the Music City, join **Walkin Nashville** (walkinnashville.com), which offers walking tour three times per week. Tour guides point out places long gone from memory as well as modern day landmarks.

» **Franklin On Foot** (franklinonfoot.com, 615-400-3808) showcases the small town of Franklin with walking tours, highlighting the Civil War history, food, spooky legends, and general background.

Five Unique Sleeps in Nashville and Central Tennessee

Nashville boasts hundreds of hotels, including budget, mid-range, and luxury options. But for a more local experience, stay in one of the Music City's trendy neighborhoods.

» Don't let the name fool you as **Urban Cowboy B&B** (1603 Woodland St., Nashville; urbancowboybnb.com/Nashville; 347-840-0525) is not your average bed and breakfast. Started as a chic rental home in Brooklyn, the owners expanded into East Nashville with their eight-room Victorian mansion. Each room is stylishly decorated and they also have their own restaurant.

» Spend the night in a former train station at Nashville's **Union Station Hotel** (1001 Broadway, Nashville; unionstationhotel nashville.com; 615-726-1001), which has been completely restored into a 125-room property. Rooms have Music City touches such as cowhides while the hotel offers an in-house restaurant and proximity to the city's top attractions.

» An unlikely place for a campground, **Loretta Lynn's Ranch** (8000 TN 13, Hurricane Mills; lorettalynnranch.net/main; 931-296-7700) has RV and tent sites as well as cabins. While you're there, visit the Coal Miner's Daughter Museum, the Native American Artifact Museum, and the Grist Mill Museum.

» In Franklin, **Pot N' Kettle Cottages** (5527 Joseph St., Franklin; potnkettlecottages.com; 615-864-3392) rents out spaces in historic homes, including the circa 1900 Leiper's Fork Inn. Each cottage is furnished to go with the nearby Music City's themes and is within walking distance of shops and restaurants.

» You might feel as if you're staying at Hogwarts at the **Sewanee Inn** (1235 University Ave., Sewanee; sewanee-inn.com; 931-598-3568), located on the campus of Sewanee, University of the South. The stone building provides unrivaled access to the sprawling grounds as well as luxury amenities.

Memphis and West Tennessee

The city of Memphis, located on the banks of the Mississippi River, can feel as equally a part of neighboring states Mississippi and Arkansas, especially when it comes to the music and cuisine. Founded by Andrew Jackson in 1819, it got its name from the Egyptian city and was later a Union stronghold during the Civil War. Local industry brought in immigrants from Germany, Ireland, Italy, Russia, and Greece, who brought their cuisines and cultures in the 1900s to mingle with what we know as "Southern." The city's most notable foodstuff is barbecue, and specifically ribs, which can be served "wet" (doused in sauce) or "dry" (coated in a signature blend of spices). The Bluff City has also long played a role in music history, raising artists such as Aretha Franklin, Elvis Presley, and W.C. Handy in the integrated clubs of Beale Street while Nashville was developing its country roots. The Civil Rights Movement also made its mark on Memphis, where Martin Luther King Jr. gave his famous "I've Been to the Mountaintop" speech at the Mason Temple. Memphis and the nearby towns such as Paris and Colliersville are accessible by the international airport or the local bus and rail hub.

ALL HAIL THE KINGS

Memphis is perhaps most associated with Elvis Presley, who was born in nearby Tupelo, but lived much of his life in the city. In honor of the King, Elvis Week, an event that includes a candlelight vigil at Graceland and an Elvis tribute artist contest, is celebrated every August. If you've never seen an Elvis tribute artist, not to be confused with an impersonator, it is quite an experience. Performers from all over the world dress up as "The King" and sing his greatest hits for audiences. The tribute artists have their own sets of loyal fans who follow them to competitions around the country. Past artists of the contest have hailed from England, Brazil, and beyond!

⊙ Can't-Miss Landmarks

» As the second-most-visited American home behind the White House, **Elvis Presley's Graceland** (3734 Elvis Presley Blvd., Memphis; graceland.com; 901-332-3322) first opened for tours in 1982, not long after his death. Visitors can tour his quirkily designed home, including the famous "Jungle Room," as well as his former recording space, his collection of cars, and his airplanes. Presley's grave is also here. And thanks to a multi-million dollar expansion, visitors can learn about what life in the city was like during his time at Elvis's Memphis with dining, shopping, and entertainment.

» The legacy of Martin Luther King Jr. is remembered at the **National Civil Rights Museum** (450 Mulberry St., Memphis; civilrightsmuseum.org; 901-521-9699), located at the Lorraine Motel, where an assassin ended King's life. A wreath marks the balcony where King stood for the last time. Inside, visitors can learn about the movement and what led up to that fateful day.

» Countless artists recorded their hits at **Sun Studio** (706 Union Ave., Memphis; sunstudio.com; 800-441-6249), which is now a museum. It was here that modern music was formed through a combination of blues and country, coming from the Mississippi Delta and Nashville, respectively. Sam Phillips fostered acts such as Howlin' Wolf, Elvis Presley, Johnny Cash, and Jerry Lee Lewis.

» Established near the former homes of Aretha Franklin and Memphis Slim, the **Stax Museum of American Soul Music** (926 E. McLemore Ave., Memphis; staxmuseum.com; 901-261-6338) details the work that was going on alongside the more mainstream Sun Studios. The museum details the beloved songs to come out of the studio, including those by Otis Redding and Booker T. and the MGs.

» The name synonymous with some of music's greatest guitarists, the **Gibson Guitar Factory** (145 Lt. George W. Lee Ave., Memphis; gibson.com/Gibson/Gibson-Tours.aspx; 901-544-7998)

offers tours of their Memphis facility. One-hour tours run throughout the day and allows fans to see the process of how their guitars are made.

» It's easy to make a whole day of the city's music attractions, as a free shuttle runs between the **Memphis Rock 'n' Soul Museum** (191 Beale St., Memphis; memphisrocknsoul.org; 901-205-2533), Graceland, and Sun Studio. At the former, a Smithsonian affiliate, visitors learn about the people who founded the city's music genres.

» In addition to its role as the city's finest accommodations, **The Peabody Hotel** (149 Union Ave., Memphis; peabody memphis.com; 901-529-4000) is an attraction in its own right. Considered to be the starting point of the Mississippi Delta, the hotel closed for a period but was reopened by enterprising locals. Don't miss the Parade of Ducks, which started as a drunken joke but is now a beloved tradition. There's also a small hotel with memorabilia from the hotel over the years. And at Landry's, a clothing store, you can see where Elvis purchased his famous suits. The King signed his recording contract in the lobby.

Peabody Rooftop

Peabody Ducks

» And no visit to Memphis is complete without seeing some live music on Beale Street and beyond. **Mr. Handy's Blues Hall at Rum Boogie Cafe** (182 Beale St., Memphis; rumboogie. com; 901-528-0150) and **BB King's Blues Club** (143 Beale St., Memphis; bbkings.com/memphis; 901-524-5464) are favorites, along with **Hi Tone** (412 N. Cleveland St., Memphis; hitonecafe. com; 901-490-0335) and **Young Avenue Deli** (2119 Young Ave., Memphis; youngavenuedeli.com; 901-278-0034).

» In Hardin County, **Shiloh National Military Park** (1055 Pittsburg Landing Rd., Shiloh; nps.gov/shil/index.htm; 731-689-5696) tells the story of one of the Civil War's bloodiest battles. It was here that General Johnston's Confederate troops clashed with Grant's Union soldiers. A naval battle in Memphis led to the city being overtaken by the Union. The complex, halfway between Memphis and Nashville, includes the battlefield, cemetery, and Indian mounds.

Off the Beaten Path

» **Mud Island River Park** (125 N. Front St., Memphis; mudisland .com; 901-576-7241) across the Mississippi has the Mississippi River Museum, a Riverwalk path, and family-friendly attractions that seem a world away from the party vibes of Beale Street. Access the island from the monorail that runs between it and downtown.

» Memphis's answer to Central Park, **Overton Park** (1914 Poplar Ave., Memphis; overtonpark.org; 901-214-5450) is a more-than-300-acre space in the Midtown neighborhood. Walking and biking trails, a golf course, and the Memphis Zoo are all located inside.

» **Slave Haven Underground Railroad Museum** (826 N. 2nd St., Memphis; slavehavenmemphis.com; 901-527-3427) documents slavery in America, starting with the Middle Passage, continuing into plantation life, and the anti-slavery movement that eventually led to freedom.

» Known as the "Father of the Blues," WC Handy grew up in northern Alabama but lived in this 1900s shotgun home and was influenced by the Memphis music scene. Now the **WC Handy House Museum** (352 Beale St., Memphis; wchandymemphis. org; 901-527-3427), the home has exhibits featuring memorabilia from the place where he wrote his hit "Memphis Blues."

» The **Blues Hall of Fame Museum** (421 S. Main St., Memphis; blues.org/hall-of-fame-museum; 901-527-2583) highlights the artists who have made their marks on the genre, including Buddy Guy and Bobby Rush. The museum displays artifacts related to these hall-of-famers, including R.L. Burnside's guitar and the dress Mavis Staples wore to the Grammys.

» One of the city's offbeat attractions is the **Pink Palace Museum** (3050 Central Ave., Memphis; memphismuseums.org; 901-636-2362), dedicated to the pink stone home of the owner of Piggly Wiggly brand of grocery stores. Inside, the museum has exhibits on the company and Memphis history as well as natural history and art.

» The **Memphis Brooks Museum of Art** (1934 Poplar Ave., Memphis; brooksmuseum.org; 901-544-6200) is the state's largest and oldest fine art museum, with a collection that includes paintings, sculpture, and decorative arts. The **Belz Museum of Asian and Judaic Art** (119 S. Main St., Memphis; belzmuseum .org; 901-523-2787) is another Memphis art museum, but focuses on pieces from the Qing Dynasty and modern Israeli art.

» The famous locomotive engineer from folk tales is honored at the **Casey Jones Home** (30 Casey Jones Ln., Jackson; caseyjones.com/museum; 731-668-1222) in Jackson. The 8,000-square-foot museum inside his former home has exhibits on trains and railroad history.

» Set in a former Carnegie Library, the **Legends of Tennessee Music Museum** (305 East College, Jackson, jacksoncarnegie. com) is worth a detour for its surprising ties to the Hard Rock Cafe franchise as well as American music. There are also exhibits on the Civil War and performers such as Sonny Boy Williamson.

» Another Tennessee native is recognized at Brownsville's **Tina Turner Museum** (121 Sunny Hill Cove, Brownsville; 731-779-9000). Born as Anna Mae Bullock, Turner attended school at the one-room Flagg Grove School, now full of memorabilia related to her career.

» The **National Bird Dog Museum** (505 TN 57, Grand Junction; birddogfoundation.com/national_bird_dog_museum.htm; 731-764-2058) honors the humble hunting dog with a collection of artwork and memorabilia as well as information on winners of sporting competitions.

Tours for Every Interest

» The impressive paddlewheel boat the *American Queen* (americanqueensteamboatcompany.com, 888-749-5280) is an experience you can only have on the Mississippi River. It's the world's largest of its kind, offering cruises between Nashville and New Orleans.

» **Blues City Tours** (bluescitytours.com, 901-522-9229) offers both guided and hop-on hop-off tours of Memphis and the Delta region for music fans. Tours visit the major landmarks in the city and offer transportation to the nearby casinos.

» Choose a tour according to your interests with **Backbeat Tours** (backbeattours.com, 877-230-0331), which focuses on Elvis, historic Memphis, ghosts and spooky tales of the city, and general tours. Their Memphis Mojo tour covers music history and is the most popular.

» Taste the flavors of Memphis with **Tastin Round Town** (tastinroundtown.com, 901-870-1824), a food tour company that visits the Bluff City's most notorious eateries. Choose from barbecue tours, downtown restaurant tours, and pub crawls.

» Run by two local entertainers, **Rockabilly Rides** (rockabilly rides.com, 901-264-0819) tours Memphis in classic cars like the ones Elvis drove. Tours cover Presley himself, the "Million Dollar Quartet," and general Memphis history.

Five Unique Sleeps in Memphis and West Tennessee

>> **The Peabody Hotel** (149 Union Ave., Memphis; peabody memphis.com; 901-529-4000) is certainly the most well-known, retaining its iconic lobby fountain and duck details. But the rooms themselves have been brought into the modern day with all of the amenities a traveler could want.

>> **The Guesthouse at Graceland** (3600 Elvis Presley Blvd., Memphis; guesthousegraceland.com; 901-443-3000) is as close as you can get to staying at the home of the King. As one of the largest hotels in Memphis, the design of the AAA Four Diamond property was inspired by details of Graceland itself, overseen by Priscilla.

>> To be closer to the energy of Beale Street, stay at **Hotel Napoleon** (179 Madison Ave., Memphis; hotelnapoleonmemphis.com; 901-526-0002), a restored 1902 building designed by Napoleon Hill. The sleek design makes it one of the city's first boutique hotels.

>> It's hard to miss the Pyramid (a nod to the Egyptian name), while driving into Memphis. The building was previously a sports arena and entertainment venue, but sat vacant for a decade until Bass Pro Shops opened it as a mega-store complex with dining, a bowling alley, an observation deck, and an archery range. But, it's the kitschy **Big Cypress Lodge** (1 Bass Pro Dr., Memphis; big-cypress.com; 901-620-4600) that offers an experience you won't find anywhere else. Guest rooms have sweeping views of the Mississippi River and rustic furnishings.

>> For some peace and quiet and perhaps inspiration to pen your own tune, **Lone Oaks Farm** (10000 Lake Hardeman Rd., Middleton; loneoaksfarm.com; 731-376-0082) in Middleton is the perfect getaway. Operated by the University of Tennessee, this agricultural center has rentals including an 1800s log cabin, an apartment above the stables, and an authentic South African safari tent.

Arlington National Cemetery

Virginia

Explorers arrived on the coast of Virginia in the name of France, Spain, England, and Holland in the 1400s. The Spanish set up Catholic missions in Fredericksburg, but it was Englishman Sir Walter Raleigh that named the state Virginia for Queen Elizabeth I, the "virgin queen." Native American tribes, mostly Algonquian-speaking, had been living in the area for thousands of years when European arrival brought disease and warfare. In 1607, the Jamestown colony was established, where John Smith famously met Pocahontas. Tobacco became the region's major crop, but slaves were brought over to work the plantations starting in 1619. This economy continued through conflicts such as the French and Indian War and later the American Revolution. In fact, it was in Richmond where Patrick Henry uttered the famous words "Give me liberty or give me death." The nation's capital, the District of Columbia, was established on the Potomac River in Virginia.

15 Things to Taste in Virginia

There's no way to limit the delicious dishes you'll eat around Virginia to 15 items, but when traveling through the state, be sure to brake for these.

1. Apple fritters, **Blackbird Bakery** (56 Piedmont Ave., Bristol; blackbirdbakerybristol.com; 276-645-5754)

2. Cookies and cream ice cream, **Klines Dairy Bar** (58 E. Wolfe St., Harrisonburg; klinesdairybar.com; 540-434-6980)

3. Lloyd's Famous Fried Chicken, **Southern Kitchen** (9576 S. Congress St., New Market; newmarketvirginia.com/visitors /dining/southern-kitchen-menu; 540-740-3432)

4. Famous Apple Butter Donuts, **Apple House Restaurant** (4675 John Marshall Hwy., Linden; theapplehouse.net; 540-636-6329)

5. Chili, **Texas Tavern** (114 Church Ave. SW, Roanoke; texastavern -inc.com; 540-342-4825)

6. Fried chicken, **Michie Tavern** (683 Thomas Jefferson Pkwy., Charlottesville; michietavern.com; 434-977-1234)

7. Deli egg bagel, **Bodo's Bagels** (505 Preston Ave., Charlottesville; bodosbagels.com; 434-293-5224)

8. Chicken salad, **Sally Bell's Kitchen** (2337 W. Broad St., Richmond; sallybellskitchen.com; 804-644-2838)

9. Chicken and dumplings, **Dixie Restaurant** (250 N. Sycamore St.; Petersburg; 804-732-7425)

10. Crab cakes, **Whitlow's on Wilson** (2854 Wilson Blvd., Arlington; whitlows.com; 703-276-9693)

11. Shrimp and Grits, **Bay Local** (2917 Shore Dr., Virginia Beach; baylocalvb.com; 757-227-4389)

12. Pork barbecue with slaw, **Doumars** (1919 Monticello Ave., Norfolk; doumars.com; 757-627-4163)

13. Steam pot, **Wickers Crab Pot Seafood** (4201 Indian River Rd., Chesapeake; wickerscrabpot.com; 757-351-2724)

14. Oysters, **Merroir** (784 Locklies Creek Rd., Topping; rroysters. com/restaurants/merroir; 804-204-1709)

15. Smithfield ham, **Restaurant at Smithfield Station** (415 S. Church St., Smithfield; smithfieldstation.com; 757-357-7976)

The Mountains

The mountainous landscape of Western Virginia attracts hiking enthusiasts year after year for the Appalachian Trail, Virginia Creeper Trail, and dozens of smaller paths. The climate is ideal for growing grapes and apples, thus producing wine and cider. It's here that the Blue Ridge Parkway hits its northern terminus in Rockfish Gap and becomes Skyline Drive in Shenandoah National Park. Bristol is largely considered to be the birthplace of country music, straddling the line between Virginia and Tennessee. Smaller towns such as Blacksburg and Harrisonburg are home to universities. Roanoke, Staunton, and Lynchburg have small regional airports that allow visitors to explore the Appalachian region of the state further but may require connections through Richmond or Washington DC.

ON THE TRAIL

Perhaps America's best-known long-distance hike, the **Appalachian Trail** runs up the East Coast from Springer Mountain in Georgia to Mount Katahdin in Maine. It was first planned in 1921 and completed in 1937. The trail runs through more of Virginia than any other state on its journey over 2,000 miles, much of it in Shenandoah National Park. The elevation and difficulty varies greatly during this stretch. Memorialized in Bill Bryson's *A Walk in the Woods*, some hikers choose to "section hike," or do pieces at a time with breaks in between, rather than "thru hike," meaning completing it in one trip. The hike generally takes between five and seven months, so it's not for the faint of heart!

⊙ Can't-Miss Landmarks

» The **Birthplace of Country Music Museum** (520 Birthplace of Country Music Way, Bristol; birthplaceofcountrymusic.org; 423-573-1927), which straddles the states of Tennessee and Virginia, is an important stop. It celebrates the Bristol Recordings of 1927 and the artists who made it famous, including Jimmie Rodgers and the Carter Family.

» Home to the Crooked Road Heritage Music Trail, **Heartwood** (1 Heartwood Circle, Abingdon; myswva.org/heartwood; 276-492-2400) brings together the region's best arts and music with gospel, bluegrass, and old-time music. Shop for locally made gifts and crafts in their galleries. The **Rocky Mount Center for the Arts** (220 Franklin St., Rocky Mount) is another great place to see local artisans work.

Heartwood

» The **William King Museum of Art** (415 Academy Dr. NW, Abingdon; williamkingmuseum.org; 276-628-5005) is a free attraction housed in a 100-year-old building. Inside you'll find fine art from around the world as well as contemporary works, photographs, and pottery.

» There's nowhere quite as iconic as Roanoke's **Mill Mountain Star and Park** (Mill Mountain Star Road, Roanoke; visitroanokeva. com/things-to-do/attractions/roanoke-star), which offers the best views of town. It's illuminated every night and has been since it was constructed in 1949. What started out as a Christmas decoration is now up year-round.

» Virginia has countless ties to presidential history, including the **Woodrow Wilson Presidential Library** (20 N. Coalter St., Staunton; woodrowwilson.org; 540-885-0897) in Staunton. Located at his birthplace at Staunton Presbyterian Manse, the

Heartwood

Shenandoah National Park

National Landmark is furnished with period pieces and interprets the future president's life. His wife's life is honored at the **Edith Bolling Wilson Museum** (145 E. Main St., Wytheville; edith bollingwilson.org; 276-223-3484), which documents her history as a descendant of Pocahontas and rise to the role of First Lady.

» The most scenic part of Virginia is within **Shenandoah National Park** (3655 U.S. Highway 211 East, Luray; nps.gov/shen/index.htm; 540-999-3500), which sits between the Blue Ridge and Allegheny Mountains. The famous Skyline Drive scenic highway is the best way to see the park, which boasts 500 miles of hiking trails. The nearby rails-to-trails **Virginia Creeper Trail** (vacreepertrail.org) is a favorite of cyclists, as is the **Heart of Appalachia Bike Route** (heartofappalachia.com/trail/heart-of-appalachia-bike-route-and-scenic-drive).

» Winchester is home to the **Patsy Cline Historic House** (608 S. Kent St., Winchester; celebratingpatsycline.org/visit -historic-house; 540-662-5555), where the music icon lived out her teenage and young adult years with her family. The home has been furnished to how it would have been during that time.

» Managed by the Virginia Military Institute in Lexington, the **Stonewall Jackson House** (8 E. Washington St., Lexington; vmi.edu/museums-and-archives/stonewall-jackson-house; 540-464-7704) is just one of the school's museums, located in the only home the infamous general ever owned. The **VMI Museum** (415 Letcher Ave., Lexington; vmi.edu/museums-and-archives /vmi-museum; 540-464-7334) dates back to 1856, with over 15,000 items related to alumni.

» The **Blue Ridge Music Center** (700 Foothills Rd., Galax; blueridgemusiccenter.org; 276-236-5309) hosts seasonal concerts of the genres native to this region and has a museum on the Roots of American Music. **Clark's Ole Time Music Center** (1304-1586 Ridge Rd., Raphine; lexingtonvirginia.com/directory /attractions/clarks-ole-time-music-center; 540-377-2490) near Lexington also hosts live music and dancing.

Blue Ridge Music Center

Blue Ridge Music Center

⊘ Off the Beaten Path

» Located in the town's old courthouse, the **Lynchburg Museum** (901 Court St., Lynchburg; lynchburgmuseum.org; 434-455-6226) is made up of artifacts related to local history, including the Dunbar Collection, named for the area's African-American high school, local artists and artisans, and early life in Lynchburg.

» The **Maier Museum of Art** (1 Quinlan St., Lynchburg; maier museum.org; 434-947-8136) at Randolph College was started in 1907 when the senior class commissioned a piece by William Merritt Chase. Since then, the collection has expanded to include pieces from the American Impressionism and 20th-century Realism movements.

» Named for the "House of Pestilence," better known as Lynchburg's first hospital, the **Pest House Medical Museum** (401 Taylor St., Lynchburg; gravegarden.org/the-pest-house; 434-847-1465) has exhibits on the Confederate surgeon who treated smallpox and other ailments.

Roanoke Star

» The **Legacy Museum of African-American History** (403 Monroe St., Lynchburg; legacymuseum.org; 434-845-3455) documents the stories of local African-American residents with rotating exhibits.

» **The Taubman Museum of Art** (110 Salem Ave. SE, Roanoke; taubmanmuseum.org; 540-342-5760) in Roanoke was designed by architect Randall Stout and features a permanent collection made up of works by artists such as John Singer Sargent and John Cage. The nearby **Eleanor D. Wilson Museum** (8009 Fishburn Dr., Roanoke; hollins.edu/museum; 540-362-6532) at Hollins University focuses on regional as well as international works.

» Museums don't have to be stuffy! The **Roanoke Pinball Museum** (1 Market Square SE, Roanoke; roanokepinball.org; 540-342-5746) is an interactive experience documenting the history of the beloved arcade game from the 1930s to the present. Admission includes game play.

» The **Southwest Virginia Museum** (10 W. 1st St N, Big Stone Gap; swvamuseum.org; 276-523-1322) is set inside a hand-chiseled sandstone and limestone building from 1888. Inside are exhibits on early life in the Appalachians.

» *Trail of the Lonesome Pine* (518 Clinton Ave. E., Big Stone Gap; trailofthelonesomepine.com; 276-523-1235) is the state's outdoor drama, telling of the love story between an Appalachian mountain girl and a mining engineer from the East. Based on the novel of the same name, the play is performed seasonally in scenic Big Stone Gap.

» Founded in 1995, the **Virginia Quilt Museum** (301 S. Main St., Harrisonburg; vaquiltmuseum.org; 540-433-3818) educates visitors on the arts and crafts community of the Shenandoah region. The collection features heirloom quilts and modern pieces.

» The **Museum of American Jewelry Design** (217 S. Liberty St #103a, Harrisonburg; jewelrymuseum.org; 540-574-4306) is truly a one-of-a-kind museum, established by Hugo Kohl to inform on the process of creating jewelry. Pieces of vintage jewelry are on display and there's also a station to create your own items.

Trail of the Lonesome Pine

» James Madison University's **Mineral Museum** (365 S. High St., Harrisonburg; sites.jmu.edu/mineralmuseum; 540-568-6421) boasts over 600 pieces of minerals from around the world. Private collections and donations from other museums contribute to the vast display.

» Staunton is home to the **American Shakespeare Center's Blackfriars Playhouse** (10 S. Market St., Staunton; americanshakespearecenter.com; 877-682-4236), which performs the Bard's greatest hits year-round. The 300-seat space means there are no bad seats in the house.

» The **Frontier Culture Museum** (1290 Richmond Ave., Staunton; frontiermuseum.org; 540-332-7850) tells of the early inhabitants of western Virginia, who traveled from England, Germany, Ireland, and beyond in search of a better life. The outdoor museum has reproduction buildings and artifacts. The **Settlers Museum of Southwest Virginia** (1322 Rocky Hollow Rd., Atkins; settlersmuseum.com; 276-686-4401) also tells these stories.

» The **Camera Heritage Museum** (1 W. Beverley St., Staunton; cameraheritagemuseum.com; 540-886-8535) has an impressive collection of cameras from the 19th century to the present. As the only camera museum in the US, it showcases pieces usually only found in private collections as well as the stories of the photographers.

» As one of the only original pre-Revolutionary structures in Western Virginia, **Smithfield Plantation** (1000 Smithfield Plantation Rd., Blacksburg; smithfieldplantation.org; 540-231-3947) was the home of notable Revolutionary War patriot William Preston. It's open for tours of the house, grounds, and outbuildings.

» Managed by Bridgewater College, the **Reuel B. Pritchett Museum** (E. College St., Bridgewater; virginia.org/listings/HistoricSites/ReuelBPritchettMuseumatBridgewaterCollege; 540-828-8000) has over 10,000 artifacts, including rare coins, Native American items, Civil War weaponry, and ancient Bibles from the Church of the Brethren.

» The **Valley Brethren Mennonite Center** (1921 Heritage Center Way, Harrisonburg; vbmhc.org; 540-438-1275) tells the stories of the Mennonite people who have inhabited the Shenandoah Valley for 200 years through artifacts, buildings, and story-telling. Highlights include a pre–Civil War mill and a historic meetinghouse.

» Best known for his namesake "Marshall Plan," George Marshall is honored at the **George C. Marshall Museum** (VMI Parade, Lexington; marshallfoundation.org/museum; 540-463-2083) with exhibits that focus on his childhood, the World Wars, and later years. Marshall attended VMI and later won a Nobel Peace Prize.

» **The Ralph Stanley Museum and Traditional Mountain Music Center** (249 Dickenson Hwy., Clintwood; ralphstanleymuseum. com; 276-926-8550) is set in a century-old home that shares the history of the legendary bluegrass artist. Interactive exhibits educate on his career and influence.

» And Kentucky isn't the only state with caves! The **Caverns at Natural Bridge** (6313 S. Lee Hwy., Natural Bridge; natural-bridgeva.com/the-caverns-at-natural-bridge.html; 540-291-2482), **Skyline Caverns** (10344 Stonewall Jackson Hwy., Front Royal; skylinecaverns.com; 540-635-4545), **Endless Caverns** (1800 Endless Caverns Rd., New Market; endlesscaverns.com; 540-896-2283), **Luray Caverns** (101 Cave Hill Rd., Luray; luray caverns.com; 540-743-6551), **Shenandoah Caverns** (57 Caverns Rd., Quicksburg; shenandoahcaverns.com; 540-477-3115), and **Grand Caverns** (5 Grand Caverns Blvd., Grottoes; grandcaverns. com; 540-249-5705) are all commercial caves open for tours.

▶ Tours for Every Interest

» Bentonville's **Virginia Canopy Tours** (zipthepark.com, 540-622-2000) operates three-hour canopy tours in the Shenandoah Valley, which include UTV trail rides, zip lines, high ropes bridges, a nature walk, and rappelling. Guides teach guests about area history, including native species of plants and wildlife.

» **Tour Roanoke** (roanokefoodtours.com, 540-309-1781) has any type of tour you could ask for, including downtown food, brunch, craft beer and kayaking, wine, and scavenger hunt tours. All public tours are three to five hours long.

» Outdoors lovers can take guided tours of the "Mountain Bike Capital of the East" from **Roanoke Mountain Adventures** (roanokemountainadventures.com, 540-525-8295). They also operate guided kayaking and paddleboarding excursions and offer rentals.

» Taste the flavors of Harrisonburg's Culinary District with the local experts at **Rocktown Bites Food Tours** (rocktownbites.com, 540-432-8922). The walking tours last around two hours and stop by five local businesses for samples.

» Started in 1996, **Lexington's Ghost Tour** (lexingtonvaghost-tour.com, 540-464-2250) follows in the footsteps of Stonewall Jackson and Robert E. Lee for grim tales from the Civil War.

💤 Five Unique Sleeps in Western Virginia

» Located in quaint Abingdon, the **Martha Washington Inn & Spa** (150 W. Main St., Abingdon; themartha.com; 276-628-3161) has 63 rooms and suites fitting for a First Lady, earning it the prestigious AAA Four Diamond award. Built as a retirement home for a general from the War of 1812, it later became a part of Martha Washington College before opening as a hotel in 1935, hosting guests such as Jimmy Carter and Elizabeth Taylor.

» Perhaps the only hotel in the world to be themed around shoes, the **Craddock Terry Hotel** (1312 Commerce St., Lynchburg; craddockterryhotel.com; 434-455-1500) was once an 1888 shoe factory. It retains its industrial feel while updating with cozy furnishings and includes daily breakfast.

» Built in the Tudor style in 1882, **Hotel Roanoke** (110 Shenandoah Ave. NW Roanoke; hotelroanoke.com; 540-985-5900) is the perfect Blue Ridge getaway, with over 300 guest rooms. It has been updated with green touches such as electric vehicle charging stations.

» Boasting more than 2,000 acres of Virginia landscape, **The Omni Homestead Resort** (1766 Homestead Dr., Hot Springs; omnihotels.com/hotels/homestead-virginia; 888-444-6664) has been the getaway for 23 US presidents. It has a full-service spa that takes advantage of nearby mineral springs.

» More than just a luxury resort, **Primland** (2000 Busted Rock Rd., Meadows of Dan; primland.com; 866-960-7746) has its own glamping option, the Golden Eagle Treehouse. But unlike your childhood treehouse, this comes equipped with soaking tub, WiFi, and a private vehicle to take to and from the lodge.

Central Virginia

Central Virginia runs from Washington DC to the north and south of Richmond, equal parts past and present. It was in this region that men such as George Washington and Thomas Jefferson lived and planned out what they wanted America to be. It's a region ravaged by slavery and the Civil War, including the battle in Fredericksburg and eventual surrender at Appomattox. But it's also full of modern cities such as foodie-friendly Richmond and relaxed college town Charlottesville. The capital city is also home to the regional transport hub, with buses, trains, and a major airport, but Washington DC's international airports also make the area easy to access.

 Can't-Miss Landmarks

» Visitors flock to Central Virginia to tour **Monticello** (931 Thomas Jefferson Pkwy., Charlottesville; home.monticello.org; 434-984-9800), the home of Thomas Jefferson near Charlottesville. Tours include the space he designed himself as well as the grounds, which have interpretive panels about slavery at the plantation. History buffs can also visit his childhood home at **Tuckahoe Plantation** (12601 River Rd., Richmond; tuckahoe plantation.com; 804-774-1614).

Monticello

IN VINO VERITAS

California has Napa, but Virginia has the Blue Ridge Mountains. The cool climate throughout most of the year makes it ideal for growing grapes and apples. The wineries around Charlottesville are a popular day trip from both Richmond and Washington DC. Drive the roads around Afton Mountain and you'll see countless cellar doors, begging you to come in for a glass and a view. **Blenheim Vineyards** (31 Blenheim Farm, Charlottesville; blenheimvineyards.com) is owned by musician Dave Matthews, while **Veritas Vineyards** (151 Veritas Lane, Afton; veritaswines.com) has a cafe and stunning tasting room. **Jefferson Vineyards** (1353 Thomas Jefferson Pkwy., Charlottesville; jeffersonvineyards.com) has been a winery since Thomas Jefferson gave Filippo Mazzei land to plant grapes in 1773. **Loving Cup Vineyard and Winery** (3340 Sutherland Rd., North Garden; lovingcupwine.com) is one of the few certified organic operations. No matter your tastes, you're sure to find it in Virginia wine country! But if you prefer beer or cider, there are plenty of cideries and breweries, namely **Starr Hill** (5391 Three Notched Rd., Crozet; starrhill.com) and **Bold Rock** (multiple locations, boldrock.com).

>> James Madison's home, **Montpelier** (11350 Constitution Hwy., Montpelier Station; montpelier.org; 540-672-2728), is another favorite, located farther north. It's been almost completely restored to how it was when Madison and wife Dolley lived there, but retains some elements from the family who lived there after them before turning it over to the state.

>> Just down the road from Monticello is **Highland** (2050 James Monroe Pkwy., Charlottesville; highland.org; 434-293-8000), the site of the home where James Monroe lived. Little remains from the original house, but visitors can see the outbuildings that would have existed during his time. The **James Monroe Museum and Memorial Library** (908 Charles St., Fredericksburg; james-monroemuseum.umw.edu; 540-654-1043) also informs about the president's life, located in a building believed to be his law office.

Capital Grounds

VA Capitol Rotunda

» There are a number of museums and attractions centered around the Civil War, but the **American Civil War Center** (acwm.org, 804-649 1861) is unrivaled when it comes to sheer volume of information and balanced perspectives. They operate a museum in Appomattox, the White House and Museum of Confederacy in Richmond, and another museum at Historic Tredegar.

» Not every state capitol is worth a visit, but the **Virginia State Capitol** (1000 Bank St., Richmond; nps.gov/nr/travel/richmond/virginiastatecapitol.html) was designed by Thomas Jefferson in the Roman Revival style. Guided and self-guided tours are available, and visit the sites of constitutional conventions, succession, and even where much of the building collapsed during a Supreme Court trial in 1870.

» Revolutionary War orator Patrick Henry is honored at **Red Hill** (1250 Red Bottom Rd., Brookneal; redhill.org; 434-376-2044), the home at which he lived out his later years and the site of his burial. It's open for visitors to see a reconstruction of his home as well as the cemetery. Living history days further interpret the time period.

» The campus of the **University of Virginia** (400 Emmet St. South, Charlottesville; virginia.edu; 434-924-7081) is a destination in its own right, designed like those in England. Dormitories are set around a central lawn, which is framed by Jefferson's iconic Rotunda. While wandering around, visit the room in which Edgar Allan Poe lived and the Fralin Museum of Art.

University of Virginia, Charlottesville

» George Washington's home at **Mount Vernon** (3200 Mount Vernon Memorial Highway, Mount Vernon; mountvernon.org; 703-780-2000) is right outside Washington DC. The original president's colonial mansion has been restored to how it looked when he and his wife lived there in 1799. Tours include the home, grounds, and outbuildings. Washington fans can also visit his boyhood home at **Ferry Farm** (268 Kings Hwy., Fredericksburg; kenmore.org/visiting.html; 540-373-3381) in Stafford County and his mother's house at the Mary Washington House in Fredericksburg.

» Located right outside Washington DC proper, **Arlington National Cemetery** (1 Memorial Ave., Fort Myer; arlingtoncemetery.mil; 877-907-8585) is where our nation pays respect to the people who protect them. Visit the Tomb of the Unknown Soldier and the Eternal Flame for President John F. Kennedy Jr. Arlington House, the columned building around which the cemetery is set, is a memorial to Robert E. Lee.

» Also in Arlington is the **National 9/11 Pentagon Memorial** (1 N. Rotary Rd., Arlington; pentagonmemorial.org; 301-740-3388), which remembers the lives lost during the terrorist attack on the government building. Memorial benches are set up for each of the 184 killed.

 Off the Beaten Path

» Near the site of Edgar Allen Poe's family home, the **Edgar Allan Poe Museum** (1914 E. Main St., Richmond; poemuseum. org; 804-648-5523) highlights the macabre author's career, starting with his childhood and progressing through his brief time at the University of Virginia and his later success.

» Established in 1898, **The Valentine** (1015 E. Clay St., Richmond; thevalentine.org; 804-649-0711) was Richmond's first museum, housed in an 1812 home. The collections focus on the history of the city, with textiles, documents, and artifacts as well as rotating exhibitions.

Statue of Edgar Allen Poe

» The **Virginia Holocaust Museum** (2000 E. Cary St., Richmond; vaholocaust.org; 804-257-5400) is a sprawling and free museum that educates on the most horrific time in human history.

» Tour the 1893 mansion known as **Maymont** (1700 Hampton St., Richmond; maymont.org; 804-358-7166), which now serves as a museum with tours of the mansion, grounds and gardens, farm pastures, a nature center, and even a collection of carriages. They host frequent events and classes.

» A surprising find at the University of Virginia is the **Kluge-Ruhe Aboriginal Art Collection** (400 Worrell Dr., Peter Jefferson Place, Charlottesville; kluge-ruhe.org; 434-244-0234), which is the only collection devoted to this type of art in the country. It started with a donation from an American businessman who started his personal collection in 1988.

» The city of Alexandria operates the **Alexandria Archaeology Museum** (105 N. Union St # 327, Alexandria; alexandriava. gov/Archaeology; 703-746-4399), which contains a collection of pieces found during digs such as the 1800s musket found in someone's backyard. The nearby **Alexandria Black History Museum** (902 Wythe St., Alexandria; alexandriava.gov/Black-History; 703-746-4356) is set in a formerly segregated library building and interprets local African-American history.

» Learn about the inductees of the **National Inventors Hall of Fame Museum** (600 Dulany St., Alexandria; invent.org/honor/hall-of-fame-museum; 571-272-0095), which has interactive exhibits telling the stories of the inventions. More than 500 people have become members of the hall of fame, including George Eastman and Thomas Edison.

» **Historic Port Royal** (506 Main St., Port Royal; historicportroyal. net) was established in 1652 as a colonial tobacco and supply port. Today it's been reconstructed as a living museum. Stop by the Peyton-Brockenbrough House, where John Wilkes Booth ran after the assassination of Abraham Lincoln.

» The National Air and Space Museum in Washington DC has its sister campus, the **Steven F. Udvar-Hazy Center** (14390 Air and Space Museum Pkwy., Chantilly; airandspace.si.edu/udvar-hazy-center; 703-572-4118) in Chantilly. It holds more than 250 artifacts, including a Lockheed SR-71, a Concorde, and the space shuttle Discovery.

» The **Civil War battlefields** in Central Virginia were home to some of the war's bloodiest, including **Fredericksburg** (120 Chatham Ln., Fredericksburg; nps.gov/frsp/index.htm; 540-693-3200) and **Chancellorsville** (3215 E. Broad St., Richmond; nps.gov/rich/index.htm; 804-226-1981). Both are open to visitors, along with **Richmond National Battlefield Park** (8761 Battlefield Park Rd., Richmond; nps.gov/rich/index.htm; 804-226-1981).

» The **National Marine Corps Museum** (18900 Jefferson Davis Hwy., Triangle; usmcmuseum.com; 703-432-1775) tells the stories of soldiers starting from the American Revolution and continuing to the present. The **US Army Women's Museum** (2100 A Ave., Fort Lee; www.awm.lee.army.mil; 804-734-4327) honors the sacrifices women have made in the military since its inception.

» Located near Scottsville, **Hatton Ferry** (10120 Hatton Ferry Rd., Scottsville; thehattonferry.org; 434-296-1492) is the only remaining poled cable ferry, which has been in operation for over 145 years. Cross the James River as the early inhabitants did.

» Schuyler is home to the **Walton's Mountain Museum** (6484 Rockfish River Rd., Schuyler; waltonmuseum.org; 434-831-2000), which has recreated sets from the popular series as well as some of the film equipment that was used. Nearby, you can visit the **Waltons Hamner House** (128 Tree Top Loop, Schuyler; thewaltonshamnerhouse.com; 434-831-2017), where the show's creator grew up.

» The **Pamplin Historical Park & The National Museum of the Civil War Soldier** (6125 Boydton Plank Rd., Petersburg; pamplinpark.org; 804-861-2408) was created to preserve nearby battlefields but now makes up more than 400 acres of interpretive spaces. It includes museums, antebellum homes, battlefields, and programming.

» **Longwood Center for the Visual Arts** (129 N. Main St., Farmville; lcva.longwood.edu; 434-395-2206) has a collection that highlights both regional and international artists, but shines when it comes to their folk art and Virginia artists. They also have a substantial amount of African, Chinese, and contemporary art.

» The unlikely story of the early Civil Rights movement of rural Virginia is interpreted at the **Robert Russa Moton Museum** (900 Griffin Blvd., Farmville; motonmuseum.org; 434-315-8775), which tells of the Brown vs. Board of Education Supreme Court Case. The county closed its public schools for years to avoid integration.

► Tours for Every Interest

» See what makes Richmond such a foodie city with **River City Food Tours** (rivercityfoodtours.com, 804-479-8929), which conducts walks through Carytown and the Arts District. They even have a desserts tour to indulge your sweet tooth.

» **Riverside Outfitters** (riversideoutfitters.net, 804-560-0068) is one of the top outdoor excursion companies in Richmond, leading guided rafting, kayaking, and paddleboarding trips on the James River.

» **Taste of Virginia** (tasteofvirginiafoodtours.com, 434-589-5558) operates in Charlottesville, bringing visitors to beloved local restaurants downtown and in Stonefield.

» While they're based in the capital, **DC Metro Food Tours** (dcmetrofoodtours.com, 202-851-2268) has an Alexandria food tour that highlights the history of the colonial city through its foodways.

» **Alexandria Colonial Tours** (alexcolonialtours.com/ghost
-graveyard-tour, 703-519-1749) runs a number of tours of the
city throughout the year, but their Alexandria's Original Ghost
& Graveyard Tour has been a favorite since 1982.

» Safely visit the region's best wineries, breweries, distilleries,
and cideries with locally owned **Cville Hop On Tours** (cvilleho-
pontours.com, 434-218-3565). Tours are public and the comfortable bus even has WiFi!

» Pedal your way around the capital with **Richmond Rides** (rich-
mondrides.net, 804-893-5065), which runs tours of Church Hill
that focus on its restaurants and history. The price comes with
bike rentals and helmets.

» What's better than free? **Richmond Tour Guys** (richmondtour-
guys.com, 804-215-8530) offers free walking tours of downtown,
Church Hill, Capitol Square, and Shockoe Bottom.

» Let the experts at **Richmond Brewery Tours** (richmondbrewery
tours.com, 804-404-2739) take you to the up-and-coming beer
city's finest. Samples are included with each of the stops, as well
as transportation between them.

💤 Five Unique Sleeps in Central Virginia

» Richmond has plenty of hotels, and even historic hotels, but
the **Quirk Hotel** (201 W. Broad St., Richmond; destinationhotels
.com/quirk-hotel; 804-340-6040) combines the history of a
dry goods store with the artistic details brought by art gallery
owners. Locals love the rooftop bar, but guests will adore the
loft suites.

» Escape the fast pace of Washington DC at **Salamander Resort
& Spa** (500 N. Pendleton St., Middleburg; salamanderresort.
com; 540-687-3600), the heart of horse and wine country. Onsite

Quirk Hotel

amenities include fine-dining restaurants, a full spa, cooking classes, zip lining, and horseback riding.

» Set in Crozet, a short drive from both Charlottesville and Shenandoah National Park, **Montfair Resort Farm** (2500 Bezaleel Dr., Crozet; montfairresortfarm.com; 434-823-5202) is an eco-friendly resort with uniquely designed guest cottages. The 129-acre property also provides countless opportunities for outdoors lovers.

» **The Alexandrian** (480 King St., Alexandria; thealexandrian.com; 703-549-6080) is the most stylish place to stay in the colonial city's Old Town. The 241 guest rooms are in a Civil War–era building that hosted guests such as George Washington.

» The owners of the hotel company opened the more-than-4,000-acre **Marriott Ranch** (5305 Marriott Ln., Hume; marriottranch.com; 540-364-2627), which offers a unique rural inn experience on a working cattle ranch. Take advantage of the guided trail rides to see the sprawling acreage that's a short drive from Washington DC.

Coast

Some of the first settlements in the New World were in coastal Virginia, starting in 1607, although Native American tribes were already in the area. This region is where names from history books, such as Pocahontas and George Washington, were more than just stories. That time period is still seen in Colonial Williamsburg, one of the nation's top attractions. Plantations were established farther inland along the James River, some of which can still be visited today. Maritime history is reflected throughout the coast, especially in the Navy town of Norfolk. Families love the beaches and museums of Virginia Beach as well as smaller towns such as Hampton. The state has miles of coastline, including undeveloped barrier islands, the longest string in the country, with two National Wildlife Refuges and a National Seashore. The region is also known for having some of the best oysters in the country, especially in the Chesapeake Bay. Norfolk and Newport News both have airports for easy access. Norfolk also has a thriving cruise port.

BEAUTIFUL BIVALVES

There are plenty of places known for their oysters around the US, but Virginia is quickly surpassing them all. It's an item that has been eaten since the very beginning of settlement by local Native American tribes and early colonists. The oyster roast is a beloved community event. The bivalves are grown in eight regions within the Chesapeake Bay, each with a distinct flavor in terms of brininess and finish. The state even established the **Virginia Oyster Trail** (virginiaoystertrail.com) to showcase the restaurants and "agri-artisans" who create them, giving this area the honor of being called the "Napa Valley" of seafood. Visitors can even tour oyster farms to see the oyster-growing process firsthand.

⊙ Can't-Miss Landmarks

» By far, the biggest attraction on the Virginia coast is **Colonial Williamsburg** (101 S. Henry St., Williamsburg; colonialwilliamsburg.com; 757-229-1000), a 173-acre living-history museum with interpreters dressed in 18th-century attire. It's easy to spend days exploring the structures, touring the grounds and museums, and catching a performance. Admission includes access to the Abby Aldrich Rockefeller Folk Art Museum and the DeWitt Wallace Decorative Arts Museum. Don't miss the iconic Governor's Palace.

» Similarly, **Historic Jamestowne** (1368 Colonial Pkwy., Jamestown; historicjamestowne.org; 757-856-1250) has been recreated to how it would have looked when the colonists arrived in the New World. The National Park–affiliated island is an active archaeological site, so workers are constantly uncovering new items to showcase. See landmarks such as the 17th-century church tower and monuments to colonial figures. The neighboring **Colonial National Historic Park** (I-64, nps.gov/colo/index.htm; 757-898-3400) also manages the Yorktown Battlefield.

» Hampton's **Virginia Air and Space Museum** (600 Settlers Landing Rd., Hampton; vasc.org; 757-727-0900) is affiliated with NASA's Langley Research Center and has interactive exhibits related to space and air travel. Highlights of the collection are the command capsule from Apollo 12 and early military planes.

» Norfolk's naval and maritime history is celebrated at **Nauticus** (1 Waterside Dr., Norfolk; nauticus.org; 757-664-1000), an interactive science and technology museum. It features exhibits on the Navy and NOAA and also includes the Battleship *Wisconsin* and the Hampton Roads Naval Museum.

(facing page, clockwise from the top) Colonial Williamsburg Drum Corps, the Battleship Wisconsin, Scenes from Colonial Williamsburg

» The **American Revolution Museum at Yorktown** (200 Water St., Yorktown; historyisfun.org; 757-253-4838) has more than 22,000 square feet of exhibit space, educating visitors about the lead up to the Revolutionary War as well as the role the people and places of Virginia played. The organization also operates the **Jamestown Settlement** (2110 Jamestown Rd., Route 31 S., Williamsburg; historyisfun.org; 757-253-4838), a recreation of the original colony where Pocahontas saved John Smith.

» The **Mariners Museum and Park** (100 Museum Dr., Newport News; marinersmuseum.org; 757-596-2222) has more than 150 watercrafts from around the world, surrounded by a 550-acre park. A conservation lab holds artifacts from the Civil War iron-clad *Monitor*.

» Set in a historic neighborhood, the **Chrysler Museum of Art** (1 Memorial Place, Norfolk; chrysler.org; 757-664-6200) was founded in 1933. Its collection contains early European art, including Medieval and Renaissance works; artifacts from the Ancient World; and glass art pieces that date back more than 2,000 years. Don't miss the daily glassblowing demonstrations.

» A historic home on the Norfolk harbor, the **Hermitage Museum and Gardens** (7637 N. Shore Rd., Norfolk; thehermitagemuseum.org; 757-423-2052) offers tours of the stunning Sloane family mansion and the sprawling grounds. The art collection was founded by a local woman who divided her pieces between the Hermitage and Chrysler, including Asian artifacts, textiles, and decorative arts.

» In nearby Virginia Beach, the **Virginia Museum of Contemporary Art** (2200 Parks Ave., Virginia Beach; virginiamoca.org; 757-425-0000) is the state's facility for what is happening in the art world now. Changing exhibitions, programming, and education are all a part of the museum.

» The history of our founding fathers isn't limited to central Virginia. The **George Washington Birthplace National Monument** (1732 Popes Creek Rd., Colonial Beach; nps.gov/gewa/

index.htm; 804-224-1732 x227) in Colonial Beach was where the young future president lived for a short time before moving farther inland with his family. The facility has a living history museum and interpretive buildings. The **James Monroe Birthplace** (4460 James Monroe Hwy., Colonial Beach; monroefoundation.org/monroe-birthplace.html; 804-214-9145) is in the same town and has a small visitor center that tells about his early life on the family farm.

» **Assateague Island National Seashore** (Route 175; nps.gov/asis/index.htm; 410-641-1441) and Chincoteague National Wildlife Refuge (8231 Beach Rd., Chincoteague Island; fws.gov/refuge/Chincoteague; 757-336-6122) are home to wild horses, which roam freely between the Virginia and Maryland sides of the parks. A paved biking path connects the two islands, making it a popular way to get around and spot wildlife.

» The more-than-2,000-acre **First Landing State Park** (2500 Shore Dr., Virginia Beach; dcr.virginia.gov/state-parks/first-landing; 757-412-2300) is home to the stunning Chesapeake Bay Beach as well as 19 miles of hiking and biking trails. Located on Cape Henry, it was near this site where the first settlers arrived. Visit the nearby **Cape Henry Lighthouse** (583 Atlantic Ave., Fort Story; preservationvirginia.org/visit/historic-properties/cape-henry-lighthouse; 757-422-9421), which was built in 1792.

» The **Virginia Living Museum** (524 J Clyde Morris Blvd., Newport News; thevlm.org; 757-595-1900) is a home for orphaned and injured animals as well as those that couldn't survive in the wild. The collection of more than 250 species of reptiles, mammals, birds, and fish are all native to the state. It's also a Certified Green attraction, keeping its environmental impact low whenever possible.

» Stretching between Virginia and North Carolina, the **Great Dismal Swamp National Wildlife Refuge** (3100 Desert Rd., Suffolk; fws.gov/refuge/Great_Dismal_Swamp; 757-986-3705) encompasses more than 100,000 acres. It was first protected in

1974 for its significant biodiversity. **Back Bay National Wildlife Refuge** (4005 Sandpiper Rd., Virginia Beach; fws.gov/refuge/Back_Bay; 757-301-7329) is also an important space for local wildlife, especially as a nesting habitat for migratory birds.

» **Berkeley Plantation** (12602 Harrison Landing Rd., Charles City; berkeleyplantation.com; 804-829-6018) has deep ties to American history as the home of Benjamin Harrison V, signer of the Declaration of Independence and governor of Virginia; birthplace of ninth president William Henry Harrison; and ancestral home of 23rd president Benjamin Harrison.

Off the Beaten Path

» Another Charles City historic home is **Sherwood Forest Plantation** (14501 John Tyler Memorial Hwy., Charles City; sherwoodforest.org; 804-829-5377), where President John Tyler lived for 20 years until his death in 1862. He became president after the death of William Henry Harrison. The plantation survived the Civil War and its grounds were designed by Andrew Jackson Downing.

» The **Hampton University Museum** (14 Frissell Ave., Hampton; museum.hamptonu.edu; 757-727-5308) documents thousands of years of human history and was founded in 1868, making it the oldest African-American museum in the US. Among the 9,000 objects are African-American, Asian, and Pacific art, and items connected to the university.

» The **Lightship Portsmouth Museum and Portsmouth Naval Shipyard Museum** (Water and London Streets, Portsmouth; portsmouthnavalshipyardmuseum.com; 757-393-8591) are dual attractions that educate visitors on the navigational aids and America's oldest shipyard. Explore the historic ship and see early ironclads, battleships, and other naval ships.

» Inspired by the azalea gardens in Charleston, the **Norfolk Botanical Garden** (6700 Azalea Garden Rd., Norfolk; norfolk botanicalgarden.org; 757-441-5830) was established in the 1930s. Today, it contains 53 themed gardens on 175 acres, which can be seen from the walking paths as well as from tram and boat rides.

» Located on a former military base, the **Casemate Museum at Fort Monroe** (20 Bernard Rd., Hampton; fmauthority.com/visit /casemate-museum; 757-788-3391) offers free self-guided tours of the structure that was built in 1834 to protect from attacks. The largest stone fort in America, the museum includes the room where Jefferson Davis was held prisoner during the Civil War.

» All that remains of the Gloucester mansion known as **Rosewell** (5113 Old Rosewell Lane, Gloucester; rosewell.org; 804-693-2585) is ruins, but a visitor center and self-guided tour showcase what life was like there. Signs show images of what the home looked like and discuss slavery and plantations.

» Learn about one of the native tribes of Coastal Virginia at the **Pamunkey Indian Museum** (175 Lay Landing Rd., King William; pamunkey.org/reservation/museum-cultural-center; 804-843-4792) on their reservation. It contains artifacts such as pottery, clothing, and tools as well as a shop selling traditionally made pottery.

⚑ Tours for Every Interest

» Experience the best locally owned wineries, breweries, distilleries, and restaurants of the coast with **Taste Virginia Tours** (tastevirginia.com, 757-340-8687). They operate in Virginia Beach, Norfolk, Hampton, and Williamsburg and include transportation in a comfortable coach bus.

» **Naval Base Cruises** (navalbasecruises.com, 757-627-7406) operates the *Victory Rover* and *American Rover* ships from the Norfolk harbor, pointing out landmarks along the way.

» Choose from coastal or flatwater adventures with **Adventure Kayak Tours** (adventurekayaktours.net, 757-237-8776), a Chesapeake-based operator. Excursions include all the gear you'll need to visit Smith Island, Back Bay, and Dismal Swamp.

» **Beach Eco Tours** (beachecotours.com, 757-754-8382) runs stand-up paddleboarding tours, including moonlight and dolphin-spotting tours. You can also rent a board if you're an experienced boarder.

» **Williamsburg Walking Tours** (williamsburgwalkingtours.com, 757-634-2452) literally walks you through the colonial town's history with tours focusing on general history, African-American experiences, and ghost tours.

» Sample the delicacies found in the town with **Taste of Williamsburg Food Tour** (tastewilliamsburg.com, 757-634-3602), which winds through 10 eateries around the College of William and Mary campus.

» **Alliance Yorktown Charters** (sailyorktown.com, 888-316-6422) navigates the historic waters on their fleet of schooners.

💤 Five Unique Sleeps in Coastal Virginia

» **Colonial Williamsburg** (101 S. Henry St., Williamsburg; colonialwilliamsburg.com; 757-229-1000) has numerous properties for those looking to extend their stay overnight, but a stay at the colonial homes is the most unique option. Each one has its own connection to history and is comfortably furnished in period-appropriate items.

» Set in the Chesapeake Bay town of Irvington, **Hope and Glory Inn** (65 Tavern Rd., Irvington; hopeandglory.com; 804-438-6053) is an 1889-schoolhouse-turned-boutique-hotel. The inn has cottages, but their independent Vineyard Tents feel more like tiny houses, complete with full kitchens. They also have their own bar, restaurant, winery, and spa.

» **The Founders Inn and Spa** (5641 Indian River Rd., Virginia Beach; foundersinn.com; 757-424-5511) is a four-star property named for the Founding Fathers and inspired by colonial architecture. Cozy guest rooms overlook the English Gardens and guests have access to their spa.

» **Smithfield Station** (415 S. Church St., Smithfield; smithfieldstation.com; 877-703-7701) boasts the state's only accommodations inside a lighthouse, including the top-level Captain Sinclair Suite. They also have a restaurant and marina to dock your boat.

» Intrepid travelers can stay overnight on Chincoteague Island at **Pine Grove Campground and Waterfowl Park** (5283 Deep Hole Rd., Chincoteague Island; pinegrovecampground.com; 757-336-5200), which serves as accommodations and habitat for 50 species of birds. They have RV and tent sites as well as a store selling anything you might need during your stay.

Index

H

Habersham, 110
Hagy's Catfish Hotel, 284
Halls on the River, 124
Halsey Institute of
  Contemporary Art, 262
Hambone Art and Music, 185
Hamilton House Inn, 161
Hampson Archeological
  Museum State Park, 87
Hampton plantations, 258
Hampton University
  Museum, 346
Hank Aaron Museum, 53
Hank Williams Museum, 42
Harbison State Forest, 273
Harborlight Guest House, 247
Harbour Town Lighthouse, 259
Hardman Farm, 108
Harkers Island, 243
Harland Sanders Cafe, 124
Hatch Show Print, 299
Hatfield McCoy Driving
  Tour, 126
Hattiesburg Zoo, 209
Hatton Ferry, 337
Haunted Eureka Springs, 69
Haunted Hearse Montgomery
  Tours, 49
Haunted History of the
  Shoals, 38
Haunted Knoxville Ghost
  Tours, 294
Haunted Tours of Little
  Rock, 79
Haunted Tuscaloosa Tours, 49
Haunted Vicksburg Tours, 194
Haunted Wilmington, 244
Haywood Smokehouse, 214
Hazel & Jimmy Sanders
  Sculpture Garden, 192
Headley-Whitney Museum, 140
Heart of Appalachia Bike
  Route, 321
Heart of Dixie Railroad
  Museum, 47
Heartwood, 318
Helen, Georgia, 111
Hemingway-Pfeiffer Museum
  and Educational Center, 85
Herbert's Boudin and
  Cracklins, 154
Herby K's, 154
Herman's Rib House, 60
Hermitage Museum and
  Gardens, 344
Hermitage, The, 299
Heyward-Washington House,
  258
Hickory Ridge Living History
  Museum, 221
Highland, 332
Highland Inn, 106
High Museum of Art, 99

Highway 61 Blues
  Museum, 191, 192
Historic Arkansas Museum, 77
Historic Durham Athletic
  Park, 231
Historic Jamestowne, 342
Historic Port Royal, 336
Historic Washington State
  Park, 78
History @ Hand Walking
  Tours, 224
History House Museum, 244
Hi Tone, 309
Hobbs State Park, 67
Hobcaw Barony, 265
Hofers, 92
Hogshead Tours, 68
Hollywood Café, 184
Hominy Grill, 250
Honey's Restaurant, 284
Hood Huggers International
  Hood Tours, 224
Hope and Glory Inn, 349
Hopeland Gardens, 271
Hope Visitors Center and
  Museum, 75
Hopsewee Plantation, 258
Horry County Museum, 265
Horse Farm Tours, 141
Horseshoe Bend National
  Military Park, 47
Hotel Bentley, 167
Hotel Chester, 204
Hotel Domestique, 281
Hotel Metropolitan, 148
Hotel Napoleon, 313
Hotel Rhea, 89
Hotel Roanoke, 329
Hot Springs Haunted Tour, 79
Hot Springs Historic Baseball
  Trail, 78
Hot Springs National
  Park, 12, 74
Houmas House, 172
Howlin' Wolf Museum, 202
Hunger Games Unofficial Fan
  Tours, 224
Hungry Town Tours, 245
Hunley, 255
Hunter Museum of American
  Art, 290
Huntsville, Alabama, 8
Huntsville Botanical
  Garden, 34
Huntsville Ghost Walk, 38

I

Idlewild Adventure
  Company, 48
Ijams Nature Center, 292
Incline Railway, 287
Indian Mound and Museum, 36
Indigo Coastal Shanty, 92
Inn at Carnall Hall, 71

Inn at Celebrity Dairy, 237
Inn at Ocean Springs, The, 210
Inn at Palmetto Bluff, 19, 267
Inn at Piggott, The, 89
Inn at Serenbe, 106
Inn at USC-Wyndham
  Garden, 276
Inn Shaker Village, The, 143
Institute for Marine Mammal
  Studies, 207
International Biscuit Festival, 18
International Bluegrass Music
  Museum and Hall of Fame,
  145, 146
International Civil Rights
  Center and Museum, 230
International Motorsports Hall
  of Fame, 42
International Museum of
  Muslim Cultures, 190
International Storytelling
  Center, 293

J

Jack Daniel's Tennessee
  Whiskey, 300
James Monroe Birthplace, 345
James Monroe Museum and
  Memorial Library, 332
Jamestown Settlement, 344
Jean Lafitte National Historical
  Park and Preserve, 176
Jekyll Island Club, The, 120, 121
Jenny Wiley State Resort
  Park, 131
Jepson Center for the Arts, 118
Jeptha Creed Distilling, 133
Jerry Lee Lewis Ranch, 202
Jesse Owens Museum, 34
Jimmie Davis State Park, 161
Jimmie Rodgers Museum, 202
Jimmy Carter Presidential
  Library and Museum, 100
Jockey's Ridge State Park, 240
Joe Wheeler State Park, 37
John Grisham Room, 200
John H. Johnson Cultural
  Center, 87
John James Audubon State
  Park, 147
Johnnie's Drive In, 184
Johnny Cash Boyhood
  Home, 83
Johnny Cash Museum, 300
Jo Jo's Catfish Wharf, 60
Jones' Bar-B-Q Diner, 60
Joseph Manigault House, 259
Judy's Castle, 124
Jule Collins Smith Museum
  of Art, 47
Juliette Gordon Lowe
  Birthplace, 115
Jungle Gardens, 177

About the Author

CAROLINE EUBANKS is a freelance writer from Atlanta, Georgia. She grew up road tripping to the beaches of Alabama and Florida, visiting the mountains of North Carolina, and attending school in South Carolina. After four years living in Charleston and another year abroad, she returned to her hometown for good to focus her work on the Southern region. She seeks to show alternative perspectives of an area frequently reduced to stereotypes and news clips and share her love for Delta tamales, soul music, and country roads.

She's written about her love of the South for Afar, BBC Travel, Roads and Kingdoms, Thrillist, and National Geographic Traveler. Her blogs, *This is My South* and *Caroline in the City*, focus on travel and stories from the Southern United States. She was named one of *Southern Living*'s "Blogs to Follow" in 2015.